CHRISTIANITY TODAY
A BOOK OF READINGS

LORD AND KING SERIES

CHRISTIANITY TODAY
A BOOK OF READINGS

Edited by JOSEPH A. NOVAK, S.J.

Holt, Rinehart and Winston, New York

Imprimi potest
Robert A. Mitchell, S.J.
Vice-Provincial of the New York Province
October 17, 1966

Nihil obstat
Daniel V. Flynn, J.C.D.
Censor Librorum
October 21, 1966

Imprimatur
Terence J. Cooke, D.D., V.G.
Archdiocese of New York
October 21, 1966

The nihil obstat and imprimatur are official declarations that a book or pamphlet is free of doctrinal or moral error. No implication is contained therein that those who have granted the nihil obstat and imprimatur agree with the contents, opinions or statements expressed.

COVER PHOTO: KEN HEYMAN

CONTENTS

PREFACE

Christianity Today has been prepared for use within the senior religion program of the "Lord and King Series." It is the companion volume to *Christian Witness: Response to Christ.* This volume provides material for reflection and discussion, according to the flexible plan suggested for second semester's consideration in the *Teacher's Guide* for senior year.

These particular readings have been selected as a result of my personal teaching experience at Fordham Preparatory School from 1962–1965, along with the recommendations and approval of a faithful group of senior teachers in other pilot schools who have used this material with both boys and girls. I express my sincere appreciation to all these pilot teachers who have made helpful suggestions. I wish to single out for special commendation Father Robert J. Heyer, S.J., of Fordham Preparatory School, and the members of a seminar which I directed within the Religious Education Department of Fordham University during the academic year 1965–66; their contributions have been particularly important to this work.

Finally, I am most grateful to the authors and original publishers of the articles included in this collection for their gracious permission to make available to students in one handy book the results of their composite scholarship and industry.

It is my hope that this book will prove to be both informative and stimulating. May the discussions sparked by its reading and reflection, under the grace of the Holy Spirit, lead to the formation of solid Christian attitudes and values and to the implementation of these values in the daily experience of Christian life and witness.

JOSEPH A. NOVAK, S.J.

1

UNIT I

CHRISTIAN PERSPECTIVES IN PRIVATE LIFE

chapter 1
FAITH AND RELIGIOUS PRACTICE

The general attitude of youth toward life and its goals is reflected in the particular problems which must be faced today and in the positive or the negative reaction to them. A pessimistic view of life, or a life filled with tensions of different kinds and degrees often is a force which impels young people to seek release in certain "forbidden" areas of life which hold out to them some promise of excitement and which appear all the more attractive by reason of their prohibition. Forced to conform to the adult world's view of achievement and success and to strive for it whether they like it or not, a large number of young people are launching a minor revolution in the area of belief and morals which is having far-reaching consequences. This revolution is now playing itself out in many of life's arenas! The particular one under discussion in this chapter is that of loss of faith and diminishing religious practice.

That this is a real and a growing problem, with Catholic high-school students in parochial and private schools, as well as with Christian young people generally, is readily admitted by all parties concerned — pastors, parents, teachers, and the young people themselves. How widespread the problem is, however, is open to question. Some exaggerate the situation and maintain that all young people experience crises of faith and have serious doubts about their childhood religion. Serious questioning and thoughtful consideration of one's religion is a good and sound practice. It is something which every mature Christian should do, certainly every senior in a Catholic high school. It would seem, however, that there is a minority which has serious doubts rather than the ordinary difficulties about the faith they received in baptism; but it is a sizable and a growing minority. Hence this problem of loss of faith and of diminishing religious practice deserves extensive treatment here in senior year for positive as well as negative reasons. Hopefully such a treatment will strengthen the faith of those of you who have never lost it and who still practice your religion regularly, although not perhaps always with full understanding or with proper motivation. It can also serve to forestall crises of faith, or if such are already present, perhaps it can contribute towards their ultimate solution.

Three articles follow. The first gives some examples of possible experiences of the loss of faith; the second, some observations of an adult on his interpretation of several negative attitudes of young people toward religion and its practice; the third is an interesting and thought-provoking letter written by a college graduate to the President of a Catholic university with his reflections on the religious dimensions of his college experience.

On Loss of Faith

JOHN G. MILHAVEN, S.J.

HIS HOLINESS recently exhorted the members of the Society of Jesus to combat atheism. More recently, Father Pedro Arupe, General of the Society, speaking at the Council, outlined a strategy of attack against atheism. The more serious atheism, he said, was not express and speculative, but the practical, implicit kind, found even in the lives of believers. And the best way to overcome atheism, whether speculative or practical, was not by intellectual arguments, but by truly Christian actions and lives. Thus from two points of view Father General emphasized life or action over thought. In this talk I would like to suggest how this epistemological emphasis might throw some light on two particular cases of atheism or, more accurately, of loss of faith.

Why do people lose their faith? Men with pastoral experience offer different reasons. One priest said, "Some give up their faith so as to be unrestrained in sexual matters." Another said, "Some give up their faith in order to be mothered. By taking this position they hope to draw attention, concern, sympathy." One Catholic psychiatrist, who has a great deal to do in varying capacities with educated Catholics, adolescent and adult, said this year, "Every case of loss of faith I know was basically a problem of growth." He illustrated this Delphic remark by the following case, which he felt was widespread and which is the first case I would like to discuss.

A boy, a young man, or even an older man, struggles day by day . . . to be a man. He is struggling to be responsible: to have the courage and confidence to think for himself, to make his own decisions, to answer for the consequences. Obviously, this will not dispense him from continuing to obey and believe and conform. But now he must do these things and everything else as a man. The trouble is—and here psychology confirms ordinary experience—becoming a man, becoming responsible, is a slow, difficult enterprise of years or perhaps a lifetime. It often ends in failure or a quite limited success.

FROM AN ADDRESS DELIVERED BY FATHER MILHAVEN. REPRINTED WITH PERMISSION.

These are clichés of our time, but out of this struggle for a responsible life, some Catholics become atheists (or agnostics). It starts with something of which they may not be clearly aware — their practical inability or unwillingness to take on responsibly a life of faith. Why won't they or can't they? Perhaps the life of faith that has been taught them and that they have seen about them has not been one worthy of a mature person and seems, therefore, irreconcilable with their present efforts to grow. Or perhaps the fault is more their own; their present efforts towards maturity are too weak and sporadic to assimilate the demands of a responsible life of faith.

In any case, they take a second step and become atheists. One may officially announce to himself that he is now an atheist. Another, without telling even himself, gives up the fight and simply reserves a corner of his life where a small boy will always be worshipping God and hopefully disturbing the rest of his life as little as possible. This man will be a professed Catholic and a practical atheist. Recently, an alumnus said to one of our Fathers, "Father, don't worry about the lack of religious practice among your students. Those fellows will meet a good girl some day; she'll tell them to go to Church and they'll go." But is it likely that a man who goes to his God because a woman tells him to, goes as a man to God? If not, is it likely that his belief in God, sincere as it may be, will affect his life? One can go to Church, pay bills for the Catholic schooling of one's children, and still let one's faith in Christ determine few of one's actions.

Let *God* judge such practical atheists as well as the professed ones. *Our* question: how can we prevent such atheism (or agnosticism), such loss of faith in thought or in action? If the cause of atheism is practical, the priest's action must also be practical, directed at the cause. Father General was surely thinking of cases where one maintains faith by feeding empty stomachs. In the particular case we have considered, the priest would, first of all, try to help psychologically, i.e., to support the man or boy in his struggles towards a responsible life. Imagine, for example, the College freshman reading seriously on his own for the first time, the couples coming to the C.F.M. meeting, the seminarian facing growing difficulties at prayer. How to help them?

Nowadays there is no need to prove or explain that a cardinal factor in assistance is that the directing priest grant considerable freedom. But, it is worth adding, this freedom cannot be indulgence or mere permissiveness if it is to promote responsibility. The priest must show his genuine respect and interest in the person's struggling efforts; he must prove that he takes them seriously. This normally means a continuing contact, much listening and watching, consequent response and reaction, which will range from enthusiastic to severely critical according to what the person has done. The combination of granting great freedom and yet following closely and reacting at each step is obviously exhausting and demanding, even when it is possible. The image that comes to mind is a cornerback back-pedalling and covering the pass receiver. But this is, I suggest, the most effective means of combating and preventing the potential loss of faith we've been discussing, of aiding faith to hold firm and grow. And a one-to-one apostolate, though certainly costly, does not seem foreign to the traditions of the Society of Jesus.

Our second case of potential atheism or agnosticism is the man who is no longer "sure" of his Christian faith. The faith still makes good sense to him, better sense than anything else he knows and, he says, he wants to believe. He has consulted priests, been apparently submissive and docile (e.g., reading the recommended books, praying as suggested) but, so he claims, his difficulty shows no sign of passing away. Consequently, he does not see how in all honesty he could in his mind exclude the possibility of being wrong, if he believed. And can one believe in Christ while at the same time admitting the possibility of Christ Himself being an illusion?

In answering this question, many Protestants and some Catholics go further than seems necessary. According to them, *all* mature believers must turn an intellectual critique on their faith and, at least once, call the faith in question. Moreover, the resultant mature faith, they say, is never absolutely certain; it is always a risk. In religious matters, to be dead certain is to be certainly dead.

I do not know whether this view is heretical or not. I do find it epistomologically unsound. For in this second case of ours, also, there applies the emphasis of life and action over thought with which we started. Every man has deep seated convictions (e.g., about his family or his country or what's right or wrong for him) which are much more a part of his living than something he thought out. Many a man could not even formulate these convictions, and most would be hard put, on the abstract, purely intellectual level of formulation, to prove them, even to themselves. Yet the convictions are objective, solidly grounded, unhesitatingly certain.

Christian faith can be this sort of conviction. It is true that for some people, perhaps nowadays a goodly number, there is value or even need for some intellectual introspection and criticism of their basic, lived convictions. For these people, it is valuable or necessary to see more clearly what are the solid, lived convictions they have. But even here the convictions are not made more certain or uncertain by being thus reduced to clear and distinct ideas.

However, what of the man in our case, who *has* conducted this introspective critique of his faith and now claims he can no longer be certain about it? He is tempted either to declare himself an atheist or agnostic, or to abandon any attempt to take a responsible intellectual position concerning Christ. In the latter alternative, he'll go along, playing it safe, behaving himself at least negatively, "believing" as he did when a child. But he, too, risks becoming a practical atheist, as the man in our first case.

How could one aid the man facing this dilemma? If he really cannot escape from his intellectual uncertainty, I would suggest that one could well encourage him to accept things quietly as they are for him. Accept, therefore, that he lacks the absolute certainty he wants, but accept also that there are enough indications, especially the testimony of his own *life* of faith, to give him moral certainty or high probability and thus warrant a completely unconditional and serene and definitive acceptance of God's Word for the rest of his life.

Perhaps his doubts have arisen from a scrupulosity of intellect. Or from pride. Or perhaps he is a victim of the intellectual climate of our times and can no longer recognize introspectively the basic and certain convictions he really has. In any case, our point is that he can accept, as most men must do in the important decisions of their life, to commit himself on good probability, to take a risk. The point, pastorally speaking, is to turn him from obsessive concern with his conscious state of mind and free him thus to give himself totally and peacefully to *living* his faith.

In brief: in both cases we have considered in this article it is suggested that the priest focus not so much on intellectual difficulties as on living; in the first case, by aiding the man to grow humanly into responsible life; in the second case, by freeing him from what is for him an impossible intellectual ideal.

Attitudes of Young People Toward Religion and its Practice

JOSEPH A. NOVAK, S.J.

IN THE FORMULATION and assimilation of ideas and value judgments, people generally, and teenagers in particular, are influenced in great part by the judgments and attitudes of members of their own peer group. By sharing similar ideas and ideals teenagers, especially, feel that "they belong," and they achieve a sense of personal and communal identity which is most important for them at this time of their young lives. One of the key areas of life, of course, is religion, man's personal and communal relationship with God. It seems to me that young people today, particularly in the latter years of high school and all through college, develop their ideas and attitudes towards God, faith, and religious practice very much from their association and discussion with one another.

It should be obvious, then, how important it is that boys and girls share proper experiences and attitudes and that they have some of their possibly misguided notions corrected during these years of growth to maturity of faith. That is one reason why discussion of attitudes towards faith and religious practice is so important within the framework of the senior year religion program. These thoughts must come out in the open and in that naked context be judged and critically evaluated not so much by teachers or the adult world as by the students themselves.

Here are several observations by someone who is not a member of the teenage peer-group. They give my impressions of negative attitudes voiced by some young people on the subject of religion. It is hoped that they will provide matter for critical reflection and evaluation on the part of students, individually through study, and corporately through discussion.

1. Religion Is for Children.
As a young person develops and moves from childhood into adolescence and young adulthood, he is anxious to

FROM A SEMINAR LECTURE DELIVERED BY FATHER NOVAK.

leave behind the things associated with that childhood, i.e., the toys, the talk, all the trappings of childhood. He is anxious to become a man. Some young people begin to assert their manhood by ventures into smoking and drinking in a belief that these *daring* acts are signs of their developing maturity and their emergence as an adult. Others engage in sexual activity of a progressively more serious nature. Still others "give up their faith and religious practice," or at least its "excessive" practice. For them, this is a mark of their emancipation. They are freed and no longer subject to the authority of their elders — parents, priests, and teachers — all those people who took them to church and taught them their prayers and supervised their spiritual lives of Mass attendance and frequentation of the sacraments. By no longer participating in any of these religious activities, or by lessening their participation, they feel they are expressing their independence and self-sufficiency for all the world (and particularly for their teenage world) to see and to appreciate and to judge that they are really "growing up."

Yet, such rebellious actions are really a mark of their immaturity. Growth into true adulthood is shown rather in a mature understanding of and in an intelligent participation in the acceptance and practice of one's religion. A real adult shows his independence from authority by freely recognizing his sonship to God and by humbly acknowledging his humanity before the divinity of his Creator. It is the mature son of God, and not the child, who responds to God's goodness and love with a loving commitment which goes far beyond the self-centered and often thoughtlessly uttered "thank you" of the child.

2. Religion Is a Crutch.
Young people gradually become very proud of their own growing self-sufficiency. Indeed this independence and self-sufficiency in many areas is an objective of both home and school education. In many ways, therefore, this desire and this feeling of satisfaction in "standing on one's own two feet" is to be cultivated. They should develop confidence in themselves to face challenges and to handle difficult situations, even without any assistance. But again,

this is a gradual process and it is not equally applicable in all situations. There are areas in which they will always need help and should not be reluctant to seek and to use it. They do so in many circumstances of their daily lives, e.g., going to college, getting a job, buying material possessions "on time," etc. It is ironic and tragic if they foolishly strive to assert their self-sufficiency and growing independence by refusing to recognize or to call upon God in the most important enterprise of living their divinely human lives.

We are reminded of Christ's warning. *"Without Me you can do nothing."* Religion is not intended to be a crutch for which we grope when we find ourselves falling or which can be discarded when we are old enough or strong enough to walk by ourselves. Rather it is a constant support which is to be the muscle of our very being throughout our lives (like the handrailing on a flight of winding stairs). It is a great help, and by no means a hindrance, in our growth to the fullness of manhood and womanhood. As men we still remain creatures made and sustained by the Creator. It is unfortunate that so many young people misjudge the meaning of religion and one's relationship with God, throw away this support of faith, and "go it alone" to their great hardship and sometimes to their destruction.

3. Religion Is for Women.
This belief is more common, perhaps, in European countries than in America; but there is sufficient evidence even in this country of the greater religious practice on the part of women to warrant its inclusion here. For example, women in religious life in America outnumber priests, male religious, and seminarians close to four to one. Is it possible that some men are hiding their lack of generosity and devotion to God's cause behind the convenient false judgment that religion is a woman's affair or that religion is a sign of weakness, if not of effeminacy?

As a matter of lived experience, however, the truth is that it takes a real man to follow in the footsteps of the Lord Who addresses all Christians of all generations with these words: *"If anyone wishes to come after me, let him deny*

14

himself, and take up his cross, and follow me" (MT. 16:24).
It takes an adult to respond to these challenging words
from Christ, male or female. This response, however, will
take different forms with men and with women. We must
not expect the same kind nor the same external expression and intensity of response from men as from women.
Father Karl Rahner has an interesting development of a
man's approach to religious life and practice in his book
Theology for Renewal.

4. Religion Is for Old People.
Visit a Catholic Church during Mass on a weekday morning
and, more than likely, you will find in attendance school
children and old men and women. In a sense we should
not be surprised at this fact because it is usually only these
two groups of the Catholic community which are ordinarily
free to attend weekday Mass. But on Saturday morning
why is it that the only constant group is that of the older
people?

Several explanations can be offered: the broad mass of
the working population who are free on Saturday are taking advantage of this day off in order to sleep later in the
morning (after all, they *must* go to Mass on Sunday!); the
school-children have been going to Mass during the week
and will go again on Sunday ("After all," some will say,
"we can't expect them to be religious fanatics; they deserve to take a day off from Mass"); finally, the Mass means
little or nothing to many Catholics except that it is something which we must attend on Sundays or else commit a
mortal sin.

There is another reason which is becoming more prevalent.
It is the belief that religion, in general, and Mass attendance, in particular, is something really intended for older
people. They have nothing better to do with their time.
Young people and mature adults are far too busy with the
really important things of life to be taking valuable time
out to spend in Church or to say "meaningless" prayers.
Such a mentality reflects the opinion, "You are only young
once: why waste it on things you can do when you are
old?" The young never, or rarely, think of death in terms of
themselves. Old people frequently do. Hence, they con-

15

clude, it is fitting for the old to pray more often and to spend their time in Church attending Mass. They are afraid.

Yet, the young also die and not only when they become old. But more to the point: the young are also God's children; they owe Him reverence, gratitude, and worship. The young need God far more perhaps than the old, as a matter of fact, because the young are still to fight through many of the difficult battles of life. It is a signal triumph for the forces of evil when young people convince themselves, or allow themselves to become convinced, that there is no Personal God Who is interested in them as persons, Who is in them really. They take off the armor of His divine presence within them and face the problems of life "on their own," often to their experienced sorrow.

5. Religion Is Make-Believe and Magic.
There is a growing tendency for young people to look upon, or at least to talk about, religion as a world of make-believe and magic. To be sure they do not regard it as a vital part of the very real world of every day life. They see it as a world of escape, a dream-world, where everything fits into comfortable compartments and is simple, good, innocent, and at peace. They understand from experience and from observation that the real world—their world— contains evil and is filled with strife and war. Religion, therefore, has no place in their real world. It is fantasy. Only those who are weak and unwilling to face the challenge of the real world take refuge in such religious fantasies and childish escapism. The real man of courage, in their misguided and mistaken eyes, does not create for himself a make-believe world of the nice hereafter to give him the necessary strength to live in the difficult and challenging world of the present.

For people who hold views such as this, faith and religious practice become superstition and a kind of magic. They tend to scorn such childish escapism. They want no part of it. Hence religion, which they identify with this caricature, has no part in their lives.

Yet, God and man's relationship of filial sonship to Him (which is what religion is all about) constitutes the one truly important and essential reality of this life. Nothing in life ultimately matters or makes any difference except where a man, as an individual and as a member of the community, stands in relationship to the God Who made him and Who sustains him in being and Who will in justice and love reward or punish him as he deserves and has freely chosen. It is more than poetry when it is said that God is life. Man lives insofar as he is united to God. Christ has expressed this truth most pointedly: *"Now this is everlasting life, that they may know thee, the only true God, and him whom thou hast sent, Jesus Christ"* (JN. 17:3).

NOTE. In discussing this attitude, it is certainly in place to recognize or to point out that *there is superstition* in the faith and religious practice of some, or even of many, Catholics and Christians today. Criticize these caricatures of true religion positively, but do not permit such excesses or minority extremes to become an excuse to deny the reality which is being caricatured. This is a fine opportunity for judging the honesty and validity of such criticism, i.e., whether an individual (or a group) cuts off from the trunk of faith those branches which are withering or dead, and throws them away, or whether he just cuts down the whole tree and throws it away.

6. Religion Is a Social Affair.
Through observation, and perhaps through experience, a good number of young people are forming the opinion that many Christians go to Church on Sunday merely because it is an obligation or because socially and politically it is the acceptable thing to do. To them it is something like being in favor of motherhood or having a drink before dinner. It is the thing that a lot of nice people do. It has become a status symbol which puts the churchgoer into a definite social class or a category of being one of the "good people" in the community. Indeed it can be considered as one of the tests of being a real American. Every politician who seeks higher office in our land must be known by the public to be a churchgoer. It does not make any significant difference to which church he goes, but he must frequent some church, at least on occasional Sundays, and especially during a political campaign. If not, he is politically dead or on the way to sure defeat.

Some young people in their revolt against such a travesty of churchgoing prefer not to go to church at all rather than to be part of such a system or to be accused of conforming to such a social custom. In rightly condemning such sham practices, however, such youths are falling into an equally reprehensible blindness to the truth which is caricatured by such sham.

Faith and religious practice in itself and as rightly lived and experienced in true Christians is in no sense sham. It is a necessary part of true life, and this necessity reaches far beneath the surface level of social conformity. Indeed it infuses true life, God's life, into the life of the believer. Recall the stirring statement, somewhat melodramatic but true nevertheless, of the Roman Emeritus who permitted the *agape* to be celebrated in his home in time of persecution and contrary to Roman law. In answer to the questioning judge's "Why?" he replied: ". . . for we could not continue to exist without the Lord's feast."

FAITH AS THE ULTIMATE OBJECTIVE OF THE RELIGION PROGRAM

It is important to relate this discussion of teenage attitudes toward faith and religious practice to the objectives of the whole religion program. It is possible that the vision of what true faith really is and should be in each of their lives — a personal response to a personal God revealed and encountered in the Person of Jesus Christ — has been clouded. Hence a re-examination of the whole question of faith with its emphasis on the personalist dimension as seen in the earlier years of the course, and especially in the doctrinal treatment of third year (See *The Church: The People of God*), is very much in order during this discussion. The triple dimension of faith as intellectual assent, volitional trust, and loving commitment should be developed in class once more. God, therefore, is to be seen as the object, source, and finality of this mature and personal faith response.

There are other consequences and conclusions to be drawn from this mention of faith as the ultimate objective of religious formation which deserves repetition at this time.

1. Faith Is a Matter for Adults.

This type of mature personal decision for Christ presupposes a mature person: children do not normally make such an act of the will in their earlier years. There is a progressive deepening of one's faith response. Such mature faith commitment will be the opposite of the hand-me-down sociological or social faith mentioned earlier.

2. Faith Can't Be Generalized.

The time and circumstances of these mature acts of personal faith and commitment are different for each individual person in different sets of circumstances. They are impossible to predict because of the interplay of grace and man's cooperation. Each person is unique in his faith response. It is important that religious educators do not make use of any kind of pressure which could end up doing more harm than good. What is needed is a personalized approach to help the students in this most personal part of their spiritual lives. In times of "crises of faith" it can often be an individual's faith in another human being — who himself has deep personal faith in Christ and in eternal values and gives evident witness of that conviction — that proves the most substantial support to the doubting individual's faith. A person who is experiencing the storms of disillusionment and doubt about his religion, and who is afraid, is more likely to weather the stormy period if he has met up with a person who bears testimony in his life to Christ, a testimony which includes love and acceptance of the person himself as well. In other words, if students facing crises of faith, realize that *someone* loves them and accepts them *with these crises*, this is in itself the best evidence by which we bear witness to a God Who is our heavenly Father and Who loves each of His children personally. Thus with some, faith may hinge upon another person's love; that person could well be his parent, friend, or religion teacher. They will often still continue to grope through the difficult time, but even while searching they will feel the support so necessary from a person who believes in them and who witnesses to a belief in a God Who is the source and the object of all love and belief.

3. Faith Will Always Remain in Some Sense Obscure.

Some aura of mystery will always surround, and to an extent, shroud faith. This is true not only because of the supernatural object of faith, i.e., God, but because faith is a meeting of two persons in an encounter which is beyond the powers of intellectual abstraction and vocal expression. But although faith is a mystery, it is not a puzzle. A puzzle is created *in order to be solved*; it must be solved completely or else there is a feeling of frustration experienced, e.g., one word still unknown in a crossword puzzle. A mystery, on the other hand, both conceals and reveals. It is beyond man's complete understanding, but it does invite man's exploration and partial understanding; indeed it is one of the thrills of Christian experience to penetrate the veil of mystery even for glimpses of understanding. Mysteries remain within the range of wonder, appreciation, and love for the believing Christian.

Teachers must be on their guard to warn students about a rationalistic spirit which would try to remove *all* veils from the mysteries of our faith. They must make it clear that faith is the introduction to a mystery and not a crystal clear set of proven propositions. Faith in God is not the conclusion of a rational syllogism. It is reasonable, i.e., the act of a rational man placed on reasonable grounds. A poet might speak of the "leap of faith" made from a secure foundation, but still *calling* for a leap.

4. Faith Is a Drama.
It is a drama involving a meeting of persons, the young person and Christ — with a friend, parent, or teacher sometimes being the human bridge on which the young person meets Christ. In all personal meetings and dramas there is usually a gradual revelation which takes place; persons are slow to reveal their real selves to another. It is through frequent contact and association that more self-revelation and communication takes place and ultimate real knowledge and communion is experienced between two friends, between married people, or between a man and God. God treats man as a person, as someone who is intelligent and free, as someone capable of knowing and loving. It is this free response of knowledge, trust, and love which God seeks from man, His creature, His son. A religious educator, for example, must not measure the success of his teaching by discernible standards only during the stu-

dent's high-school years. The action of this faith-response drama is not usually in evidence in the classroom. It often takes place "offstage," and the teacher may never know about it fully nor even at all; nor need the teacher necessarily know about it. Part of the entire process in which God makes use of parents or teachers as His instruments can often call for this kind of faith from His teaching instruments where they never have the sensible consolation of knowing the full effect of their teaching efforts.

5. Faith Is a Risk.

Scripture refers to faith as "the pearl of great price." A Christian must be willing, if not ready, to renounce all in response to God's call, e.g., the call of Abraham. The price is very high for the student of today who is surrounded by the fascinating attractions of this world and who is encouraged on so many sides to "get all that he can out of life." His faith makes demands upon him; sometimes it asks him to sacrifice something of these visible, tangible, most attractive realities of this world for some invisible, spiritual, somewhat dubious realities of another world. The risk is great and should not be minimized. There is need for patience, encouragement, and above all prayer for young people. In God's goodness the veil of the mystery of His reality and of His presence parts at times during the Christian's life, and he catches glimpses of God and experiences almost tangibly, the blessedness of His presence, e.g., at First Communion, on a wedding day, at the birth of a child, on profession days, during a particularly moving celebration of the Eucharist. It is because of such moments that the risk of faith appears well-founded and most worthwhile. Such moments spark and enkindle a flame of love which makes belief both possible and a privilege. Love and belief can be considered as two aspects of the same reality, i.e., faith.

If the call of faith is heeded despite its risks, then we will have within young people the *metanoia* ("conversion") of which the synoptic gospels speak (MT. 4:17 AND MK. 1:15), i.e., either a complete change of heart in order to begin a new life or, analogously, a renewal of spirit by which a Christian rededicates himself to living his faith.

6. Faith Is Not a One-shot Affair.

The full commitment of faith is an action or an event which continues in a vital way throughout one's life. It continues to grow and to deepen in response to the progressive demands made upon this faith which is lived constantly and not merely made at one moment of *metanoia*. Christians continue to penetrate the mystery of God and their relationship of sonship to Him with each experience of contact with this mystery as personalized in Christ, the Risen Lord, actively present in our midst today within the Church. God not only makes demands: He also gives. In the personal drama of faith God both calls man and responds to him.

NOTE. This development gives a realistic insight into the elements contained in this mystery of faith. Hopefully, these ideas are already familiar to you as seniors. Your role now is to recall them rather than to learn them for the first time. If these ideas are totally foreign to you, then more explanation and discussion will be required.

Letter from a graduate to the President of Notre Dame

RALPH MARTIN, JR.

DEAR FATHER HESBURGH:

For a long time I've been wanting to write to you; ever since you restored my scholarship at the beginning of my senior year. I almost made it last year at Princeton when Father ——— was on his way to meet you in South America, but for a number of reasons it never happened. It seems just as well. In the last few months, in especially the last week or so which I spent at Notre Dame talking to priests, faculty members, and students, a lot of things concerning Christianity at Notre Dame have finally come reasonably clear.

I graduated magna cum laude, winner of the Dockweiler Award in Philosophy, and went to Princeton to study philosophy on a Woodrow Wilson. At the moment, another graduate student and myself have taken some time off to work with the newly established National Secretariat of the Cursillo Movement, located in Lansing, under the Episcopal Advisorship of Bishop Green. It seems that the movement is at a critical stage in the United States at the moment and we hope we can make a real contribution to it.

The first thing that must be mentioned about my experience at Notre Dame is that as I was exposed to the best that Notre Dame had to offer a student in the College of Arts and Letters, I grew farther and farther away from Christianity; it ceased having a practical influence in my life. I grew in intellectual ability and in creativity—exposed to the best professors, the Committee on Academic Progress, writing for the *Scholastic* and the *Juggler*. As associate editor of both publications, I helped build these to the point where they won national awards, and as president of the Wranglers, I helped make possible some of the highest level thinking and writing taking place among students in the university. As I did all this, the less and less did Christ as a person figure in my life.

FROM *AVE MARIA*, APRIL 16, 1966. REPRINTED WITH PERMISSION.

It must be noted that my experience at Notre Dame was with some of the very best Christian scholars and teachers there. It was a contact which became very personal and which has turned in most cases into deep and continuing friendship. Professor ———— did open me up to the wonders of Christian art and philosophy and literature. But with me, as with most students, it wasn't an introduction to Christianity primarily, but to art and literature and philosophy. And it had the deceptive quality of providing us with a Christian vocabulary which gave us the impression of living Christianity when we were only thinking and talking about it. Fr. ———— impressed us by "clearing away the intellectual obstacles" but he left to chance what filled up the clearing. Dr. ———— made me realize that "you aren't God" but not that Jesus Christ was, or what was meant for me. Fr. ———— made me understand the relation of political structures to the transcendent; but the term transcendent left things vague enough so that I could call a number of things by that name, some of which I suspect were a transcendent selfishness. Dr. ———— helped me understand Christian commitment and involvement and Christian moralii ˙ but not the source of them, not the living God who call. us each by name and knocks on the door of our hearts. Dr. ———— and Dr. ———— made scrupulous attempts to show how philosophy was not in conflict with Christianity—but somehow that left untouched and unchanged the fact that I was. Dr. ———— ended his course with a summons from Rilke to "change your life"—and many of us did, but not to Christ.

These are the small number of Notre Dame faculty who make a serious try at relating their academic discipline to Christianity. They cannot and do not transmit the Gospel message as it must be presented; they cannot and do not confront their students with Jesus Christ in the way in which they must if those students are to accept or reject Him. These men are doing a noble and courageous work; but because of the pastoral vacuum at Notre Dame, their effect on the students often is a distorting one—and the impression is conveyed that being equipped with a set of Christian categories is Christianity—that being concerned with the theme of salvation is being saved—that thinking about Christianity is doing it.

24

Those who were really thriving on the new Notre Dame, on academic excellence, seemed more and more to be focusing precisely on that; on the university part of Christian university. Many of the national fellowship winners in the class of '64 and '65—I know almost every one personally—are not practicing Catholics. In the course of four years at Notre Dame, my own Catholicism dissolved. In junior year I stopped practicing. The vitality and honesty of that small part of the student body and faculty in the school of arts and letters who were thriving on academic excellence seemed much more attractive and alive than Christianity at the university. "All the action" seemed to be in the academics, and many of us drew the practical implications and went where the action was. In my opinion many of the best students that Notre Dame "produces" are no longer Catholics by the time they graduate.

And the same thing is true of the mass of students, whose search for truth is less conscious, and whose rejection of Christianity is correspondingly less explicit. Each year Notre Dame graduates over a thousand persons, very few of whom have been personally converted to Jesus Christ, very few of whom the Gospel message has penetrated and transformed, very few of whom are concerned with making Christ a real part of their lives and work. A practical paganism pervades each graduating class. The practical axis of most Notre Dame students' lives is "getting ahead," "being a success"—not in giving witness to their Lord—for they neither know nor follow the Lord and they scarcely ever make Him their Lord. A sentimental residue keeps most of them going to Mass and confession; but scarcely any students have a regular and deepening prayer life, a reverence for God's Word and regular reading of it, and an apostolic sense and attempt to bring this life to others.

It must also be noted, as a fundamental datum, that most Notre Dame faculty members do not or cannot make the painful attempt to relate their discipline to Christianity—and that most aren't concerned with their students' salvation, as most of the professors I had were. And apparently, with the policy of hiring non-Catholic faculty members now in force, these professors are to remain a small minority, or perhaps they'll go elsewhere. But I want to emphasize that the question of the academic secularization of Notre Dame is an entirely different question from the one I think is the crucial one. Whether the faculty are seriously Christian or not, the problem of a huge pastoral gap still remains. Not even a very strong school of theology would change the situation very much. The effect on the students, I suspect, would be much the same as the effect of the deeply Christian teachers—ambiguous and often misleading. For there's a big difference between thinking about Christianity and doing it; and students need to be shown how to do it. They need to be initiated into the Christian life, into a Christian community where the life is being lived in a serious and appropriate liturgy, in a common life of obedience and faith to God's word openly discussed and acted on, in an apostolic community which is forming men into apostles and saints.

It wasn't until February of my senior year '64 that I was introduced to Christianity the way that I and many others needed to be introduced to it. It was on the second Cursillo given in South Bend that I saw for the first time a living Christian community; that I met men who had obviously placed their lives in the hands of God and staked them on the promises of Christ; that I saw the Mystical Body expressing and manifesting itself. The Church at Notre Dame always seemed to be a dying Church, and the Holy Cross order a dying order. On the Cursillo I met life and I could no longer deny that Jesus Christ was God and the most important person for all of our lives. Men taught me how to pray, how to read the Scriptures, how to bring others to Christ, not just in the three days themselves but in the months following. They introduced me to how it was to live the Christian life in common with others. Since then I've tried with the grace of God and the help of fellow Christians to find out who Jesus is and what He's saying, and to follow Him, obey Him—to change my life. And I can truly say that I am changing; I am being changed by Christ into the new person He wants each of us to be. And I have seen the same thing happen to many others—students, priests, townspeople.

Let me draw out the lines of the trajectory Notre Dame seems to be traveling; in the not too distant future Notre

Dame will no longer be a Christian university in any way other than Yale or Harvard are Christian universities — universities whose religious affiliations once were more than in name. Whenever I look at the chapels at Princeton or Columbia I think of Sacred Heart Church on campus and wonder if the day isn't too far off when it too will be a monument or a museum rather than the center of the university. Already it is no longer the center. I think it is undeniable that this is the direction in which the university is moving. It shows up in all kinds of ways: the practical attitudes of the great majority of students, of faculty; the values which are in fact transmitted to the student body; the falloff in vocations; the demoralization of so many priests. Notre Dame is becoming more and more like the pagan and secular modern world rather than asking the world to become more and more like the Kingdom of God. It's almost as if it were becoming part of the problem rather than contributing to the solution; as if it were gaining the whole world, yet suffering the loss of its soul. It seems to me to be a fearsome responsibility before God to be entrusted with 7,000 students and give them everything but the one thing necessary — for if they die and haven't been given what they need most — to be able to call on Jesus Christ as their Saviour — everything else which will have been given to them will have been given in vain. In the time between the Resurrection and the Second Coming what ought we to be doing? What have we been commissioned to do as disciples of Christ? What is it worthwhile doing?

There used to be a time when a student coming to Notre Dame was introduced, after a fashion, to the living of the Christian life. But processions, Benediction, visits to the Grotto, the rosary, and devotion to Mary can no longer do the job. Whether this is a desirable situation is discussable, but it is a fact. These things have in fact been swept away, and nothing is taking their place. A pastoral vacuum exists, and it seems that nothing short of working out a pastoral plan for the building of Christianity at the University can deal with the problem.

One thing that is necessary is an initiating instrument along the lines of a weekend program which will confront the student with the personal call of Christ to come follow

27

Him, which will open the student up to wanting seriously to work at being a Christian. The study weekend which was developed at Notre Dame over the past few years is one such weekend. The Cursillo is another, although it can't be the key piece in the renewal at the university because it can take only a few students, priests and faculty on each Cursillo, in order to maintain the whole cross section of society. The point is that an instrument is at hand which can open up students to want to begin working at Christianity. But two things are necessary if this instrument is to be used at all effectively—a pastoral plan and a movement of priests.

Briefly, a pastoral plan is a technique for renewal which coordinates the total apostolic effort in an area. It surveys the problem, analyzes their cause, takes stock of available resources, material and manpower, allocates the resources, and sets up a scale of priorities for implementing the plan. For Notre Dame this would mean working out a plan for the university as a whole—a pastoral plan—and working out a plan for each hall and for off-campus. The plans should be constantly reviewed in light of experience, and those working on them should meet regularly to survey the progress, discuss the situations and further their own formation in apostolic techniques and in growth in Christianity.

The movement of priests is also essential for the renewal. On the priests depends the success of deepening Christianity at the university. This means regular meetings—even on a small scale—of those committed to renewal, in which the priests form themselves into a community, becoming in fact what they will ask others to become, and in which they carry on their formation in spiritual direction, in pastoral planning. It seems clear that if Notre Dame is interested in renewing Christianity on campus she must be willing to allocate many more men and resources to it than she is presently. The likeliest thing to do would be to build up a core of chaplains who were free for full-time pastoral work and who were meeting regularly together. I know that the objection is raised that a chaplain at a university must have academic credentials and must keep up in his field in order to be effective with the students. I think that certainly a reasonable education in theology is necessary. But the students are looking less for academic credentials than for a man who can introduce them to God, for a man who is holy and who has apostolic sensitivity and dedication. The same is true, I think, of the move to turn the chaplains into professional psychologists; this is neither necessary nor advisable, and rather detracts from their effectiveness with students on the fundamental things. What the students are looking for is what we're all looking for, a man who is growing in holiness, a man who has, as it were, received his credentials from God.

These are just a few brief sketches of what I think could be helpful to Notre Dame. There is much more that could be said about what is necessary, specifically, if Christian renewal is to work out pastorally at Notre Dame. There is much more that could be said about what could be done in each hall to introduce the students into the Christian life; but I hope that this gives the idea that some radical refocusing has to be done if the students are to be drawn into Christianity and that the pastoral plan and the movements of priests are key techniques in achieving this. Both of these are recommended in the conciliar decree on the duties of Bishops—and I think that the situation at the university is parallel.

I tried to write an honest letter; but it wouldn't be honest if I didn't say I wrote it out of love. Both Holy Cross priests and Notre Dame have given me much; Fr. ———— brought the Cursillo here at the cost of much personal sacrifice. Fr. ———— gave much time to us novice Christians and helped us grow, and most of the work being done by the students around here to build up the Christian community is because of the inspiration. Fr. ———— became a very close friend last year at Princeton, and there are many others. When all is said and done, "There's something about the place." I hope this letter may have a small part in making this even truer. With a promise of prayer and sacrifice for you and for Our Lady's university, with gratitude and hope,

In Jesus Christ, Our Lord,
RALPH MARTIN, JR.

A REPLY

Participants: VERY REV. THEODORE M. HESBURGH, C.S.C., PRESI-
DENT OF THE UNIVERSITY OF NOTRE DAME; REV. JOSEPH HOFF-
MAN, C.S.C., UNIVERSITY CHAPLAIN; AND FATHER JOHN S. DUNNE,
C.S.C., PROFESSOR OF THEOLOGY.

Does the letter accurately describe the pastoral-spiritual problem of today's Catholic college?

FATHER HOFFMAN: I agree with it in substance. There seems to be a consensus among both priests and students on the pastoral vacuum, but
nobody knows exactly how broad or how deep it is. One point should
be made clear, however: there are really few students who are not going
to Mass on Sunday. The pastoral vacuum refers, I believe, to the influence
that religion has on their lives. They are going to Mass, but how many
do so as a formality?

FATHER DUNNE: I would say that the religion of the college student can't
be interpreted in terms of a simpleminded idea of faith, as straight acceptance of dogmas and the like. At this stage, a young man is going
through a transition, a developmental process. He is passing from the
faith of childhood, which is not really his own faith but that of his parents
and teachers, to a faith that is his own. And this process requires a personal search, a personal quest for meaning in life. It requires a kind of
gradual weaning from the religion of childhood and its practices and a
rediscovery of that religion in an entirely new context. This is probably
true of every stage in life.

So there is a kind of apparent agnosticism that you find in colleges, which
is not real agnosticism at all. I think that our students, and especially the
bright ones, are not agnostic; they are highly concerned religiously. What
they are going through is a discovery process. I think it is all-important
for us not to be impatient with this, not to hurry them through the process.
Rather, we should help them to do just what they are doing, to help them
find their own faith and not try to wrench them back to the faith of childhood, or to urge them on too fast to what is new.

FATHER HESBURGH: I think that college experience itself has a lot to do
with the problem. A university is a microcosm, a place where all the tensions of the time tend to focus. It provides a much more complex experience than, say, the family where you have the opinions of a father and
mother and a few elders. Here everything that is being voiced in the nation or in the world is being voiced geographically in a small area. There
are people around here who would voice almost any imaginable opinion.
The fact is, it is a lively place. Couple this liveliness with the psychological and cultural excitement, plus the long tradition of the university as

a Catholic center, with this experience of growth that Father Dunne mentioned and you have all the ingredients for a kind of crisis. The experience is heightened today because things are being discussed now which were not talked about with such clarity and frankness many years ago.

Another thing I have noticed is that, in times of crisis, the depth of the faith on the campus seems to come to the fore very quickly. For example, the first thing that happened when the word came of President Kennedy's assassination was that the church filled up, automatically. Nobody said anything. Nobody urged it.

I am impressed, also, when I say Mass in one of our residence halls. Maybe to talk about a pastoral vacuum might be to use the wrong word. We are in a time of pastoral change, certainly. New forms are evolving and new symbolism: the emphasis on the Word as against the emphasis on novenas, if you will. We are going through a period which requires enormous understanding between pastor and people, priest-professor or priest-rector and student. There was a day when I think if it were known that a body was not going to Mass, he would probably have been asked to go home right away. Today most of us have the belief that we have enough here to help him through a crisis. There is no place on earth where he will better find his faith, or reconstruct his faith to a mature image, than at a place like this. I think at times when people say there is a pastoral vacuum, what they are really saying is that they are not sure how the pastoral ministration is best applied in 1966 as against 1950 or 1940.

Q. *One of the main points Ralph Martin makes in the letter is that he felt, as he grew academically, he regressed in living Christianity. Is this another way of stating the perennial problem of integrating intellectual and character formation in the university?*

FATHER DUNNE: Well, I think in a university everything moves on two levels at once: the level of thinking and the level of living. This is particularly true in the humanities, and especially in theology. Though the teaching is overtly on the level of thinking, you can't get around the fact that the relationship of student to teacher is a person-to-person relationship, and so the teaching has a tremendous effect on the level of living, too. The spirit of inquiry that exists on the level of thinking becomes, especially in theology and in some of the humanities, a kind of quest on the level of living itself. This spirit of inquiry tends to encourage a search for personal faith, for "the way, the truth and the life," to use New Testament terms. I think this is really the beginning of mature faith.

FATHER HOFFMAN: I think it is remarkable that there are very few students —say, less than five per cent of the freshmen who come to Notre Dame —who indicate that they are coming here because it is a Catholic university. Their motive for coming is primarily to get a good education. They also express their desire for some insight into themselves, or self-discovery, and I think religion is a part of this. But they don't look upon the university as a place for character formation. Now the priests living in the halls, if they approach students from this point of view, see them as persons who are trying to find themselves. Whatever help they can give them in any way—just being understanding and accepting them in a situation of quest—this is really what the students want.

FATHER HESBURGH: You will always find, I think, that many people do look on Catholic education as principally character formation. They look at priests teaching theology, for example, as preaching, in a sense. This has been a constant tension in the theology department, which has always resisted this notion. The problem, those teaching in theology feel, is to teach young men how to think theologically, how to get at the roots of an understanding of the faith, how to create an intellectual formation that won't be overturned by emotionalism or by the fad of the day.

Q. But the letter seems to point up a kind of split between intellectual formation and Christian living at the university level that comes from the nature of the intellectual life itself.

FATHER DUNNE: I tend to disagree with this. Maybe there is a more fundamental issue here—about the nature of religion itself. Is religion something that can be set apart from the intellectual life and other aspects of man's existence? It seems to me that the very idea of Incarnation is that it pervades every aspect of man's life. In a university it takes a specifically intellectual tone. I would think it a kind of distorted conception of religion that would see it as clearly apart from the intellectual life. The kind of religion I am talking about, of course, is quite distinct from blind acceptance. As I mentioned earlier, faith is primarily a search or a quest, a search for meaning in life, and a discovery, in its highest stages, of that meaning in Christ. It is a response to revelation, not a blind acceptance of authority. When you conceive of it this way you can see how it can be incarnate in the intellectual life, that it can pervade the thinking as well as the living. But when it is conceived as just a blind acceptance of authority, then it appears as something quite apart from thinking, as certainly not helped by, but perhaps hindered by, one's thinking.

FATHER HOFFMAN: This kind of explanation strikes a very responsive note in the student himself. Students are, perhaps, somewhat reluctant to follow any particular form of devotion, until it becomes a part of them. You will find students who say: "Well, I may not be going to Mass as often as I did, but religion means much more to me." This is not just the response of one man. I can't help but think that this is the kind of religious education that ought to take place in universities. It isn't just that I know more about my faith or that I observe the Commandments better, but faith means more to my whole life than it ever did before. I think there is some indication that this is what many students want to experience in going through a Catholic college. The pastoral vacuum results from their not finding religion taught this way.

FATHER HESBURGH: There's another factor, I think, that leads to the feeling that there is a dichotomy between the intellectual life and Christian formation. At an earlier age in this country, there was an enormous emphasis in Catholic universities on moral formation and this was accepted by students and parents, at times, as the very meaning of the university. And perhaps it was. Universities were often put in the same category as seminaries. Certainly there has to be an element of moral and spiritual formation in the total educational process. But at the same time one has to always hold, as Cardinal Newman did, that the primary purpose of the university is intellectual formation, involving a philosophical and theological sophistication in the total teaching and learning process.

Q. Would you say, Father, that the search in theology and its effect on students that is taking place on Catholic campuses is happening also at state and nonsectarian universities?

FATHER HESBURGH: I think that generally across the country there is a complete revitalization of interest in theology, although it often will stem from curious channels. I find it difficult even for myself to understand many of the currents of what might be called "the new theology" and the "God-is-dead theology" and that sort of thing. I have some sense of why it is happening, and some sense of how it is affecting students. I suspect that it represents in its way the same kind of crisis we have been discovering in our way, because we are in a world of rapid and very vital changes. Personally, I welcome the change. I think it is a good thing, but I think it is going to take a lot of intelligence and understanding to keep it growing toward positive goals and not let it run down blind alleys.

FATHER DUNNE: Perhaps we ought to ask the question: can this search, this quest for meaning in life, go on within the Church, or must it lead one temporarily outside the Church? Perhaps it is the task of the Catholic university to witness the fact that the quest can go on within the Church, that the Church is big enough to allow for this search for meaning, this questioning of things within itself, and this is perhaps the very thing that is being encouraged by the spirit of Vatican II, the openness toward the truth and the personal seeking of the truth, and the development not only of personal faith but also of personal conscience. It seems that it is for the Catholic university now to show by its example, by its existence, by what happens within it, that the quest can take place within the Church and should take place within it. This is the normal personal development of the Christian, that he is not content to remain a child, to stick merely to a blind acceptance of the beliefs of his parents.

FATHER HESBURGH: It's something like what Tillich always talked about, the *ecclesia semper reformanda* (the Church continually in need of reform). The trouble is that in trying to institutionalize the good things that come from the Spirit, in the very institutionalization, you tend to deaden them. How do you keep reviving them? By the Church constantly reforming itself, constantly becoming more conscious of itself, and the human persons within the Church constantly becoming more conscious of their faith and its meaning in their total lives.

Q. Do you, Father Hoffman, in your contact with students as chaplain, find, as Ralph Martin intimated in the letter, that the Church today is a stumbling block to the brighter, more creative students?

FATHER HOFFMAN: Again, I think the Church of their childhood is, because this is the Church of their parents. I think that Vatican II had a special impact on brighter students. It is new to students to have a Church that might not be quite so static as they knew it. It's a new idea for them, and, as a first response, I think they like it. Just what it is actually going to be for them is uncertain. For I think the crisis of faith has been made more difficult for them at this time. As they leave their childhood faith, they are not sure what they are grabbing onto in this new Church.

FATHER HESBURGH: I recall once meeting a young Venezuelan Communist who was studying in Uruguay. We were flying from South America. He told me he had been a Catholic at home but now he was a Communist. I asked him what were the reasons or the beliefs that led him to leave the Church and join the Communist party. He was very surprised when I told him that every one of these beliefs were things I very firmly and fundamentally believe in. They all had to do with social justice. But he did not see those things reflected in the Church in his country at that time, therefore he left it.

I think today there are so many revolutionary currents going on in the Church that the leader or the apostle or the artist—the creative type—will find plenty to do just keeping up. All types of new forms are being created.

I think a Catholic who was used to the preconciliar Church found great comfort very often in having everything in order. He went through certain practices and forms. He felt there was no point in criticizing the faith he had, because it was for him a very real thing. He felt secure in his religious beliefs. Now he feels that that security and order is being challenged. I am sure there are many people, even on this campus, with the widest range of opinions about the changes. There are probably those who say we would be better off with the campus of the 20's than of the 60's. At least everything was in order, the questions were predictable, whereas now it sometimes resembles a boiling pot.

Q. *Is the criticism in the letter reminiscent of the judgements expressed in the early 40's by the people devoted to specialized apostolates of Catholic Action?*

FATHER HESBURGH: I would think so. The early people in Catholic action gave the other Catholic people around them the idea that they were rocking the boat, that they were doing something that lay people really shouldn't be involved in. Despite a vast wealth of papal documents on the subject, there was the feeling that these people were trying to be super-Catholics and that they ought to go back and pay their pew rent and be submissive.

Today, I think the young Catholic, particularly, is living in a most exciting time. . . . I am sure we will have movements, as indeed we have now, to go back to where we were. On the other hand, you get the other extreme of the spectrum where people want to cast off, to denigrate everything that happened in the past and embrace everything that's existing today in its most total expression. . . . But, it seems to me, the most exciting of all worlds today is the world inside the Church where there are many new realities to be carved out and many directions in which to go. There is great richness to be found if one is involved in this building. But while the building is going on there is bound to be turbulence and crisis following crisis. But the crises will be caused by people on the two extremes of the spectrum, not by those who are staying inside the margins.

Q. *Would you say that in the 40's the "boat rockers" were a relatively small group, whereas today they are almost the whole body of the Church?*

FATHER HESBURGH: I would think so, including a lot of Bishops and Cardinals. I recall running into Cardinal Suenens—I have some of my most interesting conversations on airplanes—and his opening remark was: "Aren't you glad you didn't live in the 18th century?" "This is such a wonderful age," he said, "so much is happening intellectually and spiritually."

Q. *It is said that today college students express their religious convictions in social action, for example, in the drive for civil rights. Is this true at Notre Dame? What significance would you attach to it?*

FATHER HESBURGH: There is certainly an enormously greater interest in social action than there was in the past. And I would say that this is not entirely a good thing. It leads to too much of a concern for action at a time when we should be laying the intellectual foundation on which this action is going to be effective. I think many of our most promising students—and this is not just here but across the country—tend to get seduced by the alluring action that is possible today for a student and tend to get away from the hard discipline and the long years that have to be spent to prepare oneself for a 40- or 50-year life of action. It doesn't help in the long run, I think, if students are distracted from what they can do only during their college years.

FATHER DUNNE: I would agree. But I think also that many of the students do express their religious convictions in their intellectual interests—in the things they read, for example, in existentialist literature, both the philosophers and the novels and plays, all of which are permeated with the religious problem. This perhaps is a very characteristic form which religious, or ultimate concern can take for someone who is engaged in intellectual work. I find this type of interest very intense.

Q. Getting back to the specifically religious question on campus, are we in agreement that the older religious forms—the rosary or processions to the Grotto, or Benediction in the evening—are inappropriate for students in colleges today?

FATHER HOFFMAN: I think that processions, and any kind of mass religious movement, are repugnant to students. In high school, and certainly here in college, they prefer smaller groups talking about religious matters, like a short conference and a discussion afterward. Again, they reject the old retreat, where a retreat master gives a half-hour conference and then everyone retires in silence for private meditation. They want to get involved in discussion with other persons. Fifteen or 20 can do this, and it is something very effective for them. But to join a crowd for, say, the rosary or procession, no. I think right now Benediction is not so popular because of the great emphasis on the Eucharist in the Mass. There was a time not long ago when you would have a priest ready to distribute Holy Communion outside of Mass, but not any more. Yet Communion during Mass, this is meaningful for them. Again, it is possible on occasion to get large numbers for a night of adoration before the Blessed Sacrament. But I do think that before the devotion to the Blessed Sacrament, apart from Mass, is not as much a part of student life as it used to be.

Q. You are providing new kinds of retreats next semester are you not?

FATHER HOFFMAN: We are experimenting with forms used elsewhere. There are at least three forms possible. One utilizes the facilities of our major seminary, where we take students who have expressed an interest in the priesthood. Here they will meet people who are involved in this vocation. Another form takes the students out of the residence hall for a few hours at night simply to discuss religious topics and thrash out questions. A third form is highly structured, the Christian Study Weekend modeled after the cursillo but adapted for college undergraduates. Here the work is almost entirely done by other students under the guidance of a priest and assisted by laymen. In all of these types there is an attempt to

36

communicate religious concern. Each form has the advantage of taking the student as he is now for the starting point. They attend Mass, receive Communion, talk and sing together, pray aloud or in silence. They develop a sense of Christian community, that is, one founded on the awareness of God's action on them as a group.

Q. *Would you say then that the heightened understanding of his function at Mass and the heightened experience he has in participating could be the key to a solution to this so-called pastoral vacuum? Maybe this vacuum is not as serious a question as the student is posing in the letter?*

FATHER HESBURGH: If you are going to have a pastoral plan, it obviously has to be tied up with some liturgical expression, because this represents whatever is new and exciting in the postconciliar Church. The lay person is not just active from the point of view of understanding his religion better, but he is active in praying better as a part of the total community of the People of God. You can say to students at Mass today: "Let's pray for the whole world," and this means something to them. They have some sense of what the whole world needs today, with all the vital revolutions going on in the areas of human problems and equality.

FATHER DUNNE: I think no one would have said years ago when the Grotto was strong and daily Communions were numerous that there was a pastoral vacuum. But now you hear the complaints. I suspect there is more here than meets the eye. We are in a transitional period in the Church, a period, as Father Hesburgh said, that is more of a pastoral change than a pastoral vacuum. And this period of change is, in a sense, a period of destruction when old forms are being destroyed and a period of gestation and creation when new forms are being created. Thus it gives the impression of being a vacuum. But I think this vacuum is the chaos of creation. It is the "Spirit moving over the waters" before God separates the light from the darkness. And this is necessary. We have to have this freedom and this destruction before the creation is possible. What lines the new forms will take is not easy to say, but as you can see a lot of helpful indications in the techniques of group dynamics, on the group level and the techniques of nondirective counseling on the individual level. The spirit of these forms is likely to be pastoral and liturgical. The kind of community you have at Mass is, as Father Hoffman says, a real community, not just people who happen to meet in church. The type of retreat, the type of homily, the type of spiritual direction, the type of confession, everything, I think, will be in this line, which is what you might call, a line of personalism or interpersonalism. It is very hard, at the present time, to spell out these forms completely, because they are in the process of making. And it would be a mistake at this time, out of a fear that everything is getting out of control, to impose some ready-made forms upon the situation. I think fear would be a lack of insight into what is really going on.

FATHER HOFFMAN: A recent issue of *The Living Worship* was devoted entirely to reports from parishes and religious communities that are experimenting with new forms. Much can be learned from these shared experiences. Maybe a particular innovation will work with one group and not with another. This freedom is not something which you can frown on. If the new form doesn't last all right; it doesn't last. At least they can try to express what the Mass means to them.

Q. *In reading the letter, one gets the impression, while agreeing in some respects with the criticism, that the writer is not wholly representative of the university student body, but that he represents a kind of "super-apostle." Would you comment on that?*

FATHER DUNNE: I think it is fundamentally a problem about how Christianity should be communicated. There are two fundamentally different conceptions of this. One is that you should try to get a person to accept Christianity as a totality at once, through a decision, a formal commitment to Christ, in which he attempts to accept the whole package, not only what he understands and what is meaningful to him, but also everything else. The other view is to give a person as much Christianity as he needs and can use at a given time, to use Christianity to help a person with the problems that he actually experiences.

I am not sure that both approaches don't have something to commend them. But in my own way of thinking, the second approach is the valid one: that Christianity is meant to save the world and it is meant to save the individual and that an individual experiences Christianity only to the extent that it helps him with his own needs, his own human problems.

I think then that the only valid communication of Christianity is the second way, that people should not be attacked with Christianity, but rather helped with it in their own problems. For young persons this means problems of maturing, of becoming a person and of meeting other persons.

For the rest, I think one simply has to be patient and let a person find his own way in his own time. There should be a respect for the integrity of a person's intelligence, of his conscience, and no more should be offered to him than what he can use at a given time. Christ Himself, it seems, followed this method when He said: "There are many things I have to tell you but you cannot bear them now." The other method seems to be an attempt to make people accept something and it narrows the number of persons to whom Christianity can be communicated. I am not sure that it helps people to be attacked with Christianity. There is a tremendous human desire for security, to settle for something, and one can seek that security for Christianity. It is much more desirable I would say, to search for meaning in life and to accept that meaning as it is discovered, as one recognizes it in Christ, and in the Church.

FATHER HESBURGH: There's a great story about the preacher who was assigned to a small parish in the hills of Montana. He arrived on Saturday and worked all day with great fervor getting up his sermon. On Sunday he stood in front of the Church and waited. Finally, one farmer drove up in his truck. The preacher preached to him for an hour. Afterward he shook hands with the farmer and asked him how he liked the sermon. "Well, parson," said the farmer, "I'm just a poor old rancher and I've got my wagon out here full of hay and I drive around the range all day and when I find some cattle I give them some hay. But if all I find is one calf, I don't dump the whole load."

Q. *In your opinion, have Catholic college administrators taken into account the fact that today's priest-teacher, because of academic demands, may and rightly so, be less concerned, in terms of time and even interest, in the spiritual welfare of the students than in his own academic interests?*

FATHER HESBURGH: I think one tries to. You get certain priests who, like Father Nieuwland in the old days, practically live in a laboratory. You don't expect them to be a chaplain in a hall. We don't assign people to be chaplains unless they have some time to give to it. I think it is possible for a priest to witness to the priesthood and in his priestly vocation, even in the area of knowledge, and secular knowledge at that. The Church's interest, I think, is in sanctifying everything; not just those things which seem to be in themselves holy or capable of being made holy. There are many avenues in which the priestly apostolate can be expressed. I think Teilhard de Chardin expressed a priestly apostolate even when he was out in the Gobi Desert somewhere with people on a dig.

SUPPLEMENTARY READINGS

Babin, Pierre. CRISIS OF FAITH. *New York: Herder and Herder, 1963.*

Cooke, Bernard, S.J. FORMATION OF FAITH. *(With study club outline and questions.) Chicago: Loyola University Press, 1965. This excellent booklet is composed of a slightly modified text of a series of television lectures.*

Kavanaugh, James (Rev.). "FROM APOLOGETICS TO ECUMENISM," *(An Experiment in Guiding the Crisis of Faith),* THE LIVING LIGHT, *Vol. 2, No. 1 (Spring, 1965).*

Latourelle, Rene, S.J. "FAITH: PERSONAL ENCOUNTER WITH GOD," THEOLOGY DIGEST, X *(Autumn, 1962), 233–38.*

Liege, P. A. "PROGRESS TOWARD MATURITY OF FAITH," THEOLOGY DIGEST, VII, *1959.*

POINTS FOR DISCUSSION

1. What is your personal idea of faith? In what sense is it a mystery? In what sense can we say that it is a gift? What do both of these ideas really mean in the concrete experience of human life?

2. Does faith have any relation to love? What are some of the characteristics of love which shed light upon the true meaning of faith? Can a person have faith without love? Love without faith? What supernatural and natural effects does faith have upon the person who possesses it? Can you grow in faith? In what way? How do you achieve such growth?

3. We speak of the act of faith as an act of a free man, an act which gives expression to his full use of his personal freedom in a way which liberates him. The following list of contrasting ideas can serve as a basis for discussion relating to this FREE-DOM-SLAVERY theme. Perhaps examples from Scripture, history, and present-day situations can be used to develop the ideas contained in this comparison:*

* The material contained in points 3–6 has been compiled and organized by Sister Francesca Clifford, O.P., from Houston, Texas. We are grateful to Sister for her kind permission to include this material in this book of readings.

SLAVERY	FREEDOM
UNBELIEF	FAITH
HABIT OF SIN	STRIVING FOR GOOD
FEAR	CONFIDENCE
DESPAIR	HOPE
SELF-WILL	OBEDIENCE TO PROPER AUTHORITY
LOSER	WINNER

4. *Discuss the following two contrasting statements in terms of faith, freedom, and religious practice:*

STATEMENT A

"Since there is no God, there is no law of morality; there are no objective norms. Each man is completely on his own; he must decide for himself. Other men can advise him; they can try to persuade him one way or the other, but none of them can speak with authority. Hence each man becomes the supreme arbiter of values. In choosing for himself, each man experiences a sickening sense of abandonment, for there are no standards to follow, there are no guides to help. Each man is his own; he is abandoned; he is forlorn. This is pure and simple freedom."

(THOUGHTS OF JEAN-PAUL SARTRE FROM EXISTENTIALISM, TRANS. VINCENT MARTIN, O.P. WASHINGTON, D.C.: THOMIST PRESS, 1962, PP. 20–21.)

STATEMENT B

"I am the way, and the truth, and life. I have come as a light into the world, that whoever believes in me may not remain in darkness. If you abide in my word, you shall know the truth, and the truth shall make you free. Without me you can do nothing, but he who believes in me, the works that I do he also shall do, and greater than these he shall do. Then your heart shall rejoice, and your joy no man shall take from you, for if the Son makes you free, you will be free indeed. In me you may have peace. He who believes in me, even if he die, shall live; and whoever lives and believes in me shall never die. Take courage, I have overcome the world."

(THOUGHTS OF JESUS CHRIST TAKEN FROM ST. JOHN'S GOSPEL)

---

5. *Discuss the ideas contained in the following presentation:*
"There is no victory without a struggle. Great love and steadfast faith are not gained without struggle and suffering, but it is in the very struggle that success and self-fulfillment are achieved. Christ explained this shortly before he gave us the example in himself. 'Unless the grain of wheat falls into the ground and dies, it remains alone. But if it dies, it brings forth much fruit. He who loves his life, loses it; and he who hates his life in this world, keeps it unto life everlasting (JN. 12:24–26).' *An explanation of this saying of Christ could be given graphically. Dig up a tiny oak without disturbing the roots. You will find that the root begins at the side of a cracked and completely empty acorn. You can probably find in the same ground a whole, full acorn, but with no roots or sprout. The seed that has died to itself, emptied itself, is producing much fruit. It has been fulfilled. The seed that contains itself remains alone, unfulfilled. From this example class discussion can follow on the meaning of Christ's words and the application to the circumstances of the present. Elicit instances of obstacles to faith and life situations in which one must choose to keep himself alone in his selfish satisfactions or give up his own inclinations in order to follow the will of Christ and bear fruit for his own and for his neighbor's good.*
"The Paschal significance of Christian life, therefore, is evident. Christ died in order to bear fruit for us, to be glorified in his resurrection. In Christian living the many lesser deaths, the struggles to overcome our wayward inclinations, are rewarded with a sharing in the glorious life of the Body of Christ now. The final victory of faith will be a complete self-identity, for then, as the Father says, 'Come ye blessed,' we shall truly recognize our-

selves as sons of God, brothers of Jesus Christ, worthy of sitting at the table of the Lord for all eternity."

6. Discuss the significance of some or all of the following verses of Scripture as they shed light on the important theme of God's love as a basis for faith:

WHAT GOD HAS GIVEN	WHAT GOD SEEKS	POINTS OF EMPHASIS
Eph. 1:4a	Eph. 1:4b	God's love for the individual, even
Dt. 4:34–39	Dt. 4:39–40	from the beginning.
7:6–9	11:1	Identification of present with past.
10:14–15		God's free choice to love us without our having merited that love.
Isa. 44:21–23		
49:8–16		Our attitude of loving gratitude. Ex.
54:4–10		24:7b.
Jer. 3:19–22		God's patience in extending his
Hosea whole theme	Hosea 14:2	faithful love in spite of human failures.
Jn. 1:12, 14		Jesus Christ incarnate as the visible manifestation of God's boundless love and patience. The extreme to which the love of God would go for us. Christ's being glorified in us that we might be channels of his love to the world.
3:16		
10:14 ff.	Jn. 14:15	
14:21		
14:9–11, 13	15:14	
16:27		
17:11b, 23b	17:10e	Consciousness of the need to reciprocate Christ's love by bringing Him to others.
20, 26	26b	

7. Does Father Milhaven's article, in your opinion, reflect an experience which is relatively common or relatively rare with Catholic teenagers today? Do you have any additional suggestions with regard to an effective approach in helping such young people regain their faith or achieve a deeper and a more realistic faith?

8. What is Christ's attitude toward the relative importance in Christian life of: (1) religious practices (Mass, sacraments, prayer); and (2) love of neighbor as exercised in daily life? Document your statement with material from the New Testament.

9. Answer this difficulty: "Religion is okay for people who can't cope with life and who have to retreat into another less frightening world. But, outside of reinforcing conventional morality, it doesn't contribute much to the making of a better world."

10. *What is your reaction to the article by Ralph Martin, Jr., as applied to your local school situation? In making a critical study and evaluation of the religious atmosphere of your school and the formative effect of your exposure to religious programs within the school and to its faculty do not omit consideration of your own and fellow students' contribution to the overall high, average, or low religious tone of the entire school corporately and of yourself personally.*

chapter 2
MODERN ATTITUDES TOWARD SEX
AND ITS ASSIMILATION IN PRIVATE LIFE

In this chapter we consider the proper understanding, appreciation, and assimilation of the beautiful mystery of sex, God's gift to men and to women, into one's personal life, within one's particular culture, and according to one's particular character. Through an existential, inductive, student-centered approach, students and teachers, working together, should aim at establishing the goodness of sex by God's design and to discover its significance in each individual's personal and community life.

At the same time it is important to note that man's sexuality constitutes only one part of his nature. Granted, it is a very forceful part which asserts itself in many ways and is particularly strong during the years of growth through adolescence; yet, this part of man's nature must not obscure the totality of his person nor assume too dominant a role in the development of his approach to life. Man, as man, is first of all a rational and volitional being; all of his other faculties are ultimately directed and governed by these noblest of human faculties in any responsible, human act. In truth it is their presence which makes man the most perfect image of God in all creation. Man is also risible (he can laugh at himself and others, at people and events); he is emotional (he reacts to people and events with love or hatred, fear or confidence, enthusiasm or disinterest). All of these qualities are intrinsic to man's nature and are mutually helpful or harmful to man's integral personality.

The nature of man in his present state is a nature which has been wounded by sin but redeemed by Christ. It still suffers today, however, under the burden of concupiscence, that mysterious power which is a consequence of sin and which can lead to sin. In no other area, perhaps, is the pull of concupiscence more real and discernible than in the area of sex (this certainly seems to be true in the case of most adolescents, at least). Recall the words of St. Paul which are particularly applicable here: *"For I do not the*

45

good that I wish, but the evil that I do not wish, that I perform. Now if I do what I do not wish, it is no longer I who do it, but sin that dwells in me" (ROM. 7:19–20).

NOTE: It would be profitable to review the treatment of concupiscence from *Our Life and Worship,* pages 335–37. It is essential to have clear and full understanding of this fact of life in order to make proper assimilation of the powers of sex into one's personal life.

A second source of particular difficulty comes from the pressure exerted by the very relaxed attitudes and practices regarding sexual conduct current today in so many different people and places. It is always difficult to swim against the tide and the tide of current sexual morality is certainly flowing very strongly in direct opposition to traditional, and even modern, Christian attitudes and values.

Any observer of the present-day scene who spans a few generations can report on the revolution in sex attitudes and practices which has taken place in the world and in America during the decades since World War II. It takes no great powers of observation to see how strongly sex makes its presence felt in so many areas of daily life. Sex and its attractive pleasures are garishly portrayed on billboards and in advertisements; it is subtly pushed as the sophisticated male's proof of manhood; it is shrilled from jukeboxes and peddled in commercials on television.

In recent years many different sources have written on the breakdown in current American sexual standards and morals. New codes of morality are being evolved and given wide following if not credence as well. Traditional Christian morality is ridiculed in some circles. The age of any objective morality, or of absolutes, has passed in the practical moral judgments of many people. Various statements of the new morality have been formulated in the present generation. Most of them subscribe to theories whose expression goes something like this: "If the majority of the people do it and think it is right, or if no one is harmed by the act in question, or if it is mutually agreed upon by those involved in the act, or if my conscience tells me that it is all right for me—*then it is all right for me.*"

The two articles which follow will present a rounded picture of current trends. The first selection depicts the experience of a young Catholic teenager caught up in the confusion of modern attitudes toward sexual morality; the second gives the critical reflections of a trained and experienced Christian moralist regarding the trend of these modern attitudes, and gives his evaluation of them in the light of his understanding of Christian morality.

The Individual at Bay

IN THE SPRING of my third year of prep school, at the age of sixteen, I had my first love affair. I met a girl whose beauty, passion, wit and sensitivity completely engulfed me. Our first encounter was at one of those innumerable Christmas dances that the subdeb set attended. For sixteen, she had a rather full figure and a perfectly groomed bell of jet hair, framing exquisitely small features punctuated by tiny, deep, incisive eyes. We met at subsequent parties and fell deeply in love.

I believe it is possible to become more completely infatuated with another person during the throes of adolescence than at any other time of life. During that period one has a range of interests which, compared with those of an older person, more travelled and educated, is much more restricted. At that time of life it is still possible to find another person who has the same interests and who views different facets of life in the same manner. Later, with an expanded horizon, it becomes impossible for any two people to find in each other so perfect a complement of themselves. It seemed that between this girl and me there was not a subject which we had not independently considered and resolved in the same manner. And we were perfectly adjusted sexually, though in retrospect, I believe she was somewhat more experienced than I.

The only impediment in our relationship was distance. She lived thirty miles away in one of the city's pretentious suburbs.

I had no car, and my father would not permit me the use of his. We solved this problem, though, by visiting each other on alternate weekends. One weekend she would come into town and stay with friends; the next weekend I would stay at her home as a house guest. Between these times we would write letters, sometimes two a day, as well as compose some very bad poetry. She tended toward free verse with monumental Freudian symbolism, while mine sounded, I suppose, like Edgar Guest with a stomach-ache.

As the weeks passed, we became more and more infatu-ated with each other. Our physical relationship reached an impasse; we had progressed through the usual necking into very serious petting; and at that stage we had stopped. Before discussing the possibility of going all the way, I suggested that we exchange a set of letters telling each other just what we thought of pre-marital intercourse, together with justifications for our positions. Our thoughts were identical.

The next weekend, as I took the commuter train to her home, I knew that we had reached the right decision, and was very happy that we had arrived at it independently. That night, after bidding good night to her parents, we retired to our separate wings of the house. I set my alarm for two thirty A.M., but didn't need it. At that hour I tiptoed through the house and gently slipped through her open, beckoning door. Neither of us slept that night, and with the dawnlight in the halls, I returned to my room. It had been the most overwhelming, the most beautiful experience of my life. I am convinced that nothing is more rewarding than making love, again and again, in every mood, in every state of physical strength, to a person with whom one achieves a complete psychological, cerebral, and physical rapport.

Sex was like a new poetic language; we were discovering new words and phrases and new combinations of old-word rhythms. The days between our weekend meetings became too long. My father ordinarily left his keys in his topcoat pocket. So I began borrowing his car late on Wed-nesday nights and driving the thirty miles to her home. Before retiring she would leave the front door ajar. I would park far down her driveway and, in stocking feet, climb the stairs to join her.

We always left her door open a fraction, to keep an ear cocked for noises in the rest of the house. One night her mother's door opened far down the hall. I quickly snatched up my effects from where they lay scattered all over the room and leaped into the closet. My heart was beating so furiously that I was sure it could be heard all through the house. Her mother stopped outside the room, swung open the door, and glanced around. But she noticed nothing amiss. After she closed the door again, I emerged from my hiding place behind the evening dresses. It took the better part of an hour for my heart to return to normal. After that it was no good that night; we were both too frightened.

Later, as I drove home at eighty miles an hour, I was stopped by the police. I had left home without my wallet, and so the police had to call my parents. When the officer told them that a young man, allegedly their son, had been apprehended in their car driving eighty miles an hour at five in the morning, my father would not believe it: he left the phone to check my bed, sure that I was in it. When he found that I was not, and that the car was really gone, he took a taxi to the station, settled with the police, and then wanted to settle with me. As an explanation I lamely said that I hadn't been able to sleep and so had gone for a drive. Strangely, he accepted this lie. Apparently no other explanation occurred to him.

But the combination of these two traumas spelled the end of the love affair. Apparently she was severely frightened by the whole situation, and saw continuing dangers in maintaining the liaison. Her ardor soon cooled, but mine did not. She deserted me, and I was badly shaken for over a year.

Beyond the loss of my virginity, the sharp, intense love affair had repercussions on my whole Weltanschauung. My parents are Roman Catholics, and since I was attending a nonsectarian school, they had insisted that I take religious instruction at a convent one afternoon a week. For one reason or another, however, I had not taken really intensive instruction in catechism, in preparation for confirmation, until I was about fifteen. But by then it had been too late; I hadn't been able to swallow the irrationalities and inconsistencies. When one is told to accept an incredible proposition on faith, the dogma becomes meaningless if one does not already *have* faith. The others at the catechism classes had been either converts, who were already blindly committed, or people planning to marry Catholics, who were completely bored. I, for my part, had raised objection after objection. When the dull young priest had consistently ignored my sincere reactions I had finally subsided, memorized the fatuous question-and-response answers, and had been duly confirmed in the Roman Catholic Church.

During my love affair I had not gone to Communion. This seemed necessary, for I sensed an unsolvable problem: I could not make a proper confession. I remember, about six weeks after the affair was over, kneeling in the neighborhood church for hours one afternoon prior to entering the confessional. It had been a long time since I had confessed, and I was reviewing my sins of commission and omission. But I became very confused when I thought of the recent affair. Though it was over because the girl had ended it, I was still in love. According to Catholic doctrine, I was obliged to confess my sins of the flesh, say I was sorry for them, promise never to commit them again, seek absolution, and perform penance. But I could not! I was not sorry for having slept with the girl: on the contrary, it was the most beautiful experience of my life, the most rewarding, and the most satisfying. It was the high point of my life up to that time and I could see no wrong in it. I conceived of wrong quite simply: harming others or one's self. That girl and I had not wronged each other or ourselves; we had given each other an almost mystical fulfillment, an experience of beauty and depth. It seemed not wrong, but most right! And kneeling there in the church, I knew that if she should have a change of heart and wish to resume the relationship, I would be at her side as quickly as I could join her. The Church said it was wrong, but I felt, I *knew* it was right. I entered the confessional and ran through my roll of minor transgressions. When I came to the real issue, I stopped, unable to continue. Sure, in a few words I could have sketched the affair to the priest, mumbled words of repentance, and walked out absolved. But I could not abdicate my judgment to Church authority, and would not lie to God and myself. In the middle of the seance I rose from my knees and left the confessional, outlawing myself from the sacraments, and placing myself outside the body of the faithful by an act of will.

I came to the conclusion that the Roman Catholic Church had failed me. It was not so much that Church doctrine did not possess the truth, though that seemed to be the case, too, but that it was irrelevant. It had created a problem for me that had not previously existed, and then had failed to provide an acceptable solution. From my catechism I remembered that one was obliged to accept the entire body of Church dogma; the corollary is that denying any facet amounts to repudiating it all. I then denied all. Because I could not go to confession, I could not go to Communion. As all Roman Catholics are obliged to perform these ceremonies a specified number of times each year, I thenceforth began to consider myself outside the Church, as I still do.

The Search for the Real

RICHARD A. McCORMICK, S.J.

EVERYBODY IS TALKING about "the new morality" or at least the need for one. What is it all about? It is above all about the need for a new sexual morality. Voices are heard from every quarter and competence. In their Public Affairs Pamphlet *Sex and our Society,* Lester Kirkendall and Elizabeth Ogg remark: "As the light of rational enquiry continues to illuminate sexual behavior, even in its most tabooed aspects, our society can hardly hope to enforce absolutist morality that is out of harmony with the findings of science." Dr. Ira Reise points out that "permissiveness with affection" (sexual intimacy permitted where engagement or a stable affective relationship exists) is the going standard *(Premarital Sex Standards in America).* A group of English Quakers refuses to make any absolute condemnation of premarital and homosexual relationships. They insist that "Where there is a deliberate intention to avoid responsibility and all possibility of being involved and committed, then evil creeps in and the act becomes mutual exploitation. But where there is genuine tenderness, an openness to responsibility and the seed of commitment, God is surely not shut out. Can we not say that God can enter any relationship in which there is a measure of self-less love?—and is not every generalization we make qualified by this?" (*Towards a Quaker View of Sex* as cited in *America,* March 6, 1965.) Joseph Fletcher, in an address to a large group of clergymen and students at Harvard Divinity School, insisted that the core of the matter is social responsibility and neighborly concern: "One enters into every decision-making movement armed with the wisdom of the culture, but prepared in one's freedom to suspend and violate any rule except that one must as responsibly seek the good of one's neighbor."

These are the surface gropings. What is behind it all? The obsolescence of traditional morality in the face of changing circumstances, say a host of divines. We are told that the old legalisms and conformisms will no longer do. We

FROM "TOWARD A NEW SEXUAL MORALITY?" IN *THE CATHOLIC WORLD*, OCTOBER 1965. REPRINTED WITH PERMISSION.

are told to put off the traditional absolutes as reflecting blind externality and Puritanism. We are urged not to feel guilty about sex, but to affirm it in a casual warm, bursting-with-life-and-acceptance frankness. We are reminded that this is the twentieth century in which new knowledge of sexual psychology has finally gotten through to us and toppled the old certainties. This is the age of personalism and positive valuation, the age of erotic know-how, the age of freedom, responsibility, inner growth and authentic relationships. This is the age of irreconcilable opposites: static-dynamic, love-law, liberal-conservative, biological-personal, open-closed. We can no longer afford the unthinking static-legal-closed-conservative attitudes which clouded the vision of our ancestors. These attitudes just do not fit the facts any more. Thus, as *Time* reported (March 5, 1965): "What they (progressive church thinkers) propose is an ethic based on love rather than on law, in which the ultimate criterion for right and wrong is not divine command, but the individual's subjective perception of what is good for himself and his neighbor in each given situation."

Those familiar with theological discussion will recognize in some of this a vintage product: situation ethics. These persons who object to situation ethics will insist that the Pauline freedom of the children of God did not intend to and actually did not deny the validity of absolute moral norms. They will point to a false oppositionism that the new ethical theorists set up between law and love — whereas adherence to law is nothing but the concrete and necessary expression of love. Concerned with validating the natural law as an obligating force even in the Christian dispensation, they will point out that far from being inhuman and impersonal, this "natural law argument against sexual aberrations . . . indicts them precisely because in them man succumbs to his own biological inclination in violation of the primordial inclinations of reason and love" (J. C. Murray, S.J., *We Hold These Truths:* 296). These opponents, will, in short, be much exercised with the time-worn and tedious refutation of the massive nominalism (as Karl Rahner styles it) of situation ethics.

And they may waste much time in the process. While the

current ferment in some circles may often reflect situationist ethical theory, it seems to me that the problem is more basic and much simpler: at stake is the significance of human sexuality.

At first blush this seems an absurd and ridiculous statement. Few ages have been so preoccupied with sexual fulfillment and the positive values of sexuality, so ready to affirm the relational possibilities of sexual encounter. Nevertheless there is every indication that our most basic problem does not directly concern the moral norms in control of sexual conduct; it concerns the very meaning of sexuality. The fervid vehemence of our pursuit of sex paradoxically reinforces the conviction that our concern is not norms at all, but significance. And if we are seeking significance, there is good reason to think that we have lost it to some extent. Specifically, I submit that our culture has gone far along the road toward emptying sexuality of genuine significance. This is, of course, quite a feat. The insignificant is always morally problematic simply because morality concerns good and evil and the insignificant is neither. Where significance disappears so do good and evil. Our problem, then, is recovery of the significance which alone validates any dictates in control of sexual conduct.

To say that we are unwittingly succeeding in rendering sexuality insignificant calls for clarification. Recent thinkers suggest that instead of a joyous but challenging expression of total personal commitment, total personal encounter in fidelity — variously mysterious, humiliating, frivolous, refreshing, playful, hallowing, dutiful, boring, etc. — sex has too often become a mechanized, manipulatable, tabulated, microscoped thing always on call. We know all about it: its incidences, its glands, its controls, its nerves, its deviations, its selling powers. There are hundreds of books telling us which button to push and how. As Leslie Farber noted in *Commentary* (November, 1964): "Our residence in the laboratory is recent: really only since the turn of the century has the act of sex been interviewed, witnessed, probed, measured, timed, taped, photographed, judged." The process going on here he suggests is that of objectification, a wrenching from human context.

This objectification appears even in our language as Farber trenchantly observes: "Qualities such as modesty, privacy, reticence, abstinence, chastity, fidelity, shame— could not be questioned as rather arbitrary matters which interfered with the health of the sexual parts. And in their place came an increasing assortment of objective terms like ejaculatio praecox, foreplay, forepleasure, frigidity— all intended to describe, not human experience, but rather the behavior of the sexual parts. The quite preposterous situation arose in which the patient sought treatment of ejaculatio praecox or impotence and the healer sought to find out whether he liked his partner."

First, then, there was objectification, a situation where knowing about was too easily substituted for biblical knowing. It was then inevitable that such knowledge should lead to greater dominance by the human will, and that this dominance should gradually assume its easiest form, mechanization. Thus, we not only have contraceptives, but we have pills and the IUCD (intrauterine contraceptive device) which operate with minimum tax upon human intelligence. We seek the perfect rhythm regulator. The controls are increasingly external and automatic. We have become the masters of techniques, the clinicians of quality precisely in an area where quality escapes the mere clinician. The euphemism "affair," "sleeping with," "going to bed with" reflect the ultimate cultural achievement of mechanization, casualness.

This dominance-by-will and ultimate mechanization means the growing autonomy of sexuality. Thus Farber, in discussing the laboratory experiments of Dr. William K. Masters on female orgasm, sees them as symbolic of our real cultural dilemma. For those involved, "sexuality would have to be autonomous, separate from and unaffected by her ordinary world. 'World' here would have to include not only affection but all those exigencies of human existence which tend to shape our erotic possibilities."

Once there is autonomy, there is depersonalization and decontextualization of human sexuality. Depersonalized sex is simply inhuman. It is mere coupling, and eventually arrives at the point where even coupling becomes an inconvenience in comparison with the swift assurances of autosexuality. Farber concludes that "over the last fifty years sex has for the most part lost its viability as a human experience." Such a reduction of sexuality to facility led Paul Ricoeur to remark that "it may be that tomorrow's greatest problem will be to preserve the expression and meaningful value of sexuality" (*Cross Currents,* Spring, 1964). And if it will be tomorrow's problem it is already today's.

Certainly these sweeping strokes represent a caricature. But the broad lines of the process of objectification-autonomy-depersonalization are sufficiently discernible to suggest that our characteristic threat is an increasingly dim perception to the meaning of sexuality. If human sexuality is gradually losing its significance for men, then of course, a new significance must be discovered in another world. Is this not precisely what is happening? The symbol par excellence of this search for meaning is *Playboy* magazine. It presents an unreal, hence a basically anti-sexual sexuality. It is far more than a publishing phenomenon; it is a cultural symbol which presides over the communications media as they aid us in the reconstruction of values.

Harvey Cox, a member of the faculty of Harvard Divinity School, has given us a brilliant and penetrating analysis of the *Playboy* motif (*Christianity and Crisis,* April 17, 1961). Cox shows that *Playboy* wants to tell us what it is to be a man, specifically a male in our society. It provides its consumers with a normative identity image and the means to achieve it. The ideal male is here presented as one "who savors sports cars, liquor, high fidelity and book club selections with a casual aplomb. Though he must certainly *have* and *use* the latest consumption item, he must not permit himself to get too attached to it." He is told what is impeccably masculine; what real men smoke and drink; what necktie is passé; what is cool; what is unforgiveably awkward. The most dreaded sentence from this dictatorial tastemaker is "you goofed." The criterion is always a sophisticated and urbane earthiness. Being a male demands a relationship to the female, and the magazine is instantly ready to define this relation with the same sophisticated formula of detachment. Sex emerges in its pages as an item of leisure activity, something which fits the area of entertainment-recreation. "When play time is over, the playmate's function ceases . . ." In such a notion of sex is a carefully departmentalized item. It must present no danger of involvement. It is an accessory, and like an accessory it must remain detachable and disposable. The really knowledgeable treat sex with characteristic detachment. Casualness is the cardinal principle. "Never get serious about it." The female presents total sexual accessibility but demands nothing from the observer. The ultimate formula for significance: sex equals fun. Mr. Hefner is making a tremendous effort to be taken seriously and it is a measure of our confusion that he is partially succeeding.

It is extremely interesting to note how woman (and through her, sexuality in general) has been developed into a packageable item for the consumer market. As the eminent moralist from Bonn, Werner Schollgen, has indicated, everyone experiences a craving to be taken out of the ordinary, everyday world into a state of exaltation. This is particularly true of the adolescent whose basic insecurity makes the never-never world even more appealing. Escape into the imaginative provides a release from the pressures of day-to-day worries.

Schollgen points out that this release can be achieved in either of two ways: by seeing the everyday in a context which transcends and sanctifies or by flight into the sub-spiritual. It is in this latter that one finds all forms of intoxication leading to the world of fantasy. The ego exercises omnipotence in this world, "His majesty, the ego" as Freud said. The barriers of time and place disappear; one reaches goals arbitrarily. Whereas in reality there are fellow men, practical repercussions, legions of obstacles, rebuffs, failures and in general the limitation of the earthly, in the world of fantasy there is only interior stupefaction. There is fulfillment without effort; achievement without work; there is no striving, no encounter with painful situations, no conflict; no development of coping mechanisms. There is only the swift buildup of desire and immediate, exaggerated satisfaction. Quite expectedly there is also the increasing tendency to resort to this world of ego-kingship in the face of challenge. And just as expectedly there is in the real world one notable effect: lack of growth. There is, briefly, unreality.

Benjamin DeMott has pointed out (*Commentary*, August 1962) that *Playboy* and its blunter sycophants achieve their effect precisely by a process of abstraction which ends in the world of fancy. That is, they present experience, especially sexual experience, in a purely imaginative way. The only substantial merging realities are: sexual need and sexual deprivation. By thus simplifying sexual experience, one produces sexual absorption. Every means is used to block out memories of reality and any knowledge which ties one to reality. The chief means in the campaign to simplify sexual experience and produce absorption is a continuing attack on the notion that with women reluctance is the norm, eagerness the exception. The magazines' subtle attempt, DeMott insists, is to create the illusion that women burn insistently and insatiably, and that this is sexual reality. Thus the "sex-bomb" is identified with the girl next door. They include the writings of recognized authors to reinforce the illusion that they deal with reality. Once this illusion is created, one is completely in the imaginative world. The "essential woman" of the communications media is the woman of the male imagination; she it is who is then established as the *real* woman.

Thus into the growing vacuum created by the objectification-autonomy-depersonalization process, a new "significance" is being injected. Its basic characteristic is unreality. Because it is a product of the imagination it can only be discovered there. Hence it can only hasten the flight into the fanciful and imaginative—and back to the age so thoroughly vulnerable to this flight, adolescence.

It is hardly surprising, therefore, that a culture which is losing its grip on the meaning of sexuality and rediscovering it in a dream world is simultaneously one obsessed with sex. For the dream world is the adolescent world of sex-obsession. Malcolm Muggeridge remarked (*Esquire*, February 1965.: "Never, it is safe to say, in the history of the world has a country been as sex-ridden as America is today." Was he not saying that never has a country so thoroughly derived the meaning of sexuality from the imagination? Was he not saying: Never has a country been as obsessed, hence as adolescent about sex as America is today? Was he not saying, then, in effect: Never has a country so thoroughly lost its grip on the meaning and significance of genuine sexuality as America has?

"Nonsense!" say the reconstructionists. With a bagful of quotes and scientific references they consign their critics to the no-talk, no-think Puritanism of the unenlightened and inhibited past. Puritanism? Yes, indeed. But the question remains: Who is the Puritan? Actually, the basic ingredient of the Puritan outlook was and is fear. This fear assumes different masquerades. At one time it will take the form of reticence. At another it is a noisy and gaudy exhibitionism. At still another an uneasy preoccupation posing as casualness. Because modern man is progressively incapable of recognizing value in sexuality and coping with it in the real world, of taking it seriously, he shows that he is deathly afraid of the genuine article. Of course he will hide this fear, even from himself. But it is there. All his protestations notwithstanding (indeed, precisely because of them) Mr. Hefner is above all the polished symbol of this deep fear, hence of this Puritanism.

One of the most reliable signs of such abiding fear is the matter of guilt. "Don't feel guilty," we are breezily told, "Accept and enjoy sex for what it is. There is nothing wrong with that. Sin? Ridiculous. We've outgrown these unscientific, inhibited and repressive attitudes." Of course there is nothing wrong with sexuality. (One even wonders how this is an issue. Is someone protesting too much?) Indeed, there is everything profoundly beautiful and good about it. And that is precisely why we dare not dissociate it from sin. But to deprive sexual conduct of the possibility of sin is to confess its insignificance. For when there is no sin possible, clearly nothing is at stake.

We often miss the point that there is absolutely nothing wrong with the idea of guilt, the existence of guilt, the healthy feeling of guilt if one has truly sinned. Guilt is but the affirmation of value and is a sign of the freedom and intelligence of the human being as he confronts it. To attempt to remove the possibility of sin from the area of human sexuality is the equivalent of the removal of intelligence and freedom from this area—hence the removal also of love; for without intelligence and freedom, love is a hollow word. We have come full circle and arrived once more at the depersonalization of sex. The attempt to maintain significance without admitting the consequences of significance is doomed to futility. The procedure is all very logical: where value disappears, so do good and evil, right and wrong, sin and guilt. Conversely, where I resist the existence of healthy guilt, I confess to the absence of intelligence and freedom, hence to the absence of value.

The most subtle manifestation of our growing blindness to value may well be found in modern ethical discussions such as those concerned with the "new morality." It is asserted that what are really important are "genuine personal relationships, authentic and responsible relationships." Of course these are important. No one wants to deny the profound truth in the fact that the moral life is largely constituted and judged by growth in personal relationships. Nor would anyone care to assert that traditional moral imperatives have always been properly integrated into rational thinking in the past. No one wants seriously to deny that the basic structure of right and wrong, the natural law, if you will, can and should be founded on and explained in terms of these relationships.

In insisting on the absoluteness of certain moral imperatives one does not abandon this personalist structure. Contrarily he affirms its sacredness. It is precisely because premarital and extramarital sex (*if sex acts contain any meaning in themselves*) does not represent the existing relationship and offer a guarantee of continuing responsibility that it must threaten the relationship—though perhaps in subtle, elusive ways impervious to crudely clinical and reportorial criteria. Premarital and extramarital sex must be interdicted precisely for what it is, and what it *is* will certainly have much to say about what it *does* to a relationship even though this may be beyond our immediate detection. Traditional prohibitions are negative statements of course. It is easy to miss the fact that they are asserting a value and a significance for sexual acts, and that it is precisely this value which is compromised by their violation. So, far from justifying sexual aberrations, the authenticity of the relationship rather confirms these prohibitions. Refusal to judge the relationship *also* in terms of its conduct suggests blindness to this value.

It also suggests naivete. Commitment and authenticity can be deceitful criteria, transparent only after the passage of time. The real threat of sexual aberrations is rarely seen before the fact because, as C. S. Lewis noted in his last published article before his death, erotic passion makes towering, impressive and irresistible promises. To the mature adult the characteristic of these promises is all too clear. The threat is rarely acknowledged after the fact for a variety of reasons, not the least of which is our innate reluctance to admit to error, especially if it involves confession of selfishness and immaturity. Human beings can, thank God, recover from their follies and build solid relationships in spite of them. But this admission does not deny the folly or make right of wrong. It is quite possible to achieve social responsibility after two murders and fifteen years in jail. But because the murders have led to irresponsible attitudes scarcely negates their unjust and immoral character. God has always been able not only to forgive sin, but to draw good from evil. But it is a mark of his omnipotence that it is *evil* that he is so often dealing with.

The new morality is above all, then, a struggle to recover significance. The apparent meaninglessness of the biblical condemnation of fornication and adultery, of the repeated assertions by the Church on the immorality of these forms of sexual expression, suggests not the need of new norms. May it not rather suggest our clouded perception of the values validating the old?

SUPPLEMENTARY READINGS

Cox, Harvey. "PLAYBOY'S DOCTRINE OF MALE," CATHOLIC MIND, 61 (December 1963), 10–14. The author gives a very telling critique of the "playboy" image of manhood by demonstrating that this image is really anti-sexual.

Oraison, Marc. UNION IN MARITAL LOVE. New York: Macmillan, 1958. This volume highlights the traditional Christian belief that sex has a truly sacred character and must be considered as a function of love. Severe criticism is brought to bear on the puritanical view of sex and on improper methods of sex-education. The entire book is excellent, but of special interest are pages 81–91 (importance of the adolescent stage of sexuality) and pages 101–5 (remote preparation for marriage: sex-education).

"SEXUALITY AND THE MODERN WORLD," CROSS CURRENTS (March 1964). The entire issue for this month is devoted to the exploration of this important question.

"SEXUALITY IN THE MODERN WORLD," TIME, Vol. 83, 4 (January 24, 1964), 54–9.

NOTE: In many current issues of major national magazines, some kind of article on this subject can be found which presents a detailed view of current sexual attitudes and practices.

POINTS FOR DISCUSSION

1. What is your over-all impression of the relationship between the young man and girl described in the excerpt from The Unsilent Generation? Was it love, infatuation, or mere physical attraction? Explain your point of view.

2. What kind of religious upbringing and instruction was given to this young man? How did it affect his religious attitudes and practices? Is he justified in blaming his situation on his parents, his religion teachers, and on the Church generally as it seems he does when he says: "I came to the conclusion that the Roman

Catholic Church had failed me. It was not so much that Church doctrine did not possess the truth, though that seemed to be the case too, but that it was irrelevant. It had created a problem for me that had not previously existed, and then had failed to provide an acceptable (emphasis added) solution."

3. Comment on the following important statements taken from the article making whatever distinctions and observations you feel are most pertinent: "According to Catholic doctrine, I was obliged to confess my sins of the flesh, say I was sorry for them, promise never to commit them again, seek absolution, and perform penance. But I could not! I was not sorry for having slept with the girl: on the contrary, it was the most beautiful experience of my life, the most rewarding, and the most satisfying. It was the high point of my life up to that time and I could see no wrong in it. I conceived of wrong quite simply: harming others or one's self." Although the author of these statements probably would deny it, had he or had he not, according to his own moral principle, done something wrong by harming himself and others?

4. Explain in what precise ways Father McCormick feels that what is really at stake in the modern sex revolution is the very significance of human sexuality itself.

5. How does Father McCormick define guilt? In opposition to some contemporary trends that wish to do away with all guilt feelings in the area of human sexuality, how does he establish the fact that such feelings can and do have an important and rightful place in our lives?

6. How does Father McCormick handle the key objection of the new morality which states that the only thing that is really important in the regulation of human sexuality is the existence of "genuine personal relationships, authentic and responsible"?

7. If sex is supposed to be something good and a gift from God to men and women, why is it such a problem for so many people?

8. How do you think parents, in raising and educating their children for life, can best fulfill their important role in leading their children through the various stages of proper assimilation of the powers of sex into their lives? How can religion teachers make a positive contribution toward that same end?

chapter 3
THE PROBLEM OF EXCESSIVE DRINKING AND OF OTHER ADDICTIONS

In most open discussions with seniors on this subject, there is usually general agreement that there *is* a problem with drink common to your age group and, even more so, to fellows and girls of your acquaintance in college. The problem may be great or small in different localities and under different circumstances. Basically most teenagers will see that the problem is not so much with drinking in itself as it is with drinking *to excess* and drinking *at this particular stage* of your growth to maturity. The consequences which can result from excessive drinking are becoming more and more known to you from the experiences of friends and other teenagers, from the sometimes bad example of adult society, and finally, perhaps, from personal experience.

After some discussion, too, most teenagers will admit that often enough drinking in itself is not the real problem; it is merely symptomatic of a still more basic difficulty or problem, such as boredom, tension, dissatisfaction at home or in school, curiosity, a desire for "kicks," or even rebellion against the adult world and society's conventions generally.

It is important for you as maturing seniors to face up to this problem and to inform yourselves concerning its various dimensions. Only then will you be in a position to make a valid judgment upon what you observe and learn in order to plan a *modus vivendi* for your present and future lives in its regard.

The purpose of the articles included here is to acquaint you with some of the facts regarding drink. In addition, your reflection and class discussion should include observations gleaned from current newspaper and magazine articles as well as from your personal experience.

The Forms of Drinking

RAYMOND J. H. KENNEDY, S.J.

AS PART of the Second Institute for the Clergy on Problems in Pastoral Psychology held here at Fordham just two years ago, Father John L. Thomas, of St. Louis University, participated in a panel which bore the general title: "Alcoholism and Other Factors." Father Thomas selected four categories of factors, which he called: Drink, Adultery, Irresponsibility, and Clash of Temperaments. To me it is very interesting that he used the term "Drink." He did not use the term "Alcoholism." It is also most interesting that the editors of the Proceedings of that Institute used as the title which tops every page of Father Thomas' presentation: "Marital Discord: Alcoholism." Permit me to begin by quoting two paragraphs from Father Thomas:

Drinking as such never appears alone in marriage breakdown. The excessive use of alcohol bears in its train serious consequences for the family. To be specific, alcohol in any form costs money, and its excessive use tends to hinder occupational advancement. It is not surprising, therefore, to find that drinking and non-support are frequently found together. Further, drinking often leads to abuse and physical cruelty. A good percentage of cases in this category allege drink and abuse as the main factor in the disintegration of the family. Another result of drinking is the association with doubtful characters of the opposite sex leading to the presumption of adultery. One often finds drinking and adultery linked together. At the same time, the excessive drinker tends to be a poor companion for wife and children. Although friendly when sober, his unpredictable episodes of drinking destroy the basis for true

companionship and render the wider social life of the family precarious if not impossible.

I have found that a good percentage of
these cases cannot be classified as alcoholics in the usual definition of that admittedly somewhat vague term. Rather,
they are periodic drinkers or "weekend-
ers" capable of holding fairly steady jobs.
Many of them boast that they have never
missed a day's work! However, some
spend much of their after-work leisure in
taverns with the "boys"; others act as if
they had an inalienable right to a "drunk"
whenever they felt so inclined. In some
cases, home conditions are such that the
husband remains away as long as possible
and eventually falls into the habit of drinking with the gang.
(THOMAS, 1958, P. 47).

Your attention is called to the fact that the word "Alcoholism" does not appear at all in those two paragraphs and
that the word "alcoholic" appears only once, and then in
the cautious sentence: "I have found that a good percentage of these cases cannot be classified as alcoholics"—
and he adds "in the usual definition of that admittedly
somewhat vague term."

The accuracy of Father Thomas and the nodding of the
editors points up the reason for this paper, whose title is
not exactly a happy one. I have not been asked to discuss
for you Scotch, Rye, Bourbon, Gin, or Rum, nor a Wine
List or Cocktail Menu but rather to endeavor to distinguish
for you those forms of drinking which can be classified
under the term Alcoholism and those which cannot. This
distinction is by no means merely academic, but rather
one of major importance in counseling.

Alcohol problems are often lumped together in the public mind with considerable resultant confusion. People think of pathological drinking and of getting tight at the Senior Prom and of drinking at all, for that matter, under the one comprehensive heading of "alcoholism." But the problems of pathological drinking, of occasional excess, and the possible problems involved in drinking at all, are very different and require entirely different approaches. It is a mistake to consider them all together, merely because they have one element in common, the use of beverage alcohol (FORD, 1958, P. 1).

It is my understanding that those who are participating in this Institute, clergymen all and of different denominations, are here to increase their competence as counselors, advisers, spiritual directors, and confessors. And it is basic in the field of alcoholism that we have defined in our own minds, as sharply as is possible with the present knowledge available, just what alcoholism is, and what are other forms of drinking which may be causing the difficulty which brought the counselee, client, or penitent to us.

With an interdenominational group such as this happily is, I should start, I think, by calling attention to the fact that the various churches have basically differing attitudes toward beverage alcohol. It is not my assignment here to assess, evaluate, praise, or condemn any of them, nor to defend or explain the Catholic teaching on this highly controversial subject. Whether your church is found in the camp of the Drys or of the Wets, whether you personally are a total stranger or an occasional drinker, in guiding souls you have the obligation to improve your competence as a counselor in this very important subject and your very presence here is witness to your desire to do so.

Meaning of Alcoholism
We begin then with the fact that approximately 75 million Americans, 15 years and over, indulge at least occasionally

in beverage alcohol. It is estimated that of these, some 5,200,000 have developed alcoholism. But what is alcoholism and what are other forms of drinking? Oddly enough, the second part of this question is far easier to answer with accuracy than the first. But let us tackle the more difficult problem of endeavoring to come up with at least a working definition of alcoholism and in the light of that definition, endeavor to evaluate other forms of drinking.

It has been said, not with cynicism but with obvious exaggeration, that there are as many definitions of alcoholism and the alcoholic as there are speakers and writers on the subject. The truth behind the statement is that our knowledge of alcoholism, though greatly advanced today over what it was a quarter of a century ago, is still far from the point where a truly accurate, scientifically established, and philosophically satisfactory definition is possible. Bear with me then while I propose to you some of the better and more widely accepted descriptive definitions which are used today.

Dr. Robert Straus, author of the study Alcoholism:

Alcoholism can be described as a complex progressive syndrome, characterized by the chronic uncontrolled use of alcoholic beverages and by various symptoms of psychological, physiological, and social maladjustment (STRAUS, 1951, P. 1).

Dr. Selden Bacon, Professor of Sociology at Yale and Director of the Yale Center of Alcohol Studies:

What is an alcoholic? Alcoholics may be distinguished from other drinkers primarily by the purpose for which they drink. Some people drink to fulfill a religious ritual, others in order to be polite, still others for a good time, or to make friends,

69

to experiment, show off, get warm, or cool, quench thirst, or because they like a particular alcoholic beverage as a condiment or because they want to go on a spree. None of these is the purpose of the alcoholic, although he might claim any or all to satisfy some questioner. The alcoholic drinks because he *has* to, if he is to go on living. He drinks compulsively; that is, a power greater than rational planning brings him to drink and to excessive drinking. Most alcoholics hate liquor, hate drinking, hate the taste, hate the results, hate themselves for succumbing, but they can't stop. Their drinking is as compulsive as the stealing of a kleptomaniac or the continual hand-washing of a person with a neurosis about cleanliness. . . . From this statement alone it can be seen that alcoholism and drunkenness are different phenomena. All alcoholics exhibit drunkenness but many who get drunk are not alcoholics. For example, a college boy on a spree or a member of a group which drinks regularly (and usually to excess) on specific occasions such as holidays, reunions, Saturday nights, may or may not get drunk, but they are not alcoholics unless their drinking is compulsively brought about by some inner need or an unresolved conflict (BACON, 1951, P. 4).

In the Manual on Alcoholism, *prepared by the Committee on Alcoholism, Council of Mental Health of the American Medical Association, Dr. Jackson A. Smith of the Nebraska Psychiatric Institute and the University of Nebraska College of Medicine, writes:*

Any individual who relies on alcohol to meet the ordinary demands of living and continues to drink excessively after alco-

hol has caused him marital or occupational difficulty is an alcoholic whether he
drinks only in the evening, has never taken
a drink when alone, or has not touched
anything but beer for five years (SMITH,
1957, P. 53).

The Subcommittee on Alcoholism of the World Health
Organization defines the condition as covering:

---

those excessive drinkers whose dependence on alcohol has attained such a degree that it shows a noticeable mental
disturbance or an interference with their
bodily and mental health, their interpersonal relations, and their smooth social
and economic functioning, or who show
the prodromal signs of such development
(WORLD HEALTH ORGANIZATION, 1952, P.
16).

Dr. Oskar Diethelm, Psychiatrist-in-Chief, the New York
Hospital, and Professor of Psychiatry of the Cornell University Medical College, New York, states:

A patient suffers from chronic alcoholism
if he uses alcohol to such an extent that it
interferes with a successful life (including
physical, personality, and social aspects),
and he is either not able to recognize this
effect, or is not able to control his alcohol
consumption, although he knows its disastrous results (DIETHELM, 1955, P. 568).

To these five definitions, I will add one more, not by a
sociologist, psychiatrist or man of medicine, but rather by
a moralist whose reputation and eminence in this special
field are internationally recognized, Father Ford. He offers

71

the following definition in the article on alcoholism in the Supplement to the *Catholic Encyclopedia*:

Alcoholism can be described as the condition of those whose excessive drinking creates serious problems in the management of their lives, and yet who usually are unable to stop drinking, even if they want to, without outside help.

Summarizing these definitions and adding a thought from that masterpiece of successful therapy in this field, the book *Alcoholics Anonymous,* I would say then that the characteristic elements of alcoholism are: 1) a pattern of excessive drinking, usually over a long period of time; 2) a physiological reaction to the ingestion of beverage alcohol which sets up a strong, even at times overpowering craving for more alcohol; 3) an intellectual obsession, present even when the person has no alcohol in his system, that life without liquor is either impossible or totally undesirable; and 4) serious problems of living.

It is evident, I think, that the condition spoken of by these various authorities, representing many different disciplines, is a pathological one which lies frequently within the competence of the medical practitioner, sometimes within the area of the psychiatrist, but always within the province of the priest and minister.

Father Ford in his pamphlet, Church Goals in Alcohol Education, *has written:*

There are millions of heavy drinkers whose use of alcohol exceeds clearly the bounds of moderation but who have not become involved in a degree of difficulty or degree of dependence which would classify them as alcoholics. They are an extremely difficult group to reach, partly, perhaps, because so many of them still seem to be getting more pleasure than pain out of alcohol. What can be done to reach them? We have a responsibility not only to alcoholics but to these other millions. . . . One of our goals should be to work out a practical program for reaching these heavy drinkers and bringing them back to the practice of sobriety. . . . It must be remembered that just as the total abstainer never becomes an alcoholic as long as he remains a total abstainer, so it is equally true that no truly moderate drinker ever becomes an alcoholic as long as he remains a truly moderate drinker. Obviously he is in greater danger of excess and of subsequent alcoholism. But it is not quite true to say that all alcoholics started as moderate drinkers. Actually all alcoholics started as total abstainers and some drank excessively from their very first drink. . . . I am convinced that it is the excessive use of alcohol itself which is the principal cause of alcoholism in any given case. It is the repeated toxic dosage that eventually results in alcoholism. If this is true, then prevention of excess, the mere practice of the virtue of sobriety, will result in preventing a great deal of alcoholism. This may sound rather obvious but apparently it is not obvious to everyone (FORD, 1958, PP. 3–4).

OTHER FORMS OF DRINKING

Apart then from the pathological condition known as alcoholism, the counselor or spiritual director should have clear notions of other forms of drinking. We hear the terms Occasional Drinker, Social Drinker, Weekend Drinker, Spree Drinker. We also hear of the neurotic drinker, the psychotic drinker, and occasionally we hear the term "Plateau Drinker." A few comments on each is in order, for certainly the advice to be given to one who has alcoholism will be worlds apart from that to be given to the others.

The Occasional Drinker

This term can be taken in two senses, first, referring to the man who drinks only on special occasions, such as weddings, christenings or when a toast is offered, and secondly, to the man who drinks rarely or, as we say quite indefinitely, "on occasion." Such a person will seldom if ever seek the advice of the clergyman unless both are members of a Church which condemns drinking entirely. It is obvious, I think, that such a person is not suffering from alcoholism.

The Social Drinker

This person has a drinking custom quite different from the rather abstemious drinker just mentioned. I would like to call attention here to the superb publication of the Joint Commission on Alcoholism of the Protestant Episcopal Church published within the past year under the title "Alcohol, alcoholism and social drinking." Under the caption "Social Drinking and Changing Customs," we read the following:

> With rare exception, drinking in America is a custom involving more than one person. Solitary drinking is outside the limits of the custom and does not come within the definition of social drinking. Customs of this sort, requiring interpersonal behavior, must, if they are to persist, carry mutual rewards to the participants. In other words, if drinking is to be social, then the drinking by Mr. Jones must be rewarding to Mr. Smith and the drinking by Mr. Smith must be rewarding to Mr. Jones. The fact that Mr. Jones finds relaxation or a feeling of happiness from his drinking is secondary and almost irrelevant to this social function. . . .
>
> This view may help one judge the degree of "socialness" in a drinking situation. If the drinking by one person in the two or ten drinking together does not reward but even renders anxious one or more of the others, then to that degree the social char-

acter of the drinking is reduced. The party or the group is then tending to become a number of non-integrated persons, each involved in individualistic drinking practices. Drinking that occurs in a group is not necessarily social drinking.

It is also true with occasional exceptions that the drinking custom in America is connected with some other social activity which is primary to the interests of the drinking group. Ordinarily people who drink do so at a wedding, at a meal, when greeting a friend, at a party, after a meeting, or with some other leisure-time activity. In these instances the drinking is definitely secondary. In other words the function to be served, whether it is celebrating or eating or commiserating or playing, is the major function and it could be achieved, though perhaps not with such rewards for these persons, if no drinking occurred at all. . . . On the American scene drinking as the central purpose and the main function of a gathering may be viewed, with rare exception, as a deviation from custom. But customs change, and persons with a Christian concern for alcohol problems may well ask themselves if the customs of using alcoholic beverages in America are tending to change from a secondary position to a primary one. For example, is the cocktail offered prior to a business luncheon becoming the major item of that luncheon instead of an introduction? At an evening party at home for relaxation with friends, is the host becoming more and more of a bartender, continuously and anxiously filling all glasses during the party and urging one last libation at the time of departure so that he hardly completes a conversation and at the evening's end has found no relaxation at all? When friends gather together, is fishing, golfing, bowling, dancing, or listening to music the main purpose for the occasion, or is drinking being pushed forward to the point where it starts earlier, where it readily interrupts the previously major function, or where, if it were omitted, the joint activity would be considered a failure? When asking the question "What is social drinking?" it is useful to keep in mind the relative importance of alcoholic beverages to these and other similar social customs. It is not enough to state that offering cocktails to people coming to one's home for dinner is "social drinking." One must also state the degrees of purpose, of duration, of amounts, of timing, of emotional investment by participants, even of cost, and of many other aspects of the drinking in comparison to other concurrent activities of the gathering. If, as seems the case to many observant Americans, the custom of drinking is changing, then the opinion one might have held about social drinking twenty or one hundred years ago is hardly pertinent to the current situation (Protestant Episcopal Church, 1958, pp. 13–15).

Certainly, regardless of our ecclesiastical affiliation, all of us should feel gratitude to the Joint Commission of the Episcopal Church for this excellent statement. I would strongly urge all participants in this Institute to obtain a copy of this publication. All counselors, spiritual directors and confessors will profit by its attitudes and suggestions.

Father Ford has expressed deep concern about our American drinking customs:

Education in true moderation would help to change some of the dangerous drinking customs which exist in this country. A degree of excess which is definitely contrary to the virtue of sobriety, and would be excluded even by social standards of good taste and civility in other parts of the world is still socially acceptable and rather taken for granted in many circles here. The immature search for excitement, thrills and the more violent effects of alcohol has, in the opinion of many, a causative relation to our high rate of alcoholism. Our social customs sanction or at least tolerate the habitual use of an easily available chemical in toxic quantities. The medical scientists tell us that such customs are incompatible with sound bodily and mental hygiene. The theologians tell us that such customs are incompatible with the practice of the Christian virtue of sobriety. There is remarkable agreement between the principles of hygiene and the principles of morality. Here we have an immense and fertile field for religious education (FORD, 1958, P. 5).

The Weekend Drinker

When we come to the Weekend Drinker and the Spree Drinker, we are beginning to approach once more the area of alcoholism, if not actual, at least potential (or, to put it less technically, if not obvious, at least suspicious). Through the research done at the Yale Center and through many excellent popular publications of the National Council on Alcoholism, it is a fact becoming more and more widely known that the vast majority of the alcoholics of America are still working and living with their families. Their alcoholism has not advanced sufficiently as yet to have cost them the loss of their jobs, their homes, their families. They comprise the many thousands of "Monday Absentees" who so plague our industries today and they have been referred to in many lectures and articles as "The Hidden Alcoholic" and "The Half-Man in Industry." On both the executive and the labor levels they are the men who start their drinking on Friday afternoon or evening, and maintain it, with varying rates, over Saturday and Sunday. As this pattern continues and progresses (as it inevitably does, if true alcoholism is developing), Monday absenteeism begins to appear, of if they report to the plant or office, their efficiency is so lowered and impaired that they might as well have been absent. The term Weekend Drinker almost always means excessive drinking and (particularly if there is some underlying personality problem present also), the Weekend Drinker can usually be properly suspected of being at least in the pre-alcoholic phase of alcoholism, if not already in its early stages.

The Spree Drinker
Oddly enough, the Spree Drinker may be in an entirely different situation. Obviously, the Weekend Drinker is a Spree Drinker, in a sense, but this latter term is usually applied to those whose pattern of drinking is quite different. They remain drunk for days at a time, and then, sobering up on their own, return to normal living. They usually are impulsive personalities, not infrequently moody, who show an immaturity of emotional development in that they cannot make a normal adjustment to unusual situations. They get drunk deliberately, and so, cannot be excused of guilt, and they rationalize their episodes with such fatuous statements as "Every man is entitled to a drunk once in a while." Though they offer a problem to themselves, their families, and their employers, it is usually merely a problem of patience with an otherwise hardworking man of normal habits. The danger of developing alcoholism is always there, particularly because of their personality maladjustments, and the spiritual advisers should warn them of it, in addition to calling attention to their sin of excess and the consequent injustice and suffering which they inflict on their fellow-workers, on whatever level, as well as on their families and dependents.

The Neurotic and Psychotic Drinker
The Neurotic and Psychotic Drinkers pose special problems. The former in that the spiritual director or counselor should be adept enough to recognize a neurotic condition when he is confronted with it, and if he finds the neurosis

such that it is beyond his competence, he should make the proper referral to a trustworthy psychiatrist. The psychotic, of course, is entirely beyond his competence and should receive medical and psychiatric care at once. In both cases, should there be a drinking problem the advance toward true alcoholism is almost inevitable.

The Plateau Drinker
This is a relatively new term in the field of alcohol problems, but one which has a very real meaning which should be clearly understood by all counselors and spiritual directors. It is a known fact today that most of the habitués of the Skid Rows of our great cities are Plateau Drinkers and not alcoholics. These are those unfortunate individuals frequently referred to as "social misfits," insufficient personalities who have adopted Skid Row as a way of life. They cannot face the realities of life without the anaesthetic effect of alcohol and have developed a technique whereby they can bring themselves to a semi-intoxicated state and maintain that state throughout their waking hours. They rarely, if ever, have a bad hangover, and are, even less rarely, completely drunk. Theirs is a state of being constantly "high," frequently "tight," but seldom drunk. Theirs is a state for which the true alcoholic longs but can never attain. They have no family or employment problems for the obvious reason that they have no family or employment. Panhandling is their practice, Welfare their Utopia. How many real alcoholics learning of their proficiency have sighed "They have it made!" They are known to get deliberately drunk with the advent of the first frost so that they might get heat, board, and lodging for the winter months at city or county expense, and they usually end their relatively placid days in the city or county home, where, their need for mingling with the normal population being absent, they spend a pleasant old age in the understanding fellowship of their peers. From a counseling point of view, they offer no problem for they never come for spiritual direction or advice, or if they do, it is for a rather obvious ulterior motive at the Salvation Army or the Rescue Mission. Otherwise "the man in black" meets them only with hands outstretched. I merely commend these unfortunate yet placid souls to your kindly prayers. Should any of the participants in this Institute desire further informa-

tion on this point, a wealth of material can be obtained from the Homeless Man Committee of the National Council on Alcoholism and from the studies which are published occasionally in Yale's *Quarterly Journal of Studies on Alcohol.*

A rather interesting and somewhat unusual example of the Plateau Drinker is in the employ of a Catholic religious house of my acquaintance. The man in question works alone there in the laundry, and has charge of the washing and ironing of all the linens, domestic and personal, of the thirty priests who reside there. For the five years of his employment he has never been drunk, never sober. He puts in a rather easy day's work, due to modern washing and ironing equipment and throughout the day maintains his placid way by regular drafts of wine. He has come to the state that he feels he cannot work or live without this; he has his steady job, his furnished room, his blessed bachelorhood, and never reflects on the futility of his life. There has been no progression in his drinking habits; he is no problem to himself or others; he smiles his pleasant smile through his alcoholic haze and does satisfactorily the work for which he is employed. What a blessing that a kindly Providence did not give him an analytic mind to apply to his own condition or he might have taken his own life years ago! Dr. Jellinek of the World Health Organization has suggested that the Plateau Drinkers be classified as "habitual symptomatic excessive drinkers" and clearly distinguishes them from "addictive drinkers."

Returning now, full cycle, to the man who has alcoholism, it is obvious, I hope, that he is the only addictive drinker in the group. It follows as a corollary, then, that the technique of the counselor will differ entirely in his case from the approach to be used with all the others.

SUMMARY
Summarizing, I would say that Problem Drinkers fall into three general categories: the alcoholic, the plateau drinker, and the others. The techniques to be used with these others are known to all of us. Primarily the help to be offered them is spiritual and the proven use of the pledge is certainly in order, making, of course, the usual allow-

ances and taking the usual precautions of prudence. For the Plateau Drinker little can be done, since he is perfectly satisfied with his state and will rarely seek any spiritual advice or rehabilitation. But with the man who has or is developing alcoholism, a very specialized type of approach is required. Exhortation, scolding, threats, and pointing out the great harm which the drinker is doing and has done to himself, his family and his job—all these are not only out of place but positively dangerous. They lead the person to further drinking. The pledge has no place here at all. The immediate goal in therapy here is recognition of the fact that he *has* alcoholism. Yet, oddly enough, no one can point out that fact, so obvious to all others, to the alcoholic himself. There must be a process of self-diagnosis. For this an extremely useful tool for the clergyman has been worked out by a priest of the Diocese of Rochester, which he calls "The Priest's Do-It-Yourself Kit for Alcoholic Counseling." The kit contains a transcript of a lecture on alcoholism written by a doctor who is a specialist in this field, together with a step-by-step procedure for the counselor to follow in his interview with the alcoholic. I most strongly urge all participants of this Institute to obtain a copy (Collins, 1957). The steps in this procedure are: first, self-diagnosis of alcoholism; second, frank admission of the condition; and third, a sincere desire to do something about it. With these three steps behind him, the alcoholic is usually well on his way to rehabilitation and a life of happy sobriety.

Permit me to conclude this presentation with one more quotation. In the beautiful surroundings of the White Mountains of New Hampshire there assembles every June a group of clergymen of all denominations for the North Conway Institute on Problems of Alcohol and Alcoholism. Each year the group issues a statement of their conclusions and convictions concerning the subject of that particular Institute. Two weeks ago the Institute discussed the topic: "Pastoral Care of Alcoholics and Their Families" and I am sure it will be of great interest, possibly a real inspiration, for the participants of our Institute to hear a paragraph or two from this year's statement which was subscribed to by 69 men and women, clergy and laymen representing Catholic, Jewish, and thirteen Protestant groups from all over the United States and Canada. The statement reads, in part, as follows:

Whether alcoholism be called disease, sickness, addiction, social problem, or sin, it demands attention. Recognition of the reality of the situation and effective means of meeting it are imperative, far more important than terminology because alcoholics and their families are worthy of compassion and in desperate need of help. . . . We have discovered that whether we believe it right or wrong to drink, we are agreed that alcoholism presents a special problem and that the alcoholic suffers from a situation from which he cannot escape without help. We can, therefore, regardless of our ecclesiastical ties, work together in our communities to provide hope and help for the alcoholic and the members of his family. We have learned that our congregations and clergy can effectively provide much of what the alcoholic and his family need. . . .

The ministry of the church and synagogue is not limited to counseling but includes the utilization of all their resources — worship, the sacraments or religious duties, preaching, exposition of the Scriptures, the fellowship of the congregation, and pastoral visitation — for the assistance of the alcoholic and his family. Responsibility for providing hope and help for the alcoholic and his family does not, however, rest solely on the church and synagogue. Alcoholism is a community problem, and part of the function of the clergyman is to stimulate community action where it is lacking and support its maintenance and extension where it exists. . . .

> We recommend that clergymen assist in
> the formation of work with local commit-
> tees on alcoholism. Pastor and rabbi can
> work with Alcoholics Anonymous, the
> most effective of all the ways in which
> alcoholics are being helped, and with the
> Al-Anon Groups, which provide similar
> assistance for families of alcoholics, al-
> ways respecting the anonymity of their
> members, and we urge that parish houses
> and church buildings be made available
> wherever desired for A.A. and Al-Anon
> group meetings. . . . (NORTH CONWAY FOUN-
> DATION, 1959, PP. 1–2).

In the name of all who are active in this fascinating field
whether in research, therapy, or education it is most encouraging to find such institutes as these for clergymen
of all denominations multiplying in so many parts of our
country. I conclude by quoting once again from this year's
North Conway statement:

> As we respond to God's love for us by love
> for and service to all men, we of the church
> and synagogue must include in our con-
> cern the alcoholic and his family. Because
> a primary need of the alcoholic is aware-
> ness of God's love for him, we have a
> special responsibility to minister in God's
> name to him (NORTH CONWAY FOUNDATION,
> 1959, P. 1).

REFERENCES

Bacon, S. D. *Alcoholism, nature of the problem.* New Haven: Yale
Center of Alcohol Studies, 1951.

Collins, V. *The Priest's Do-It-Yourself Kit for Alcoholic Counseling.* Hornell, N. Y.: Hornell Committee for Education on Alcoholism, 1957.

Diethelm, O. Current research on problems of alcoholism. VI.
Report of the Section on Psychiatric Research. *Quart. J. Stud.
Alcohol,* 1955, 16,565–574.

Ford, J. C. (S.J.) *Church Goals in Alcohol Education.* Concord, N. H.: New Hampshire State Department of Health, Division on Alcoholism, 1958, Publ. No. 21.

North Conway Foundation. *Statement of the Fifth Annual Institute.* North Conway, N. H.: North Conway Foundation, 1959.

Protestant Episcopal Church, Joint Commission on Alcoholism. *Alcohol, Alcoholism, and Social Drinking.* Greenwich, Conn.: Seabury, 1958.

Smith, J. A. "Psychiatric Treatment of the Alcoholic." In American Medical Association, Council on Mental Health, Committee on Alcoholism, *Manual on Alcoholism.* Chicago: American Medical Association, 1957.

Straus, R. *Alcoholism.* New Haven: Yale Center of Alcohol Studies, 1951.

Thomas, J. L. (S.J.) Factors in marital discord: alcoholism and other factors. In W. C. Bier, S.J. & A. A. Schneiders (Eds.) *Proceedings: Second Institute for the Clergy on Problems in Pastoral Psychology.* New York: Fordham Univer., 1958, 45–51.

World Health Organization, Expert Committee on Mental Health, Alcoholism Subcommittee. Second report. *World Hlth. Org.* tech. Rep. Ser., 1952, No. 48.

"Booze and You"

THIS CHAPTER is not going to be a sermon on the horrors of alcohol. Each of us knows dozens of respectable people who drink and enjoy it. Liquor has never been a problem to those people, and it never will be. They have never lost a day's work because of drinking — although an occasional hangover may have made them wish they had put the cork back in the bottle a few drinks earlier.

These respectable social drinkers live useful and productive lives. And they will probably die of natural causes without having seen even one pink elephant.

From the beginning of recorded history man has used alcohol. Using certain roots and herbs, or berries and fruit, he found that through fermentation he could produce a liquid which made him "feel pretty good." This elixir was believed to possess magical powers because those who drank it behaved as if they were under a spell. It was used primarily in religious ceremonies to drive out evil spirits.

After a while people began to work up their own little mixtures for personal use. Obviously, the idea caught on, because in 1962 (in the United States alone) more than five billion dollars was spent on hard liquor.

Let's face it. Liquor is here to stay. For those who hoped otherwise, the signal rang out loud and clear when the Prohibition Act of 1920 laid one of the biggest social eggs in history.

The Eighteenth Amendment, forbidding the manufacture and sale of intoxicating beverages (except for medicinal and sacramental purposes), did not change people's drinking habits. It drove people underground. They couldn't drink legally, so they drank illegally. "Moonshine" by the barrel was manufactured in backyard stills. Bathtub gin was downright fashionable. Thousands of people went blind from wood alcohol.

FROM *ANN LANDERS TALKS TO TEEN-AGERS ABOUT SEX*. COPYRIGHTED BY PRENTICE-HALL, INC., 1963. REPRINTED WITH PERMISSION.

The Prohibition Act fathered a billion-dollar business, bootlegging. Rival gangs pumped each other full of lead, and many a rum-runner wound up at the bottom of a river —wearing a cement kimono.

The sale of liquor was clearly against the law, but everybody knew where to get a bottle, or a couple of jiggers of Scotch served in a coffee cup. Finally, our Legislative leaders were forced to concede that Prohibition was a national joke. Not only did Prohibition fail to reduce drinking, but probably it had increased it. A new attraction had been introduced—glamour. Americans who otherwise would not have dreamed of getting drunk were lured into speakeasies "just for the heck of it—it might be exciting."

In 1933, to the surprise of few Americans, Prohibition was repealed. The electorate decided that in a free country people have the right to get slopped to the eyeballs if they want to—that it is both undemocratic and impossible to dictate to adults what they may or may not drink. The Eighteenth Amendment was repealed, and the bootleggers had to go back to legitimate work.

Although the sale of liquor to minors is still illegal, every high school kid knows how and where to get it. So, like every other question that involves human behavior, to drink or not to drink must be resolved at the personal level. Each of us must decide for himself what to do about it. People who lead well-ordered and productive lives think ahead. They anticipate situations and problems, and they decide in advance how these situations and problems will be met. If you have some vague, half-baked notions about whether to drink or not to drink, it is likely that you will fall victim to your own indecisiveness.

It would be unrealistic to write a book on teen-agers and sex and ignore drinking, when thousands of teen-agers have told me that liquor was one of the major causes of their sexual involvements.

Before we explore the effects of alcohol on the personality let's examine some of the evidence that tells us what alcohol does to the body. Moderate drinking (and by moderate I mean two or three drinks on a Saturday night) will have no permanent, damaging effect on a normal, healthy person. Two drinks may interfere with vision and coordination just enough to cause a serious auto accident, but this is a different matter.

Moderate drinking will not rot the liver, the stomach or the kidneys, nor will it lead to deterioration of the brain. Remember I am using the word moderate, and I refer to normal healthy people. This does not include those who are allergic to alcohol. Some people should have no liquor. They are alcoholics. For the alcoholic one drink is too many and one hundred is not enough.

The drinker who starts early in life multiplies his chances of becoming a problem drinker. A Yale University study on alcoholism shows that at least two-thirds of the known alcoholics began drinking while in high school, or even sooner.

What then is liquor good for?

A medicine? The folklore that liquor is useful for medicinal purposes is for the most part scientifically incorrect.

More folklore: Liquor can cure a cold. The fact: It usually makes a cold worse.

The old wives' tale that alcohol should be kept on hand in case of a snake bite is malarkey. In this emergency I suggest the liquor be poured on the snake. (Just remember that if you are ever bitten by a snake, don't take a drink, because alcohol will dilate your blood vessels and spread the poison through your system more rapidly!) These facts are not folklore:

Alcohol is useful as a sedative. It slows up the body processes, induces drowsiness and sleep.

Alcohol is also useful as a pain-killer. In fact, alcohol and ether are similar in chemical composition. The formula for alcohol is C_2H_5OH; the formula for ether is $C_2H_5O\ C_2H_5$.

Some physicians recommend a drink before dinner to stimulate appetite. But this scarcely would be of interest to teenagers, since most teenagers have appetites which could usefully be curbed not stimulated.

I have asked hundreds of high school kids why they drink, and these are the most common reasons among both boys and girls:

"When everybody in the crowd has a drink I don't want to be different. Some kids call you chicken if you're the only one who won't join in."

"When I take a drink it makes me feel grown-up."

"A drink releases me and makes me more friendly. I guess you might say it loosens me up socially and I'm not so self-conscious."

"When I'm in a blue mood or disgusted about something, a few drinks give me a lift and make me forget."

Let's examine this magic elixir and how it works to produce these feelings. Almost everyone who drinks will swear on a stack of Bibles that liquor stimulates him. Exactly the opposite is true. Liquor unquestionably produces a superficially stimulating effect, but the exhilaration is only temporary. Liquor is a depressant—as any doctor will attest.

Why then, after a few drinks, do people often become friendly, lively and even boisterous? How can a few ounces of liquid produce feelings of exhilaration, superiority, self confidence, power?

The answer is simple, once you understand the chemical nature of alcohol.

Alcohol goes to work on the area of the brain which controls reason, judgment and our inhibitions. That area of the brain then tends to become less effective than it normally is. It is "frozen." If a dentist has ever given you a shot of novocaine you are familiar with the feeling of numbness that follows. The dentist can extract a tooth after an injection of novocaine, and you will feel nothing. Alcohol works in much the same way.

The personality changes that occur as a result of excessive drinking mystify and terrify relatives and friends of problem drinkers. They don't know what to make of it or what to do about it:

"Dear Ann Landers:

"Can you tell me how two drinks can turn a lovable, intelligent, well-mannered, considerate young man into a crude, vulgar boor? The person to whom I refer is very dear to me. It breaks my heart to see this frightening change in him. From a gentle soul he is transferred into an incorrigible trouble-maker. Last week he was arrested for disorderly conduct. He started a fight in a public place.

"If he drank a great deal of liquor I could understand it but he goes crazy on two highballs. What can I do to help him? Thank you for any advice you can give me. I am desperate.

MYRTLE"

I replied:

"The young man you are writing about is an alcoholic. With these sick individuals the amount of alcohol consumed makes little difference. Some alcoholics go off the beam after one drink. An alcoholic should not have even one drop of liquor. Urge him to get outside help. Alcoholics Anonymous and Portal House are excellent organizations. Look under Alcohol in the telephone book."

Frequently a person who drinks is under the impression

that liquor brings out his attractive and admirable qualities, unleashes his flashing wit and transforms him into an interesting conversationalist. Liquor can indeed produce some radical personality changes, but whether these changes are for the better can be decided more accurately by a sober (and objective) observer. Alcohol cannot improve talent nor can it bring out hidden genius. It can only fog the judgment and display a raw, uninhibited personality.

The feeling of being on top of the world is temporary. When the drinker moves past his threshold of tolerance the rosy glow fades and the drinker often becomes depressed, miserable, ill — and sometimes loses consciousness.

The aftereffects of a booze blast can be devastating. Although no one has ever died from a hangover, a great many people have wished they could. The morning-after feelings of nausea, weakness, remorse, and guilt can be overwhelming. Added to the physical misery of a hangover, the anxiety of being unable to remember what was said or done is pure torture. Many worthy people have lost fine jobs and destroyed valuable friendships because of boorish and revolting behavior triggered by too many drinks.

Some unconscionable males who are aware that liquor breaks down resistance will try to get girls to drink so they'll be more amenable to suggestion. Dorothy Parker's couplet is well-known to the wolf pack: "Candy is dandy, but liquor is quicker."

This is how the booze trap operates. The shy girl will take one drink to conquer her self-consciousness. She tells herself, "I need something to relax me. I'm all tied up in knots. One drink will help." And that one drink may jolly well help a bit. She becomes friendly, even affectionate — sails about the room buoyantly, saying delightful things. Through her Scotchtinted glasses the world looks glorious.

If one drink can produce such lovely feelings, she reasons that two drinks will make her feel even better. So she takes a second drink — and a third. The outcome of the evening is anybody's guess, because after four drinks the poor girl is no longer in control of her senses. This pathetic letter from Oklahoma City describes such a situation:

"Dear Ann Landers:

"I am so sick of myself I could just die. Please tell me if there is any way I can repair the damage I have done.

"Last night one of the greatest guys in school took me to a party. It was my first date with Jim, and I had been hoping for six months that he would ask me out. Jim travels with the best class of kids in school because he is tops in athletics, has a car of his own and is a big wheel. I wanted to make a knockout impression on Jim as well as the other kids who were there.

"I was nervous, naturally, so I thought one drink would loosen me up a little and give me the courage to speak to people. Well, I overdid it. I drank a little of every-thing—first a couple of martinis, then I switched to scotch and soda. I don't know how many drinks I had, but pretty soon I began to feel weak and dizzy. I couldn't make it to the bathroom and got sick right in the hall. I heard the hostess say to Jim, 'Don't ever bring that rum-bucket to my house again.' He answered, 'No danger. After tonight I wouldn't take the idiot to a dog fight.'

"I don't remember much that happened after that. I recall putting on my coat, and Jim took me home. The next day at school I saw some of the kids who were at the party and they were sort of cool. Jim drove by when I was walking home. I'm sure he saw me but he kept right on going. I'm so ashamed of myself I'd like to fall

in a hole and stay there forever. How can
a person live down such a terrible mis-
take? Is there anything I can do to square
things with Jim? Please help me.

Of course it is impossible to undo what has been done, but no "terrible mistake" is without value if you learn a lesson from it. The tragedy of too many drinkers, however, is that they don't learn a lesson. Their compulsion to drink is stronger than their decent intentions. Their insecurities compel them to reach for a crutch. They go right on drinking, telling themselves "I can handle it." And they hate themselves in the morning.

Why are liquor and sex frequent and natural bedfellows? Because liquor has the power to break down the will and paralyze the judgment. Teen-agers (and adults) who write me often confess they first became involved in illicit sexual relations while under the influence of alcohol. They say, "If I hadn't gotten tanked up I wouldn't be in this mess. I'm really not that kind of person—and never have been. After a few high balls I lost my head completely."

Let's explore the link between sex and liquor. The sex drive is one of the most powerful and persistent drives known to man. Through the centuries civilized man has learned to control his primitive urges. This is one of the basic differences between human beings and the lower animals. But when liquor gets into the act, the inhibitions melt away and animal instincts take over.

The sex urges are present whether you are married or single, drunk or sober, deeply in love of just cruising around in search of a little excitement for the evening. The biological drive is concerned only with reproduction and is ever alert for the opportunity.

Frequently I receive letters from young girls who think they may be pregnant but are unable to remember if they had sexual relations. This letter from Buffalo is typical:

92

"I'm worried to death and I can't talk to anyone else about this problem. I think I am pregnant, but I can't remember if I did anything wrong. I always thought beer was harmless and that a person couldn't get drunk if he stuck to beer. I know I had three cans of beer but after that things got hazy. My boyfriend was drinking beer with vodka chasers. I remember arguing with him about the wild way he was driving. The next thing I knew I woke up at home, and I can't recall another thing about that night. I've tried to find out from my boyfriend what happened, but he doesn't remember anything either."

How can a teen-ager best handle situations which might result from excessive drinking? This is how I dealt with the problem when I was a teenager.

I looked around at the kids in my school who were drinkers. Some of them were fairly well thought of, they came from respectable families and were not what you'd call hoodlums. But they were, for the most part, the hell-raisers, not the leaders or the kids I admired.

Then I observed what went on at parties. I believe this, more than anything, led me to the final decision. The top-notchers, I noticed, were navigating under their own power. They were having every bit as much fun as the kids who were getting stoned, but there was no sweat. They avoided liquor without making a point of it.

I watched the kids who were drinking. Their antics ranged from the amusing to the revolting. As the evening wore on, moods changed. Some of the kids became depressed and sullen. Others became pugnacious. The girls who drank too much were the saddest sights of all. Their hairdos collapsed and makeup which had been painstakingly applied was smeared and running. I often thought if someone would take candid pictures and show them to these girls the following day, it would dry 'em up forever.

An appropriate caption for the panel of photos could be the words of Robert Burns:

OH WAD SOME POWER THE GIFTIE GIE US
TO SEE OURSELS AS OTHERS SEE US«
IT WAD FRAE MONIE A BLUNDER FREE US,
AN' FOOLISH NOTION.

The big problem in drinking seems to be knowing when to call a halt. I concluded it was a lot easier not to take that first drink than to burden myself with deciding when to quit. So my drink was always ginger ale, or tomato juice, or orangeade. And it still is.

Did being an abstainer label me a square? (In those days the term was "wet blanket.") Did it interfere with my popularity? I don't think it did. I always had plenty of boy friends — in fact, I suspect being a nondrinker increased my popularity because I was a "cheap date." The boys didn't have to spend much money on me because my liquid intake for the evening was two ginger ales.

Now and then there was a little needling . . . somebody would ask if Carry Nation had brought her hatchet. But I never took the digs seriously, and I doubt that anyone else did. I have never felt that being "dry" made me better or worse than anyone else. My decision not to drink was based on reason. I noodled it out, and the choice had nothing to do with religion or moral principles. I believe the decision was a good one and that perhaps it saved me some unhappy moments and even some grief.

The teenager who decides not to drink owes neither an explanation nor an apology. He is in effect saying, "This is my way of meeting the situation and it's my own business. I like the way I am. I don't need to search for confidence or self-assurance at the bottom of a bottle. I don't need liquid assistance to pep me up, to enhance my personality or to make me one of the crowd."

Some teenagers — and surprisingly enough, more adults — feel compelled to drop a cherry in their 7-Up so that it will appear to be a Tom Collins. They feel they must cover up the fact that they are drinking nonalcoholic beverage. On occasion it has been suggested that I use this decoy so the ginger ale will look like the "real thing." I've been told it will "make others more comfortable."

Nonsense.

I refuse on the grounds that if their drinking doesn't bother me, my not drinking shouldn't bother them.

I've given you the facts on drinking, as I see them. It's up to you to decide whether to take the wet road or the dry. To those who choose the dry route, I hold my glass of ginger ale high and offer a toast, "Congratulations, and welcome to the Club."

SUPPLEMENTARY READINGS

Bier, William C., S.J. *(ed.).* PROBLEMS IN ADDICTION: ALCOHOL-
ISM AND NARCOTICS. *New York: Fordham University Press,
1962. These proceedings of the Institute of Pastoral Psychology
held at Fordham University in June 1959 contain many excellent
papers which treat the various aspects of this national problem,
i.e., excessive drinking, social effects, moral aspects, legal implications, children in an alcoholic family, teenage drinking, Alcoholics Anonymous, etc.*

Greeley, Andrew. STRANGERS IN THE HOUSE. *New York: Sheed
and Ward, 1961, pp. 79–89, "Why They Drink."*

POINTS FOR DISCUSSION

1. Alcoholic drink is at times described as being a stimulant *and
at other times it is described as a* depressant. *Which description
is more accurate? Explain.*

*2. What would you feel are the most common reasons for which
teenagers drink alcoholic beverages? One well-known sociologist has said that they drink "to kill the pain." What do you think
he meant by that statement? Do you agree? Disagree? Why?*

*3. Name and discuss some of the possible consequences of ex-
cessive teenage drinking. Of excessive adult drinking.*

*4. What insights do you draw from basic Christian truths such as
the goodness of creatures, their use and abuse, charity, justice,
scandal, mortification, responsibility, etc., as applied to this question of drinking?*

*5. Distinguish between several of the more well-known types of
drugs used by addicted people today, i.e., heroin, LSD, marijuana,
barbiturates, etc. Describe some of their effects. Are they habit-
forming? What do you think motivates young people to begin
using such drugs? What do you think is the proper attitude and
practice to form in their regard in your daily life?*

chapter 4
GENERAL ATTITUDES OF MODERN YOUTH

Under the general heading of this chapter, the opportunity is given each class, according to particular interest and need, to range rather widely across the field of modern youth's attitudes and approaches to the realities of today's world. Several particularized areas have already been considered in previous chapters. The leading thoughts which are suggested for development here concern ideas regarding college and career, conformity, apathy, insecurity, non-involvement, and the use and abuse of freedom. One purpose of such discussion is to provide you with the opportunity of analyzing through study and discussion these problem areas of personality development in order to discover to what extent and in what ways you are affected by these ills of a secular society.

In discussing these attitudes of modern youth you must be on your guard not to make the discussion too general and abstract; you should particularize these attitudes as found in real people within your class, school, and home environment. Each person is greatly influenced by the attitudes and experiences of those who are close to him, of his parents, and of his friends. This can be both helpful and harmful. In either case, the individual should make his own assimilation of ideas and experiences which he observes or learns and should not uncritically accept and conform to ideas and patterns set by either the adult world or the world of one's peer group. This is the proper use of one's freedom—after having been informed about a situation or some plan of action to choose for oneself, for good and valid reasons, what one will think, say, and do.

The general subject matter under consideration in this chapter will not require as much background reading before profitable discussion can begin. Your own experiences provide much substance for such dialogue. The three articles by Father Andrew Greeley offer a critical observation of the changing world of the young adult and his attitudes and actions over the past several years.

Whether you agree with his observations or not, they must be taken seriously into account as the mature evaluation of a perceptive and professional sociologist. They will also serve to spark much honest soul-searching on the part of members of all forms of the breed — new, old, and half.

A New Breed
ANDREW M. GREELEY

IN A FOOTNOTE to his new collection of essays, *Abundance for What?* David Riesman notes that he has observed a change in college graduates in the last seven or eight years. The cool and apathetic senior of the middle 1950's has not vanished but a new and very different kind of person has appeared on the scene.

Riesman is not too specific about what the new graduate is like, but I think I know what he is trying to describe. Several years ago I wrote a book about young American Catholics, which, in a burst of pessimism, I called The Age of Apathy. A certain sympathetic churchman suggested to me that with all the changes going on in the Church I might regret the title in a very few years. I am happy that I followed his advice, for the title finally used *(Strangers in the House)* enables me to compose much more gracefully the "change of emphasis" in this article.

There has risen up a New Breed that was all but invisible five years ago. There are not very many of them; they might not show up in any sample; the majority of their classmates in the colleges, the seminaries, the juniorates of the country continue to be listless and indifferent. But the New Breed is making so much noise that one hardly has time to notice the majority. Almost any college president or seminary rector will admit their existence and will confess puzzlement about what they want.

All I can report about the New Breed are my own impressions, and the impressions are often confused. There are many things about the New Breed that I like, but many things that baffle me. I think I understood the "Strangers in the House" of whom I wrote half a decade ago; but the New Breed are different, and I fear I do not know them.

First of all, they are greatly concerned about things like honesty, integrity and authenticity. They must know the reason why. They do not refuse to obey, but before they

FROM *AMERICA*, MAY 23, 1964. REPRINTED WITH PERMISSION FROM *AMERICA*, THE NATIONAL CATHOLIC WEEKLY REVIEW, 106 W 56th STREET, NEW YORK, N.Y. 10019.

obey they want to sit down and discuss the reasons for orders; they are confused when those in authority feel threatened by this desire for discussion. As a Jesuit college administrator observed: "For four hundred years we have been in the apostolate of Christian education, and now we suddenly find that our seminarians are demanding that we justify this apostolate." And a confrere added: "Jesuit seminarians are the most radical people in the American church—bar none." Neither of the two was opposed to the New Breed, just puzzled by them.

With this concern for integrity and honesty there comes an inability to be devious or opportunist—or even diplomatic. One generation of Catholic radicals (at least the variety I know in Chicago) accomplished their modest goals by infinite tact, patience and political skill. The New Breed will have none of this. All issues, minor or major, must be brought into the open and discussed. Truth must be spoken even if speaking it does no good and may even cause harm. To do less would be to debase one's honesty, to compromise one's authenticity. It is hard to negotiate with them, because they seem to feel that the mere repetition of what they take to be true will eventually carry the day; they seem so eager to make almost any question a matter of principle that one is tempted to feel that they are looking for a fight—though perhaps they are only looking for a cause.

With some exceptions, however, they are not intentionally disobedient or disrespectful of authority. They are appalled when their honesty is taken as disrespect and their desire to discuss is understood as disobedience; they can't see how such an interpretation can be put on their intentions. They think that they are being much more open with their superiors than those who comply with an external show of docility and then complain bitterly about authority when authority's back is turned. They contend that their desire for understanding is much to be preferred to a literal obedience that deliberately sabotages the goals of authority. They argue that superiors are much better off with the consent of free men than the compliance of automatons. They cannot understand why many superiors do not seem to agree with them.

They are greatly worried about "fulfillment." Their predecessors saw a job that had to be done and did not ask whether the job was going to fulfill the needs of the people who did it. But the fierce personalism of the New Breed will not tolerate such "nonhuman" approach. They feel that they can help others only if they can relate as persons and that they cannot relate unless there is a possibility of "fulfillment" in the relationship. They are not attracted by a task that seems to rule out the possibility of an "I-Thou" dyad.

They are anxious about loving and being loved—or more precisely, with whether they are able to love. It is not at all unusual for young people to be concerned with love; but it is surely new for youth to question its own ability to love, especially when to the outside observer it often seems that those who are the most able to love are the most likely to doubt their powers of love. They do not identify love with sexual romance, and indeed this latter aspect of love is much less a source of worry to them than friendship, encounter, relationship. They have no doubt that they can be sexually stimulated, but they are not sure that they can be "friends," that they can "encounter" a sexual partner or anyone else.

As a result their "radicalism" is not likely to have anything to do with "causes"; they are more interested in people than in ideas. Their predecessors on the picket lines of the 1930's were quite unconcerned with whether they were "liked" or not; there were enemies to be fought, principles to be defended, wars to be won. The New Breed wants to help people and wants to be loved by them. Hence they are not political ideologies; they are not "radicals" in the traditional sense of the word, since they are almost completely without a coherent political philosophy. While they work for civil rights, and may periodically throw up picket lines (sometimes, one thinks, for the sheer hell of it), they are not very active in the militant civil rights organizations or in the peace movement and studiously ignore the ideological overtones of these movements. Neither do they find much but amusement in the radical conservatives who are shouting so loudly. The New Breed is not, by any means, uninterested in politics; they are fascinated by the political game, may be active at the precinct level, and are tempted by governmental careers. But, like their heroes of the Irish Maffia, they are pragmatic rather than ideological in their approach.

Unlike the "Strangers in the House" of whom I wrote five years ago, the New Breed does more than talk about human suffering. It is from the ranks of the New Breed that volunteers are recruited for the Peace Corps, Pavla, the Extension-home missions, and especially the various inner-city student programs that are spreading across the country like a prairie fire. Such work is with people; it is nonideological and "fulfilling." One hears the volunteers observe: "We're getting more out of it than the people we are supposed to be helping."

While such statements may not be true, they furnish a very revealing insight into the New Breed. But whatever their views as to the nature of the work, make no mistake about it, they are proceeding with a cool and nonchalant competence that is often quite disconcerting. The Northern Student Movement and related tutoring programs are anything but amateur. The New Breed knows how to work with committees, write brochures, give speeches, raise money, utilize community resources and issue press releases. CALM (Chicago Area Lay Movement), the innercity movement I am most familiar with, was a going concern almost before those of us who were watching it closely were conscious that it had even started moving. Indeed, it managed to get stories into the newspapers about its work before it had begun to work — which is surely the height of something or other. This competence should not be too surprising, since the New Breed is composed of the young people who have been student leaders through high school and college and know all about organizations. As one full-time worker put it: "After running things for eight years, it would be terribly dull just to sit in a classroom and teach school." Nor does the New Breed seem inclined to view its involvement in the inner-city as a passing phenomenon. Grace Ann Carroll, the cofounder of CALM, spoke for most of the New Breed when she said: "Before we're finished we're going to think up a lot more things to do, so that everyone who wants, no matter what their age or responsibilities, can get involved."

We may be witnessing a major social change as the future members of the upper middle class return to the inner-city from which their parents fled.

The non-ideological coolness of the New Breed does not make them easy to deal with. Those who have positions of authority and responsibility over them surely deserve sympathy. The New Breed are frequently groping and inarticulate about precisely what they want, but they know that they want change. Often they seem almost to be hoping that their superiors will refuse their requests so that there may be a clear issue about which to fight, a definite change around which they can rally. They want freedom now— whatever that may mean.

The "radical" Catholic youth of the past never expected to win. They did not think that in their lifetime they would see the ideals of the social or liturgical teachings of the Church become a reality. They were resigned to being a despised minority fighting for a lost cause. But the New Breed is not going to play the game that way. They have tasted enough change in the last few years to want much more. They are quite confident that they are going to win and that they will live to bury those who stand in their way.

The New Breed is not flexible, it is not gradualist. It wants a Church that is relevant to its own needs and the needs it sees in the world, and it wants it now, not next week. Unfortunately, it is not able to say exactly what that relevance involves, and at this stage of the game neither is anyone else. Thus the New Breed is a trial to its elders; we cannot understand them and they can't really understand themselves. They are the product of a revolution of expanding expectations, and in the midst of such transitional situations, friction (and occasionally very serious friction) is inevitable. As much as we are annoyed by the inconsistencies and irrationality that the New Breed often seem to display, we must not overlook what they are trying to tell us; they are trying to say that you cannot have a half-souled aggiornamento, that if you open the window you are not going to be able to close it again and that the wind that blows in is likely to bring all sorts of strange things with it.

I have a hunch that the New Breed is basically gradualist; if it sees progress being made it will be content with a moderate pace of change and not demand everything all at once. Their present resistance to the gradualist approach may be merely an objection to a pace of change that is so slow as to be almost imperceptible. They may oppose a gradualist aggiornamento because many of them feel that almost no change has filtered down to their level. As the pace of reform and renewal accelerates at the grass roots, they may be much easier to deal with. This view however, could be the wishful thinking of a member of the older generation, hoping that in a few years the New Breed will start acting like them.

Yet it would be a terrible mistake to think that they are going to leave the Church, either by apostasy or alienation. It is their Church and it would be difficult even to drive them out of it. They have been told that they are the Church so often that they now believe it, and while they may dislike many of the things they see in the Church today, they are sophisticated enough to know that these things can be changed and young enough to think that they are going to help change them. They are restless with the Church, but they are restless with it as the fair bride that they love. Nor are they anticlerical, even though they may object to many of the policies they take to be "clerical." Indeed, anticlericalism may well decline among the New Breed since its lay and clerical members share so many common problems and hopes. It often seems that the most "anticlerical" of the New Breed are those who are seminarians; and while a very few of the ex-seminarians have, temporarily at least, left the Church, the majority of the "ex's" simply become leaders of the New Breed laity (as do the "ex-postulants" and "ex-novices"). No, the New Breed is not going to leave, nor is it going to be quiet. We are going to have to put up with it for a long time.

How has the New Breed come to be? How can we explain it? The answers are not easy. The New Breed has known neither war nor depression, but only cold war and prosperity. It lives in the midst of a psychological age when even the Sunday magazines talk about existentialism. It has read the philosophy and literature of the day, with its heavy emphasis on significance and personalism. It hears of the aggiornamento in the Church and can follow in detail the progress of reform in journals of the Catholic Establishment. Its prophet is Fr. Teilhard (in one New Breed college apartment I saw a shrine to Teilhard), and it has found its patron saint in John Kennedy, who, with his youthfulness, his pragmatism, his restlessness, his desire for challenge and service, his vision of new freedom, reflected in so many ways what the New Breed wants to be. Perhaps there are other explanations too. It is too early to say whence the New Breed has come; we will have to wait until they can explain themselves.

What will come of them? We have said that few will leave the Church. Some will become cynical and alienated. Others will bow to pressures of family and friends and settle for the good life; yet others will dissipate their energies in romantic dreams or confused and futile love affairs. Not a few of them will marry people who are not of the New Breed and endure lives of agony or frustration. Some will mellow with age. But it is a fair bet that enough of them will remain. They will mature with time, but we will be kidding ourselves if we think they will mature in our patterns. They are different now and they will be different twenty-five years from now.

They are a paradoxical bunch, supremely self-confident, yet anxious and restless; they are organizationally efficient and yet often diplomatically tactless; they are eager to engage in dialogue and yet frequently inarticulate in what they want to say; they are without ideology and yet insistent on freedom; they are generous with the poor and suffering and terribly harsh in their judgments of their elders and superiors; they are ecumenical to the core and yet astonishingly parochial in their tastes and fashions; they want desperately to love but are not sure that they know how to love. They want to scale the heights yet are mired in the foothills. I am sure there is a resolution of these paradoxes, that the New Breed has some principle of inner consistency, but because I am not one of them I cannot discover this principle.

It should be clear that I am ambivalent about the New Breed. I am fascinated by them and I admire their courage; yet they frighten me. In another quarter of a century they will be taking over the American Church. They will be the bishops, the mothers general, the rectors, the pastors, the provincials, the superiors, the scholars, the politicians, the organizers, the editors, the leaders of lay organizations. I don't know quite what their Church will look like and I wonder how much room there will be in it for someone like me. The New Breed has reason to be confident. Everything is on their side—their youth, time, the wave of history, and, one suspects, the Holy Spirit.

The Temptation of the New Breed

ANDREW M. GREELEY

A YEAR AGO in AMERICA (5/23/64) I tried to tie together some impressions about modern youth under the label of the "New Breed." I must confess I was overwhelmed by the reaction. All sorts of people announced—some of them validly—that they were members of this New Breed and happily proclaimed that at long last there was someone who understood them. (Alas, it is not true; I do not understand them.) On the other hand, many of those who had identified in the New Breed a dangerous enemy blamed me for the New Breed phenomenon—on the same principle, I suppose, that ancient kings invoked in executing messengers who had brought bad news: he who announces bad news is the one responsible for its coming to be.

Not having learned my lesson from this experience, I am now venturing back into the land where the New Breed dwell, with some new impressions. I have not changed my mind about the New Breed. I still like them; I am still sympathetic, puzzled and hopeful. But I think now I understand more clearly what their problems are and what is the crucial temptation they face. My friends in the New Breed must excuse me for sounding more critical in this article than in the previous one; but a year ago I was talking *about* the New Breed, and at this point I am talking *to* them. If I may borrow a tactic from their own approach to life, I would say that honesty compels me to write the things that I am writing here.

First of all, I feel that the New Breed are increasingly handicapped by a lack of ideology. What I mean by ideology is something rather different from what the New Breed mean by it. I mean a coherent and specific set of goals, a consistent series of norms according to which society is to be remade.

We ask the New Breed what they want of us, or what they want of society, and they say: "We want you to love us,

FROM AMERICA, MAY 22, 1965. REPRINTED WITH PERMISSION FROM AMERICA, THE NATIONAL CATHOLIC WEEKLY REVIEW, 106 W. 56TH STREET, NEW YORK, N.Y. 10019.

we want you to permit us to make something of the world where you have failed." But then if we ask: "How have we failed, and how do you want us to love you?" their words become vague. They tell us simply that we have failed because there is not enough love or freedom in the world.

"Freedom," "self-fulfillment" and "love" are for them the only ideology necessary. These are ends sufficient in themselves, and they need not be specified any further. When you ask them: "Freedom for what?" "Self-fulfillment toward what goals?" "Love in what systematic fashion?" they look at you as though you were a relic of another era.

Secondly, the lack of ideology interferes in many instances with the critical social analysis and the systematic commitment to work that is necessary to accomplish a change. The "radicalism" of the New Breed is too often a kind of free-floating social concern. There are all sorts of things wrong with society, and the New Breed are going to do something about these things; but they are not very specific about what is wrong with society—or what must be done about it—aside from saying that they do not feel free in it to be themselves. As one very honest member of the New Breed put it: "It's not just that we don't know the answers to what is wrong with the world; we don't even know the proper words to phrase the question."

It is relatively easy to throw up a picket line, or to tutor a culturally deprived child in the inner city, or even to join the Peace Corps or go to Mississippi. But these actions, while they demonstrate concern and, in some instances even heroism, deal generally with the symptoms of social problems and not with the roots. All the picket lines in the world will not resolve the difficulties of segregated education in the large urban centers unless the tax structures and the revenue codes under which these giant cities must operate are drastically reformed.

Young people ask me what organization they should join if they wish to accomplish social change in the Chicago metropolitan area. They wonder if it ought to be CORE, or SNCC, or the Catholic Interracial Council. When I reply that they ought to consider becoming precinct captains or assistant precinct captains in the Cook County Regular Democratic Organization, they look at me as though I were insane. The New Breed seem to have little taste for acquiring the knowledge and the skills necessary to deal with the causes of social problems. They have no taste at all for the complicated details of revenue codes or the grubby day-to-day work of a political organization.

Thirdly, the New Breed, for all the skill they can display when they finally commit themselves to organizational work, are basically suspicious and distrustful of organization of any kind.

They just want to love, and they think that love and interpersonal relationship more or less by themselves are enough to solve the problems of society. Organizations cramp the style of the human spirit: they restrict the spontaneity and creative love of the individual person. The New Breed want no part of this. They find it hard to believe there was a time in the not too distant past when young people could enthusiastically dedicate themselves to an organization—whether the Young Peoples' Socialist League in the 1930's or the Young Christian Students immediately after World War II.

It seems to me, however, that in the absence of carefully planned organizations, human love will, in the final analysis, become weak and ineffective. Even the most elemental kind of human love only becomes really effective when it is put into the organized structure we call the family. To be able to love at all effectively, the New Breed will have to overcome their distrust of organizations. They must learn to distinguish between those organizations that stifle the human spirit and those that create a situation where the human personality can flower much more fully than it could if left to itself. Unless they do so, they will pass from the scene without having accomplished much besides stirring up quite a bit of noise and excitement.

Here, then, is the crucial temptation facing the New Breed: either they acquire at least a provisional and concrete ideology and the ability to commit themselves to organizational work, or they expose themselves to becoming disenchanted and disillusioned idealists.

One hears that some of the young people coming back from the Peace Corps, or from PAVLA, or from Mississippi, are disappointed in their experience. They have left the comfort of their homes to help others, to love them, and they have found that many people don't seem to want their love, won't cooperate with them, won't accept the values that these young Americans bring. Those who were to be helped will not "relate" in a satisfactory fashion and will not behave like upper-middle-class white Americans. Love is just not enough; to re-evaluate everything that has been done in the past does not furnish automatic answers as to what must be done in the future. Our social problems are more complicated than they thought.

Feeling rejected, discouraged, disillusioned, the member of the New Breed is strongly tempted to give up, to re-treat, to find some comfortable ivory tower where he can "relate" to a small group of like-minded people. Thus, the disillusioned New Breeder often thinks he will find in the academic life the love and freedom he is seeking. (Yet, in a year or two, he will undergo the even worse disillusionment of discovering that the academic life is the last sanctuary of the inner-directed man—the last of the "jungles" to be found in the Western world.

The alternative for the New Breeder is to drastically change his style—to become concerned with the technical, the political, the organizational; to acquire the com-petencies and the skills necessary for the complicated grubby work that must be done if the social structure of the world is to be even slightly modified. For whether the problems are in South America, or Mississippi, or the inner city of Chicago, solutions cannot be discovered without profound understanding of law, government methods and the economics and social organization of modern life. The New Breeder, too, must fashion for himself a highly specific set of goals and norms; without these, any human effort is likely to flounder in the sea of well-meaning but ineffective good intentions. If he is to manage to keep alive the bright enthusiasm of his early days in the New Breed, he must abandon the cheap clichés and slogans of the books of existentialist philosophy and become hard-nosed and practical. As yet few have attempted this.

110

The problem of disillusionment is aggravated by the fact that the New Breed seem to have their own built-in variety of mental disturbance in the "identity crisis" syndrome. There isn't much doubt to any of us who have tried to work with the New Breed that they go through tremendous mental anguish in the process of growing up. The basic problem is that the very best young people we have simply are not sure *who* they are, *where* they are going, or *what* they want out of life. Erik Erikson's phrase "identity crisis" serves only to give a name to an experience that especially torments the members of the New Breed.

As Erikson has pointed out, it is essential to the weathering of this phase in the struggle for maturity that the young person be able to fashion an ideology that will guide the rest of his life. Part of the New Breed's problem arises because they do not know what they want, because they have no ideology. But part of the problem, too, comes from the "honesty" and self-consciousness of the New Breed. Young people today have discovered, to a greater extent than any of their predecessors, that they have an unconscious. They feel compelled to question and examine constantly their motives and their emotional states. As one fairly cynical New Breeder put it: "The trouble with us is that we must make a great big hairy deal out of all our problems." The difficulties that previous generations might have dismissed as minor take on major importance with the New Breed. This is especially true of "problems of faith." Religious doubts are not new, but the seriousness with which they are pondered seems to be much more intense with the New Breed.

The result of this intense emotionalism is that psychological ups and downs are greatly magnified. New Breeders seem to be manic-depressives. This is why it is so difficult to work with them. For all their organizational skills, one can never be quite sure that, when the chips are down, the young person may not find himself in a paralyzing emotional crisis. One finds oneself in the position of saying: "Follow me. We are going to storm the barricades!" and then looking around and finding one's followers sitting down and pondering the latest phase of their identity crisis. Again, their moods force them into taking extreme positions. Many of them leave college or seminary because, as they say, "I will be destroyed if I stay here any longer." Perhaps, indeed, they *will* be destroyed, though one wonders if the problem may be, more simply, that they lack the emotional fortitude to stick out a difficult situation.

I cannot help feeling that, for all their rejection of "phoniness," the New Breed's emotionalism has just a bit of the phony about it, too. The problems they have can be solved with intelligent effort; it is possible for the New Breed to take counsel, to put their life in order. What I find almost inexcusable is the tendency of so many of them to drift. It seems to me that in their lives there are, indeed, just too many "great big hairy deals."

Surely I am too harsh in judging the moods and identity crises of the New Breed. For New Breeders have grown up in a very different world, a world that I do not know and cannot really understand. No doubt I have permitted myself to become embittered because I have seen so many of their efforts collapse under strain. I know such a great number of young people going through these intense emotional crises. I wish there was something I could do to assist them, but having failed so many times, I fear there is nothing I can do. Sometimes I am tempted to believe that all that any of us from the older generation can do is leave them alone and let them work things out by themselves.

Thus, the final element in the temptation of the New Breed is the almost total misunderstanding between them and their predecessors, a misunderstanding perhaps more acute than has ever before separated an older and a younger generation. The older generation interprets the constant questioning of established traditions, the incessant demand for explanation, the persistent and often apparently unreasonable criticism as being signs of revolt. But this revolt is one that can neither describe what it opposes nor make clear what it wants to substitute for the present order of the Church and of society. Superiors, parents, teachers, advisers—all of us find it exceedingly difficult to communicate with these young people. The New Breed will have to excuse us of the older generation if, in the absence of a more articulate description of their goals, we say that we simply do not understand them. We would like to enter into dialogue, but there seems to exist an almost insuperable barrier to communication. Even those of us who admire them, who are sympathetic to them, who want to help them, find the languages we speak, the cultures from which we come, discouragingly different.

And so the New Breed feel, in the words of one member of the Free Speech Movement, that "you really can't trust anyone who is over thirty." The New Breed want to start all over again; they want to remake the world into a place of love and freedom. This desire of theirs to remake the world is a laudable one, indeed, but it seems to me that they will never accomplish their goal unless they can reestablish communication with those who have gone before them. In the absence of communication, we cannot help them and they cannot help us — and I think that they're going to need our help if the temptation to disillusionment and discouragement is not to overwhelm them. Nor do I think they can resolve their problems of identity unless they find at least some of the older generation who can, in some vague fashion, understand what they are trying to say.

These are dark days for the New Breed. They are going through a particularly unpleasant form of hell — a hell that they have made for themselves but that results also from the misunderstanding of those who are older. For the New Breed, the future still looks bright. They shall overcome — someday. The older generation, we Old Breeds and Half-Breeds, are no problem in the long run. But the crucial question is: can the New Breed overcome themselves, their own inarticulateness, their own confusion, their own uncertainty? At times, I confess, I have my doubts. But I am certainly not prepared to bet against the New Breed. Everything is still on their side.

A Farewell to the New Breed

ANDREW M. GREELEY

I DOUBT IF ANYTHING I have ever written has created quite the volume of reaction that my two essays on the New Breed did. Like anybody who writes, I am always pleased with evidence that people read what I say, but I was astonished by the scope and the vigor of the reaction to the New Breed articles, and I must confess there were two elements of the reaction that surprised and appalled me.

First, it was demanded of me that I take a stand for or against the New Breed.

There were those who thought that the first article was in praise of the New Breed and that the second represented a reversal of my original position. Such an interpretation, it seems to me, could only have been arrived at by those who read the articles very hastily. Neither article was for or against the New Breed. Both made commitments of sympathy and hope for them; both expressed reservations about certain problems that seemed to be implicit in the New Breed phenomenon. But neither article took a conscious stand for or against the New Breed. The moralizing influence of American Catholicism is so strong, however, that such a stand is simply not tolerated. If one attempts to observe a phenomenon like the New Breed and write about it with some sympathy and understanding, he is immediately asked: Do you like the New Breed or do you dislike them? Have you changed your mind about them? What do you think about them now?

The moralizing tendency is bad enough, but it becomes practically unbearable when it is linked with simplism. To the simple-minded, whether they be of the New Breed or the Old Breed, the phenomenon of contemporary youthful enthusiasm is something essentially monolithic and unitary. There is no room for complexity, for pluralism, even for apparent contradictions. The New Breed must be all good or all bad. One must be either totally enthusiastic

FROM *AMERICA*, JUNE 4, 1966. REPRINTED WITH PERMISSION FROM *AMERICA*, THE NATIONAL CATHOLIC REVIEW, 106 W. 56TH STREET, NEW YORK, N.Y. 10019.

or violently opposed. There seems to be no realization that reality is multi-faceted and our reactions to the whole of reality or to any segment of it, if they are to be at all intelligent, must be nuanced and selective. At the risk of repeating something I may have said too often before, I both like the New Breed and am puzzled by them. I am sympathetic toward them, and yet I do not fully understand them. Anyone who demands a reaction more moralistic or simplistic than that is simply not going to get it, at least not from me.

The second thing that upsets me about the New Breed controversy is that the phrase very quickly lost all meaning. I can't particularly object to this, since I didn't think up the phrase but stole it from a television program that expired several years before the original article was written. (The steal was suggested to me by my colleague, Fr. John Hotchkin. When he discovered that the New Breed controversy was great fun, he then joined with me in public debate over it. A good number of serious and sober people had the mistaken notion that the debate was to be taken seriously. Anyone who knows the relationship between Fr. Hotchkin and myself will be aware that, of course, everything we say to each other is to be taken seriously and nothing we say is to be taken seriously.) But if the phrase was not mine particularly, it became mine temporarily—at least by appropriation. And it pained me somewhat to see how what was essentially a descriptive label became a snide comment, a battle cry, a cliché, and, worst of all, an "out" phrase—all in the space of about six months. No self-respecting and authentic member of the New Breed would ever dream of using the word to describe his own concerns; indeed, every true New Breeder now treats the word with visible contempt. Well, so be it. But it was a terribly useful label and I am sorry to see it go. I firmly promise that this essay will be the last in which I use it. I also cheerfully relinquish to someone else—with more skill in phrase-making than I have—the obligation to find a substitute label.

But before I withdraw from the fray to the security of my crutches and wheelchair, I must make some concluding comments on the New Breed. First of all, it seems to me increasingly clear that personalism is the essential note of the New Breed phenomenon. Everything else—the opposition to ideology, the rejection of formal organization, the emphasis on freedom and love, the great concern for other people as persons, the desire for service, even the inarticulateness and dissatisfaction with everything that has gone before—is essentially the result of the New Breed's intense concern about the human personality: both their own personalities and the personalities of those around them. It could well be that this represents a decisive new element in human culture.

The philosophical, psychological and literary innovations of the last half-century have been greatly concerned with human personality. The New Breed may represent the first generation of young Americans who have completely assimilated these personalist values, at least on a mass scale. Such a change in human attitudes may well be the most decisive cultural event of the 20th century. It may portend great revolutions in the style and organization, and in the goals, of human life. If the members of the New Breed actually represent the avant-garde of the society where the human person will be not only in abstract theory but in concrete practice the most important value in society, then I, for one, say more power to them. This kind of cultural prophesying, of course, is extremely hazardous. The New Breed may be only a passing phenomenon, but if one overlooks the emphasis on the human personality, one runs the risk of not understanding at all what the New Breed really stand for.

Secondly, I very much doubt that the New Breed can be identified with the New Left. I think these are related phenomena, of course, springing from the same social and cultural factors. The New Breed I take to be much more extensive than the New Left—and perhaps much less concerned with social protest and with practical though vague attempts to create a new political order. I am not attempting to deny that the New Left, even at its most paranoid moments, is an extremely significant phenomenon in American society, but I think it represents a very tiny minority of young people, while the New Breed, even though a minority, is a considerably larger one. Nor do

I deny that there is an overlap between the two and that a fair amount of passing from one to the other goes on. The essential difference, I think, is that although both groups agree there are many things wrong with contemporary society, and both groups are uncertain as to how specifically society ought to be reformed, the New Breed's uncertainty is such that it is much less inclined to active political demonstration than the New Left. By reason of personality or family background, the members of the New Breed have much less confidence either in their own judgment or in political campaigns, which often seem to them to be ill-conceived and concerned with peripheral issues.

A good example of what I am driving at occurred at the meeting sponsored recently in Washington by the Brookings Institution for returned Peace Corps volunteers. One of the observers who attended the meeting wrote a letter afterward in which he expressed shock and regret that the returned volunteers displayed so little political radicalism. He dismissed their political and social concerns as being of the PTA or Rotary Club variety. That many of the other observers felt much more sympathetic toward the returned volunteers at the meeting seems pretty clear from comments that the Peace Corps volunteers were respectable, middle-class young Americans when they went abroad and respectable middle-class young Americans when they returned. Their vision has been substantially broadened, and their social concerns substantially deepened; their dedication to social change and progress was intense before they went and was probably more intense upon their return. But they were not revolutionaries, they were not radicals, they were anything but beatniks, and it was most unlikely that they would spend much time on the picket lines in years to come.

Whether you prefer the New Breed to the New Left depends considerably, I suppose, on your own point of view. But it seems to me that, speaking realistically, the New Breed is a middle-class phenomenon and will remain, as long as it lasts, essentially a middle-class phenomenon.

My third point is that, should the New Breed phenomenon

continue, it may have considerable impact on American society. It has been observed by Peace Corps administrators that by 1970 there will be some 50,000 returned Peace Corps volunteers in the United States. While the Peace Corps returnees have thus far quite properly resisted any notion to form themselves into a "new American Legion," there doesn't seem to be much doubt that their experience of two years' service in a foreign culture has notably influenced their own lives and collectively could exert a substantial influence on the whole of American society. When one adds to the Peace Corps returnees the tens of thousands of young people who have been involved in other kinds of personal service during their college or graduate school years, we can see that by the end of this decade there will be a substantial segment of the American population that has had experiences in personal service that previously were limited to the very few.

It seems hardly questionable that these young people will have a major impact on American society and indeed an impact for good. If most of them go into academic life or government service (as at present seems likely) the impact may even be out of proportion to their numbers. It is too early in the game to say that New Breeders are in a position to reshape either American society or, from the Catholic point of view, the American Church. Minimally, it seems to me that the New Breed signals the end of the Puritan ethic that looked on social injustice as either a necessary evil or as the result of laziness and indifference. It could be that the last conflict for social welfare legislation and government involvement in healing the personal and social ills of the disadvantaged has been won. It might even be that through the New Breed, the New Deal will have won its final battle.

Another point that might be mentioned is that it is not at all clear which way the New Breed will go. Increasingly, I find myself persuaded that the radicalism of the New Breed is a passing phenomenon. I am not as much afraid as I was when I wrote the article "The Temptation of the New Breed" that most of them would eventually become conservatives because of the practical difficulties they encountered in institutionalizing the love and concern they feel for their fellow men. I guess this is a way of saying I am now more persuaded than I was at that time that the temptation of the New Breed is going to be resisted.

As a result, the New Breed are quite likely to end up as rather respectable, moderate liberals. Considering the fact that at present the more vocal among them violently reject the notion of liberalism as being a compromise with the establishment, this prediction is not likely to be well received. And yet, in the absence of any clearly articulated left-wing philosophy or ideology, and with their increased sophistication about the nature and complexity of social problems, I see no other course for the New Breed save down the path of moderate liberalism.

I think such a path is an almost inevitable one, especially since the New Breed phenomenon is essentially a middle-class one (with personalist overtones previously not to be found among the middle class). Like all other members of the middle class, the New Breed, while wishing to be radical, also wish to be respectably radical. The difference between a respectable radicalism and moderate liberalism seems to me to be minute, if indeed it exists at all. Thus, one cynical but perceptive observer of the New Breed phenomenon has suggested to me that their patron saint will finally turn out to be not Karl Marx, or Franz Kafka, or Holden Caulfield, or Mario Savio, or Martin Luther King, but rather Msgr. George Higgins. I'm not sure whether such a delightful event will occur. But I suspect if the New Breed patron saint is not Msgr. Higgins, he will be somebody rather like him.

This is not to contend that the liberalism of the New Breed will be the same, either in content or in style, as the liberalism of my own generation—the lamentably Half-Breed. What I am suggesting is that however different the styles may be, the general posture and position of the New Breed, ten years from now, will not be too different from that of the much smaller group of liberals of my own age who managed to survive through the McCarthy-Eisenhower years. The maturing New Breed may have somewhat more global concerns. They will certainly be much more committed to the dignity of the human personality. They will use many more existentialist words than we do. They may, in fact, be far better organized than we are and far more concerned about belonging to "meaningful communities" than we are. They will certainly be less inclined to go along with slogans and clichés than some of our number in the liberal establishment are today. They will talk at least as much as we talk, though they may be inclined to take more action than we are. Finally, it is even fair to suggest that in 15 years the New Breeders of today will be puzzled by the complexities of the generation that comes after them.

Yet another question that might arise about the New Breed is what they want from the Church. It is pretty clear, of course, what they don't want. They don't want legalism; they don't want outmoded forms and silly regulations. They are often utterly appalled at the "Mickey Mouse" nature of much of what is taken to be important within the ecclesiastical structure. I remember one charming young woman who discussed the possibility of a meaningful Christian community apart from the present parish structure, exclaiming joyfully: "Good! I can hardly wait till we start pulling down all those silly parish boundaries." The New Breed find organized Catholicism today to be at best silly and at worst disgraceful. What they want from their Church is relevance, vitality, encouragement, love, stimulation, support, community, meaningful worship, exciting ideas, values they can tie into the daily problems of their life. This does not seem to be a terribly unreasonable demand on their part.

Nor does it seem very likely, in the final analysis, that many of them are going to leave the Church because the present structures meet few, if any, of these demands. What is much more likely—and those in positions of ecclesiastical authority may as well resign themselves to the fact—is that if the Church does not provide in its present structure for the New Breed, they will build the structures on their own. These structures will not be built up against the existing ecclesiastical institutions; they will certainly not have in mind revolution or overthrow of the present institutions. They will in no sense be anything but Catholic, though in the absence of official support they may be unofficially and informally Catholic.

The New Breed's present attitude toward ecclesiastical structures, as I understand it, is this: "If those in positions of power aren't smart enough or intelligent enough to change these, then we aren't going to bother them; we will be happy to let them continue with their present involvement in trivialities. We will simply build Christian communities of our own that are not irrelevant or trivial. And eventually the rest of the Church will learn from us and integrate our informal communities into their formal structure." This is not a terribly revolutionary idea, and indeed a vast amount of historical precedence can be found for it. If anything at all is new in this New Breed approach to ecclesiastical structure, it is the utter refusal to take the existing structures seriously. Previous reformers either wanted to overthrow or drastically change the existing structure. The New Breed, on the contrary, are content simply to ignore it and go their own way. Their confidence in their eventual victory, at least in this particular matter, seems to be quite unshakable.

The last observation I would like to make with regard to the New Breed may, in some sense, be considered my last observation on my work with young people, which is now, for all practical purposes, over. Indeed, this essay might just as well be entitled "Confessions of a Retired Youth Worker." I suppose the best way to approach the problem is to ask the question: what does the New Breed need most?

Several years ago I wrote two books, *And Young Men Shall See Visions* and *Letters to Nancy,* in which I contended that what young people needed more than anything else was a vision of the world as it ought to be – a vision of their own place in the world and the Church, and of the possibility of their making a significant contribution to the growth of the People of God. More recently, in my article, "The Temptation of the New Breed" (AM. 5/22/65), I seem to have suggested a variant of the same theory, namely, that what the New Breed needed was conviction and a program. I am not prepared to say that either vision or program is unimportant. They surely are, and young people growing up in American society must have both. But as I reflect back on my years of working with young people, and as I come to know at least some of them better now that they have reached adulthood, I regretfully conclude that during my decade or more of working with them I tended to miss the point completely.

What young people, especially those who are in some fashion members of the New Breed, need more than anything else is encouragement. Their biggest problem is simply that they don't trust themselves and are afraid to trust others. They do not have enough faith in their own goodness, their own dignity, their own value, their own promise. My blood chills when I think of all the young people whom I might have encouraged, whom I might have assured of their own dignity and worth, in whom I might have made an act of faith, but failed to encourage because I did not see that this above all else was what they were seeking in their priest. I surely pointed out the goals for them and paid lip service to their own ability to reach them. But in many, many instances I failed to understand that the fact that they did not strive for the goals was no indication that they did not value them or did not want them, but simply showed that they did not have enough faith in their own ability to reach the goals, or enough faith in their own goodness to achieve what the goals imply. I admit in all honesty that it will be a long, long time before I am able to excuse myself for this failure. Perhaps if my own training and background had prepared me better for working with young people, I would not have missed the point for so many years. But what is done is done, and there is no point lamenting the past.

If one looks for excuses, they are easy to find. Most upper-middle-class young people are poised and self-assured. They seem to be articulate, confident and quite able to handle ordinary human relations. In addition, in most instances their family lives seem to be warm and reassuring. And it would be difficult to believe that beneath these smooth, polished exteriors there is often a combination of emptiness and terror. For at least a good number of the New Breed, the real problem is that they do not accept themselves, that, on the contrary, they loathe themselves as quite incapable of living up to all the promise that they have shown and to all the energies that have been invested in them. I suppose the root of the problem is the manipulation that takes place so often in middle-class family life. Young people, perhaps mistakenly, draw the conclusion from parental actions that they are not loved in an unconditional way, but rather are loved for what they can do, for their ability to produce certain kinds of actions that are approved by their parents. There is nothing more damaging or diabolic in American middle-class culture than the giving or withholding of love to secure satisfactory behavior from young children.

To make matters worse, when these same children are in their adolescence, society conspires to deprecate their efforts and to call in question their promise for the future at the very time when their emotional training makes them most vulnerable to this sort of threat. On a somewhat larger level, the attitude of the *Wall Street Journal* and indeed of Gen. Eisenhower on the Peace Corps when it first came into existence, and the repetition of this attitude toward VISTA in more recent years, show that for all the effort we put into their rearing and education, we American adults simply are not capable of making an act of faith in the intelligence, the dignity, the strength and the wisdom of our younger generation.

In the same fashion, the tremendous parental opposition to volunteer service organizations, one of the great scandals in American life (and in American Catholic life especially), is another proof of our lack of confidence in the intelligence and intuitive instincts of our offspring. We have created in them personalities that are easily discouraged and defeated, and then as they grow up we do everything we possibly can to shake their confidence even more. The ultimate temptation of the New Breed is indeed a temptation to despair. But it is not, as I once thought, the despair of the possibility of reforming society; it is despair of one's own value, despair of oneself. He who would work with the New Breed must first of all be prepared to love them, and love them in a completely unconditional way; love them with a love that does not require them to fit into his patterns or do what he wants them to do, to progress along the path he has chosen for them or adopt the values he thinks they ought to adopt. He who chooses to love a member of the New Breed in this fashion should be prepared to make the astonishing discovery that he is the first one who has ever loved the young person that way in that young person's whole life.

Such, then, are my absolutely final thoughts on the New Breed (until, of course, I get another idea on the subject). My work with young people is indeed over; which is to say, it is over until the next time I encounter some of them. After all, Don Hutson retired from the Green Bay Packers every year for at least a decade. And if the New Breed cannot remember Don Hutson, it has at least heard of the Green Bay Packers.

SUPPLEMENTARY READINGS

Greeley, Andrew. AND YOUNG MEN SHALL SEE VISIONS. *Notre Dame. Ave Maria Press, 1963.*

—————. LETTERS TO A YOUNG WOMAN. LOVE IS A CHALLENGE. *Notre Dame: Ave Maria Press, 1963.*

TIME-LIFE *Special Report.* THE YOUNG AMERICANS: UNDER-STANDING THE "UPBEAT" GENERATION. *New York: Time-Life, Inc., 1966.*

POINTS FOR DISCUSSION

1. *What is your reaction to Father Greeley's progressive description of the "New Breed?" Do you feel that today's teenagers are victims of conformity to mob rule, more active and militant in word than in deed, distrustful of institutions, reluctant to make a total and lasting commitment to some ideal or cause? Describe those qualities of the "New Breed" which are particularly attractive and indicative of great hope for the future.*

2. *Father Greeley makes a big point of the need which all human beings, and particularly, young adults today, have of the full and unconditioned love and trust of other persons. Do you think that this observation is verified by your experience? Indicate some concrete ways in which this love and trust can be shown effectively to young adults by their elders.*

3. *Is conformity necessarily a bad quality? Can the term be distinguished? Indicate concrete instances of positive and negative aspects of conformity and non-conformity. A commonplace today is to speak of "the man who dared to be different." In what way could this statement be applied to a Christian teenager?*

4. *What do you feel to be the basic causes of the apparent indifferentism towards the needs of others, with a corresponding self-centeredness which seems to be present in many young people (and adults) in the modern world? Why doesn't the gospel message of Christ, "Whatever you do to the least of these my brethren you do unto me," exert a more powerful influence upon* the attitudes and actions of many Christians? Is the gospel message of love irrelevent in the modern world? Why? Why not?

5. The following questionnaires will provide some solid substance for reflection and discussion. Whereas the reflection can and should be personal to each student, the discussion in class can remain on a more generalized level, which will reflect the attitudes of broad segments of the teenage population with which you are familiar.

QUESTIONNAIRE I

Directions: Think carefully about the following statement and then answer the questions below.

The Irish people have a saying: "Love me if you will; hate me if you must, but for Heaven's sake, don't ignore me." Life would be a dull affair if no one took any notice of anything we said or did.

1. List some of the unjustified criticisms of young people which adults sometimes make.

_____   _____

_____   _____

2. Now list some of the uncalled for criticisms that young people often make of adults.

_____   _____

_____   _____

3. If you were an adult, would you allow teenagers to act as they please? Give a reason for your answer.

_____

_____

4. What do you think adults can do to make life more livable for teenagers?

_____

_____

5. If you were a teacher, a priest, a nun, or some other responsible person, what would you allow students to do that you are not allowed to do at present? Give reason for your answer.

_____

_____

6. What would you forbid students to do which you are allowed to do now? Give a specific reason for your answer.

_____

_____

QUESTIONNAIRE II

Directions: _Answer briefly the following questions._

1. What do you think is the worst single influence in your life? In the lives of most teenagers of your acquaintance?

_____

_____

2. Do you feel insecure as you face life in today's world? Why?

_____

3. What do you feel is the most important reason for going to college? Why?

_____

4. "The problem which seems to concern a teenager most is his own *apathy.* He cannot understand his lack of involvement. He has rationalized this dull state as a virtue to be commended."

Do you think this statement is true? Give a reason for your answer.

_____

_____

5. What can be done by an individual teenager to overcome the difficulty of a destructive or a negative conformity? Explain by concrete example.

_____

_____

chapter 5
FAMILY ASPECTS OF PRIVATE LIFE

As we explore the areas affecting and influencing the lives of each of us, it is obvious that the home situation and family relationship are most important subjects for consideration. The various topics which can be discussed at this time include the roles and responsibilities of father, mother, and children, family relationships (husband-wife, parent-child), and selected family problems such as use of authority by parents, communication within the family, divorce, and broken homes.

Throughout such discussion it will be helpful to keep in mind the fact that in the exploration of these ideas and situations you are to think of yourselves both in terms of the present and of the future, i.e., as children of the family now, and possibly *as parents* at a later time. It may be a source of added insight and enlightenment if at times in such discussion you assume the role of the responsible parent in making evaluations and judgments regarding concrete home situations and personal cases, especially in matters concerning parental guidance and authority.

The first article which follows deals with the role of the father in the family. Although this article was written some twenty years ago, it is included here because its basic thesis seems to have been borne out by the experience of the past twenty years so that the message remains equally sound in the '60s as it was in the '40s.

The second article deals with the concept of woman's evolving role in the modern world. It is most interesting to read this article while keeping in mind the thoughts expressed in the previous article by Ed Willock.

The third article develops the question of the conflict between conscience and authority. Primarily, it emphasizes the individual Catholic's relationship to Church authority and, vice-versa, it also sheds light on the authority-freedom conflict existent in the parent-child relationship.

The Family Has Lost its Head

ED WILLOCK

The rhyme about Mr. and Mrs. Jack Sprat and their divergent tastes in meat is a refreshing relic from some earlier day when it was considered more important that mates should be complementary than that they should be similar. The fact that Jack could eat no fat, and the Mrs. could eat no lean is as apt and typical a condition of marital dissimilarity as one could find. My wife abhors sugar in her tea, whereas I dislike cream. My friend's wife loves brilliantly colored furnishings, while he prefers neutral shades. This divergence in tastes rather than making married life difficult, makes for beauty. In the modern scheme of things the concept of unity is not that which one finds in an organism such as a flower or vine, but rather that kind of unity found in a heap of ashes. Instead of dissimilar things brought to a common fruition by a sharing of functions, the modern unity is achieved by the reduction of all things to their elemental form. The relations of persons is no longer a meeting of minds, but a wedding of valences, or in marriage, the reconciliation of metabolisms. Consequently the solution to divorce is not the marriage of likes, but marriage based upon a concept of life that finds order and beauty in diversity. The sole requirement for pairing off under such a concept, would be that the man be manly, the woman womanly, and both more or less willing to accept the fact that the children would be childish. All that needs to be common to a man and wife, is a common faith, common sense, a common bed and board, and common children. Beyond this, all other common interests can only cement the marital bond, if they are interests normally common to either sex.

To the peril of the institution of the family, men are seeking to build the common bond upon those habits of the man and the woman, which by their nature should remain autonomous. Rarely sharing a common faith, the marital expert insists that the mates read the same books or smoke the same brand of cigarettes. Commonly lacking common sense, the man and wife are counseled to share

FROM *INTEGRITY MAGAZINE*, MAY 1947. REPRINTED WITH PERMISSION.

the same intellectual prejudices. Frequently lacking a normal quota of common children, the couples are advised to baby each other and play the same games. Now if the basis of marriage harmony is playing the same games, you may be sure that it will be a losing game, and one in which it will be more and more the custom for one child to pick up the marbles and look for another playmate. To say that marriage is companionship is the same kind of lie as saying that Christ was a good man. If that is all that He is, or all that it is, then the human race has been victim of a malicious fraud. If marriage is a question of a man leaving a number of male companions to cling to one female companion, then marriage is a mad institution indeed. It is just a mad kind of card game in which the dummy has the children; it is a kind of tennis match in which the children are balls, and love is a way of keeping score. It is a race in which the human race is bound to lose.

Marriage is a wonderful thing that only God could have invented. The Church compares it with the union between Christ and His Church, for there is no other comparison on earth to do it justice. This should serve as warning to us that we should approach a study of marriage with great humility, realizing at the outset that this institution has only the faintest resemblance to the modern substitute falsely classified under the same title, and listed in the same book at City Hall.

Saint Paul has something to say about marriage which is of more than passing interest. The Church in her wisdom has incorporated it into the nuptial Mass. The good saint says, "Let women be subject to their husbands as to the Lord: for the husband is the head of the wife, as Christ is the Head of the Church. He is the Saviour of His body. Therefore, as the Church is subject to Christ, so let the wives be to their husbands in all things." On the basis of this testimony, with that nasty dogmatism so characteristic of Catholics, I present the statement without debate that "the man is head of the family." This is a conclusion hardly substantiated by statistics. Generally speaking the American male is not the head of the family. This difference between the counsel of St. Paul and the evidence of our senses in the matter of masculine headship is of prime importance, if we are intent upon reforming the family. The restoration of all things in Christ must include, well up on the agenda, the restoring of the man to his proper position within the family economy.

The Differences Between the Sexes

The most obvious fact and consequently the one most overlooked except by simpleminded Christians, is that marriage is a happy relationship because of the difference between the sexes, and not because they are similar. The proper end of marriage is the propagation of children and depends, it has been whispered, on functions peculiar to each sex. This evokes a problem very upsetting to the equalitarian. Difference of function implies difference of status. You cannot say that a woman is the equal of a man, any more than you can say that an apple is the equal of a peach, unless you have a different definition of equality from the rest of mankind. This difference between the sexes is not only physical but psychological, and it is because of these natural differences and not because of any ecclesiastical decree that man is the normal head of the family.

Man's physical qualifications for the job of headship are seldom questioned. His superior physical strength makes him the logical breadwinner, and for obvious reasons the breadwinner should be the head of the family. Women, during long periods of pregnancy, and while nursing, are dependent. This dependency indicates the function of the man. The head of the family must be independent. Adequate as these reasons may be for the establishment of headship, it is more the psychological peculiarities of the man which indicate his proper function as husband and father.

The outstanding male tendency is to be objective. The man can more readily stand off and consider a thing apart from its relation to himself. In a woman this quality, though possible, is rarely developed. She, on the contrary, is personal and tends to measure all things with her heart. For that reason she is more readily sympathetic and willing to serve. It is this tendency, when brought to virtue, which makes a woman the warm, pulsating heart of the family.

132

When she is free to do so, a woman gravitates to certain interests and occupations different from those which capture the fancy of a man. Seldom is she interested in those sciences which demand the utmost in objectivity. The fields of theology, philosophy, mathematics, and academic law have been and always will be the fields of the man. Anything which requires human sympathy and selfless friendship will be most attractive to women. Women succeed as novelists, on the whole, because of their easily stimulated sympathies, and wherever the male novelist is superior it is usually because of philosophic content. Since man's objectivity makes him more interested in universals than particulars, the composition of music, and the making of art objects in their purest form, will always be predominantly male occupations. It is neither by accident nor conspiracy that women have always been homemakers, nor is it male arrogance to say that that is their proper place. The female temperament is most happy surrounded by particular and familiar creatures on which she may be free to exercise her tremendous capacity for loving devotion.

To tell a man that he is illogical is as much an insult as to deny a woman's intuitive abilities. Wives will always say, "John Jones, you make me mad. You're always so coldly analytical!" The husband will eternally retort, "But you are always jumping to conclusions!" This is the method proper to each for attaining a deeper understanding of truth. The combination of the logical genius of man and the intuitive genius of woman is one of God's most beautiful syntheses, and it is the natural gift upon which the parents' authority to teach their children is based.

Man's other tendencies are a consequence of his objectivity, and his physical prowess. He is by nature aggressive and direct. It is his to initiate and to envision. The woman is by nature more retiring, satisfied to find strength in her husband's protection. She is circumspect, using devious methods to gain her ends, resorting to tact or diplomacy as expedient instruments. All of these innate characteristics help us to determine man's proper place in society and in the home.

Difficult to Prove

What I have said here, is not all that can be said about the relation of the man and wife in marriage, and you can't prove any of it by the isolated case of John Dee or Mary Daa. It would be difficult to prove the aptness of categorizing male and female temperaments in this way, by taking a poll among your friends. That is the sad part of it! There is a condition in modern times which, for a lack of a better word, I will call feminization. It is a condition both in the family and in the community which is the result of preponderance of feminine virtue being exercised under circumstances that demand the masculine approach. The blame, if there were any advantage to placing it anywhere, is upon the man. The women are not usurping the places of the men, nor would denying that questionable privilege solve anything. Wives and mothers are being forced to take over the throne from which the husband and father has abdicated. The man has become inoperative.

Where it is the function of the woman to be heart and center of the family, it is the function of the man to relate his family to the rest of society for the mutual benefit of all. This relating of the family to the community is the root foundation of the married man's vocation. This is his field, his domain. If the man does not control this field then the woman must, and the result will be a disregard for the common good and an over-emphatic concern for the well-being of the individual family. Since the well-being of the individual family should proceed from the common good and not merely be a sum total of all the individual goods an over-concern for the individual family's welfare will bring about a state of affairs spelling chaos for the whole society. There is a normal tension between the man and wife in regard to the question of the common good. It is the kind of tension that makes for balance. The woman will usually place the good of her family first. For her to do so is normal. The man, if he is truly the head of the family, realizes that his family's well-being depends upon the common good and this will make the common good the first end of his work. With him that sense called social consciousness will not be merely a part-time hobby, but the motivating force in everything he does. When called upon to do so, he will even jeopardize his family's welfare in order to serve the common good. Men have always done this in time of war. It may sometimes be asked of them in time of peace. Today, faced as we are with the need for reorganizing the social order, this responsibility to serve the common good cannot be shirked if we are to avoid complete disaster.

As it was of St. Joseph, the greatest praise for a man is that he be a "just man." The masculine temperament, being objective, logical, and direct, is a fitting occasion for the virtue of justice. This is the virtue most lacking in persons and their affairs today. We have evidence of charity, good will, emotional sympathy on the part of many people, all of which fail to compensate for the lack of justice. It is typically feminine to be sympathetic for the lot of the impoverished. It is typically masculine to crusade against the injustices which are the root causes of the deprivation.

Matriarchy
The average American family is approaching a matriarchy. Sons are adopting the virtues of their mothers for lack of a substantial display of masculine virtue by the fathers. The movies, radio scripts, and comic strips have all adopted this theme of masculine inferiority in the home, and it rings appallingly true to life. Among the faithful in the Church it is as evident as elsewhere. The expression of the Faith today is primarily private devotion and not public apostolicity, and it is the former that appeals most to women, and the latter which appeals most to men. Even the parochial men's groups have taken on a feminine flavor hardly relieved by an occasional "Sports Nite." Not the least misfortune that results from this feminization is that these male parochial groups act as buffers between the clergy and other men who, though possibly less pious, possess an aggressive masculinity ripe for conversion to the apostolate.

The constant and endless regard of today's good husband for the well-being of his family, so that he saves from the time of their birth for the education of his children while his neighbor's children starve, or while his local political system grows corrupt, or his Faith goes unchampioned, or his brother is exploited, is a sign of the times. It is goodness measured by the standard of the wife, and thus she is the actual head of the family. This is not good headship measured by an objective standard. Such a father may leave an inheritance of wealth to his sons, whereas what they need most is masculine virtue lived out for their emulation. The son in such a matriarchy of predominately feminine concerns, becomes one of those lads whose lack of masculine virtue has been called "momism." Under stress he becomes inoperative for lack of the soothing hand of a tender woman on his brow. He is of little use to the army, and is poor material for Catholic Action. Unless he mend his ways, the son of such a father will prove to be a greater handicap to his future wife than his dad. He will be just another child for his wife to care for. Until men go back to the masculine pursuits of devotion to the common good, relating the talents of their children to that end, they will fail to fulfill amply the office of the head of the family.

The Causes
The cause of a lapsed fatherhood is not difficult to find. I think there are two root causes. The first is immodesty on the part of women and incontinence on the part of men. The second is intellectual irresponsibility bred by modern methods of work.

Modesty and continence go hand in hand. Without either or both virtues men become the slaves of women. The natural tendencies to sexual promiscuity and feminine coquettishness as consequences of original sin, have been aided and intensified by the popular use of contraceptives. Previous to their wide-spread distribution, male continence was encouraged by women if not by the moral law, for fear of the social tragedy of bearing illegitimate children. Nature permitted to take its course rendered a punishment that few women would dare risk incurring. Thus for reasons of respectability as well as morality certain social precautions were taken to save men from themselves. The most effective of these was modesty in dress. Another was the custom of chaperons, both good Christian customs. The manufacture of contraceptives (made possible by mass-production methods) changed all this. There was nothing to fear now but God, (which is ironic, because if God were generally feared neither contraceptives nor mass-production would ever have come into existence!). Women set out to be attractive, and men gave up trying to be continent. The whole social attitude toward woman changed so that today a pious virgin can dress to the point of being indistinguishable from a harlot without evoking any comment more adverse than a whistle.

This change in the character of womanhood drastically revised the common attitude toward marriage. Having children became arbitrary. The female instrument of contraception placed the decision for having children on the shoulders of the mother. It became her prerogative to say how few children she should have. When you add this fact to the obsolescence of the male virtue of continence it is no wonder that the modern male has become subservient. We would be astonished to discover how many kept women decide the policies of our nation, due to the judicious use of their wiles and the extreme vulnerability of incontinent men.

Wherever the Catholic family continues to maintain the Christian principles of morality in relation to the marriage act, it has to be done unaided by social customs and habits of the same order. Although a wife may be of good will, she may still subscribe to the current social views on female decorum wherever they do not obviously clash with morality. She may still feel that children are arbitrary and encourage the practice of Catholic (?) birth control indiscriminately and for motives hardly sufficient to warrant so dangerous a practice. The man may consider his wife an exception while continuing to hold the current views of womanhood. This will not only try his fidelity but also make him unfit to guide his growing sons and daughters. Private virtue in regard to chastity will always be seriously threatened until it is accompanied by public customs of morality.

The second cause of the loss of male headship may very well be a remote consequence of the first. It is otherwise difficult to explain why men have for so long tolerated a social system so detrimental to the fulfillment of their vocations. The concentration of productive property in the hands of a few has left the average husband no alternative but to let himself out for hire. He no longer possesses either the skills, the property, or the tools to set his own motives or standard of work. Returning home from an office where all his conquests have been of doubtful merit to the community at large, or from a factory where his efficiency is measured by mechanical standards, he can maintain dominion' over his family only by reversing the habits which have characterized his day. What virtues he does possess can only be revealed to his children under home circumstances much more favorable to his wife. He finds himself helping her in tasks of her own invention, doing work which she initiates. In the eyes of the children and his wife, he soon assumes a subordinate role. It is small wonder that the suburban husband in more cases than one seems somewhat less formidably masculine than his wife!

TO REASSURE THE LADIES

A casual glance at the foregoing arguments might lead my lady readers to arm themselves against a turbulent and bloody revolution espoused by the menfolk. Housewives might run to the drygoods store for scarlet draping material to match the color of the blood soon to be shed in their living rooms. Dear old dad, they may suspect, will go about like some Charles Laughtonesque lion seeking whom he may devour. Becoming once again the head of the family might go to father's head. By contrast with the new regime the Barretts of Wimpole street will be considered a family with a henpecked father. For that reason, before jumping to such conclusions (or, if you will, arriving at intuitive perceptions), I hope that the ladies' glances will be more than casual. Whatever a male headship may add to a household will be something more satisfying than bruises or broken heads. It might be that peace of mind so vainly sought by neurotic matrons in the book of that same name. At any rate, it will be a state of affairs which a more sane people than we considered normal.

Whatever the specific remedy may be, the general prescription is this. Men must return to the concept of manhood in which each man is considered to have a mission to fulfill. This mission is related to: first, the honor and glory of God; second, the common good; and third, to his specific contribution to each. In the work of fulfilling this mission some men take a helpmate, so that in one flesh, and one mind, and one heart, they may more effectively accomplish this mission. As a result of this holy union children are born. These children in turn are educated by word and deed to a physical, intellectual, and spiritual maturity so that they too may take up the mission to which God has called them. And you can also see that it calls for a kind of apostolicity, and more than that, a conversion. Without this Christian concept the family has only half a meaning, and that is the women's half. When only this half-meaning is known the children are all dressed up with no place to go. They are prepared but no one knows for what. Everyone is getting ready for a great occasion which never happens. The meaning that the man gives to the family is purpose, direction, motive and end.

When groups of families get together to discuss these things, Christ will be there in the midst of them, and so too, Mary and Joseph. The job of the men will be to discover what their specific missions are. The job of the women will be to discover how they can best assist their husbands in the accomplishment of their missions. As time goes on with corporate discussion and personal meditation the men will see, as their Holy Father, that their vocations must be part of the Church's crusade to restore the affairs of men to Christ. This will become the end which gives meaning to every act. What was first an evening spent in companionable and neighborly discussion will become for them a new way of life. As they look back on their lives they will see as its milestones, not their first pair of long pants, or their school graduation, or the first dollar they earned, or the first time they met their wives but rather, they will see those magnificent steps to maturity in Christ, Baptism, Penance, the Eucharist, and Matrimony.

The work which fills the days of these men will fall under greater scrutiny. They will reform it to coincide with the laws of charity and justice courageously without fear of consequence, knowing how ridiculous and imprudent it is to seek security elsewhere than in the furtherance of God's will. They may conclude that the work they are now doing is without merit and directed solely toward the profit of the owners at the expense of the common good. Then they will consider ways and means to abstract themselves from that job, so that they may better use the talents that God has given them for His purpose.

These are the things that men can do to regain the headship of the family. You may wonder that I have said little about religious practices or the cultivation of virtue. Can it be that I am putting too much emphasis on the social problem and not enough on the problems of the spirit? This is not my intention. Once men have become aware of the magnificent mission to which they have been called, they will hunger for the Eucharist as they have never hungered before. Their virtue will not be cultivated merely by quiet spiritual exercises but rather come as the consequence of Christ acting through them in their daily apostolate. With new purposefulness, the new Christian man will lift his fellows from the quiet desperation of their lives, and in acting Christ-like, he will be setting for his children an example which is the crowning glory of fatherhood.

The New Catholic Woman

A new set of talents, traits, opportunities and attitudes characterizes the women who are influencing the life of the Church in America today. Generally, these characteristics are those which identify the American woman of this generation.

The image of the "good Catholic woman" which is in the thought of churchmen, writers, and sometimes in the minds of the women themselves, often describes the virtuous woman of an earlier time. The goodness and the Catholicity of today's woman need to be understood in terms of her own circumstances.

The questions for the first discussion were of this nature: What is "new" about the Catholic woman of today? How would she be compared with her mother or older sister of the years before World War II? What about the benefits and problems of her advanced education?

Does this woman feel a special need for personal identification — before or during her marriage? What has happened to the model of the religious woman who lives only for her family? Are the problems and pressures of the modern woman who wants to live a full Catholic life resolved — even in theory?

What are the open questions that need further thought and research?

THE PANEL
VIRGINIA BECK SMITH was born in Denver, received her college education at Mt. St. Joseph-on-the-Ohio in Cincinnati and a master's degree in journalism from Marquette. She is the mother of five children ranging from 18 years to 3. Her husband, Dr. Vincent E. Smith, is director of the Philosophy of Science Institute of St. John's University.

ROSE LUCEY with her husband, Dan, has been at the center of the Christian Family Movement since its earliest days. Their family owns and operates the San Ysidro Shop for Catholic books and art in Canoga Park, California, and a second one in Torrance. Nine children — one daughter from Korea, another in the Peace Corps. Rose is a member of the Democratic State Central Committee, on the board of directors, NCCJ in San Fernando Valley, and a member of the mayor's advisory board.

FROM *AVE MARIA*, SEPTEMBER 19, 1964. ADAPTED FROM A SYMPOSIUM. REPRINTED WITH PERMISSION.

MEROPE KERSTEN from Fort Dodge, Iowa, majored in English and speech at Mount Mary College in Milwaukee. Married to attorney Don N. Kersten and the mother of three children, she is active in CCD work. She also carries a part-time teaching assignment in the parish school.

MARY HOLUB is, in a sense, married to the Catholic press. Her husband, Bill, now General Manager of *America* magazine and publications, has worked in Catholic publishing throughout his career. Mary graduated from Marquette's College of Journalism, is a "book evaluator" for the Virginia Kirkus Service (which is used as a guide by libraries, bookstores and schools), and lectures on aspects of Catholic reading. The Holubs have five children, all teen-agers except Mark who is 11. They live in Summit, N.J.

MARY HOUCK has appeared in *Ave Maria* a number of times as a substitute columnist for her mother, Kate Dooley. Before marriage, she graduated from the College of St. Catherine in St. Paul and worked as a nurse in South Bend. Her husband, John, teaches in the College of Business Administration here at Notre Dame. They have two children and have served as a foster family for fourteen infants over a period of 2½ years.

PAT SOMERS CRONIN, after a career as a reporter and copywriter, married a family of five — her husband, Jim, and his four children. The Cronin family now ranges from nine weeks to 20 years (five girls and five boys). Mrs. Cronin graduated from Rosary College in Chicago, studied at Laval in Quebec, and is now a graduate student at the University of Chicago. In her spare time she writes explosive articles for Catholic publications.

HELEN YOUNGPETER did the first seven contributions to this symposium as she was readying her family of five children for a move to Germany. Her husband, Don, is an Army captain. Mrs. Youngpeter worked in public relations after getting her degree in journalism from Ohio State. She has been doing some free-lance fiction writing, with sales including the Italian magazine, *Cosi*.

SALLY LEIGHTON, too, is familiar to readers of this magazine. Her articles on aspects of family life have been short and sharp. She lives in Chicago, was educated by Mercy nuns "and self" — Adult Education centers, Great Books, local ecumenical series. She has been married for 20 years and finds much of the source material for her writing in her eight children, ranging from 2½ to 19.

DR. LENA EDWARDS was one of the 30 Americans singled out by the President to receive the 1964 Medal of Freedom. Dr. Edwards, now 63, gave up a successful practice in New Jersey to serve the migrant workers in Texas. She herself is a Negro and she had planned to work among the underprivileged Negroes in the South, but the sight of the migrant families in Texas prompted her to donate her equipment, her money and her service to their needs.

SISTER JACQUELINE GRENNAN, S.L., is the vice-president of Webster College, Webster Groves, Mo.*

Several of the panelists, somewhat surprisingly, denied that there is a radical change in the Catholic woman of today, but then most recognized that her circumstances are radically changed.

. . . we can find differences in the woman, but we can find no significant differences in the "Catholic part of the woman." She is one who conscientiously practices her Faith—works at it—and tries for deeper communion with God. But today's society will not permit her to live as she would have lived 30 years ago. Then she reached her family with faith—"The Church says"—whereas today she couples this faith with reason. Today's well-educated woman, with a strong foundation in Faith, also asks for reasonable answers. This leads her to one of her biggest problems—doubting with intellectual honesty.

. . . the basic role of women remains the same as it was when my mother, and when her mother before her, were my age. But the opportunities open to me are radically different. *This writer stressed the widening range of opportunity and the increased organization of the works of charity in the succeeding generations. Also the effects of family mobility.* For example, when we lived in Georgia, I realized for the first time that segregationists could be well-educated, thoughtful and gracious—our friends.

. . . Outside of the fact that the women of my mother's age seemed more secure than we do, I wonder how different we are . . . just as before World War II, the Catholic woman is far too insular—generally. She hasn't been encouraged to stretch out beyond the confines of her neighborhood (I hope she has managed to get beyond the confines of her own parish, in some things!) or her own social sphere. If, here and there, a cherished teacher tried to open her mind to a wider world, social and family pressures—except in the rarest cases—promptly closed it again. (Sometimes I think the really adventurous girls are all in convents!) Listen to a group of average Catholic women

* *EDITOR'S NOTE:* SISTER JACQUELINE IS PRESENTLY THE PRESIDENT OF WEBSTER COLLEGE.

talking; it's not the papal encyclicals or the Council they're discussing—or social conditions, or civic affairs or international events . . . it's almost certain to be the ordinary domestic or gossipy (and I don't mean malicious) chitchat one hears at parties.

. . . the newest thing about today's Catholic woman is her field of vision. Education and experience indicate to the modern woman, who is again creeping out of the "protection" of home life, that the world needs her.

. . . There is a limit to the effects she can have on her children, and she sees that if she is not careful to observe healthy limitations, she will overdo her maternal role and cause immaturity rather than development and growth.

One writer, Virginia Smith, takes a stronger position than the others on the fact that there is relatively little change in the basic problems and challenges facing the Catholic woman of today. She said:

> . . . Today's woman is being sold a bill of goods by the Betty Friedans, the Simone de Beauvoirs, the Marion Sanders, and by the Sunday supplements, the ladies' mags, and the spate of books on the WOMAN PROBLEM. . . . The Apple of Discord is being dangled before the new Eve in Madison Avenue blowups of the goods and glories which are just within her reach and forever eluding her. . . . With every door now open, woman is nonetheless supposedly trapped by her biological function.

New Insights—a New Identity?
To all intents and purposes free, she is still enslaved by that monster, "male-man." With the best living conditions, as far as material comforts and satisfactions of desires are concerned, her discontent is massive.

To the extent that they live in this pluralistic society and are seduced by secularism, Catholic women have discovered their nerve-endings are also exposed to this discontent which, if one believes what he reads, has become a national feminine trauma.

Echoing an earlier comment, Mrs. Smith adds: "What makes modern woman different from her mother and grandmother is serenity—that is, if she doesn't manage to sit down and think the whole problem through and come up with the only sane answers there are. And these answers involve the truth that her female ancestors, while they might have been dour examples of duty, submission and Victorian subservience, had achieved the deeper satisfaction with which selflessness endows any human being, man or woman.

The tension is described at some length by another writer, Helen Youngpeter: They want childbirth not to be something that happens to them, but something they do, a creative accomplishment . . . they accept their maternity with a new joy . . . the old false shame at their "delicate condition" is gone. The old female tendencies to self-pity —woman's work is never done . . . slaving over a hot stove all day, etc.—so prevalent in our mothers' and grandmothers' day seem to be disappearing. Mother Machree, with her careworn hands, is dead. And women are developing a sense of humor that enables them to laugh at themselves. (This seems part of an over-all sociological pattern. When people see no hope of recognition as full and equal human beings, it's difficult for them to see anything very funny in their situation. Note the recent rise of the Negro comedians, Dick Gregory, Godfrey Cambridge, and the like.)

On the other hand . . . statistics show a growing number of divorces among Catholics. There is more alcoholism, neurosis, adultery and unstable children. More and more Catholic women are entering the job market, and there is a groundswell of protest against the Church's stand on birth control. There is a growing restlessness and dissatisfaction with the housewife's role.

145

And the young ones . . . talk to some school supervisors. Indifferent, apathetic to either scholastic or spiritual goals, cynical, materialistic, more interested in looking like a miniature Jayne Mansfield than being a good woman, ravenously intent on getting a man, the sooner the better, going steady at 12, and perhaps pregnant and/or married at 16.

But look a little closer, back there in the stretch, coming up fast, a little band of rebels, Father Greeley's "New Breed," fiercely intent on integrity, honesty, and most of all, freedom. They want freedom and they want it now. They want answers to everything:

"Why should I have a large family? Why shouldn't I have a life of my own? Why shouldn't I get the same satisfactions from my job as a man?" And when they say "Why?" they mean just that. They're willing to go along with Church law and with the moral code. They may even be more conscientious about obeying it than their more passive sisters, but they must have reasons.

And these same, rather arrogant, little rebels, who question every word from their elders' mouths are the same girls who volunteer for the Papal Volunteers and the Peace Corps, who work in the slums and teach catechism on Saturdays. They want no part of hypocrisy or mediocrity, and hell-and-brimstone motivation irritates them almost as much as sentimentality.

Are the motives and drives of these women irreconcilable? I would say that all are produced by the same set of circumstances and reflect the anguish of any sociological change.

In our mothers' time, and even more so in our grandmothers', the position of women was firmly established. . . . When she was young, her "daddy" would make decisions for her; and when she married, her husband would take over as the source of authority. . . . Even the convent was only an extension of the home situation with the Mother Superior or the Bishop making the decisions.

Mrs. Youngpeter summarizes this point; But there were

stability and security. If a woman wasn't free to take responsibility, neither was she held responsible for the problems of the day.

With World War II, women were left to make decisions at home, they were needed outside the home, they saw the importance and possibility of higher education for women: Once women had found out that it was possible to be not only John's daughter and Bob's wife, but persons on their own, it became more and more difficult to convince them that all their personal goals and dreams could be sublimated in the lives of their husbands and children.

All of these groups have this much in common — a search for personal identity, a breaking away from a goal of passivity and irresponsibility to one of creative fulfillment and a restless questioning of whether what always has been is really what always should be.

And in the same tone: While there are Catholic women who live only for their families, as there are Protestants and others who live only for their families, this is no longer a viable *model.* It is true that many women who are temperamentally unfit for any extension of themselves into the outside world manage to rear happy, useful members of society. But this is becoming more and more unlikely. A woman needs some understanding of the world if she is to send her nurslings into it (*Sally Leighton*).

A woman's sense of personal identification, *Mrs. Leighton continues,* need not depend on work in the outside world. . . . There are women whose creativity is centered on homely arts. . . . These seem to be the natural "givers" who seem richly fulfilled and very effective with those around them. They have great personal dignity and charity.

But even for this kind of woman, some kind of balance between time spent with children and time spent with adults is needed. If gossip at the Laundromat or over the checkout counter is a woman's only "adult" contact for the day, she becomes unnerved indeed . . . she finds home an isolation booth in which the sixty-four-dollar question is, how long will she survive mentally sound? (Ironically, many consider this environment the ideal for "woman, the contemplative.")

Mary Holub questions the "simple life and values" of the Catholic home at the turn of the century and during the following generations. This is presented as the ideal for families to emulate, but this nostalgic and simplistic approach is starkly unrealistic. *She mentions that in researching the history of her own parish,* I was amused to find that the Total Abstinence and Benevolent Association was the first society organized for men. Obviously great-grandfather wasn't spending every evening around the piano with his wife and children.

A woman of this day filled her life with what was available to her. When she had a very limited opportunity for education and intellectual interests, then she made home and children her entire life. Cooking, baking, cleaning and sewing filled her days which began (and ended) early. She didn't progress beyond these things and felt (except for the mavericks who, blessedly, have always been with us) that she didn't need to do so.

The New Catholic Woman, *writes Mrs. Holub,* lives for her family just as her grandmother did, but she does not feel that this is the very end of her existence. She recognizes her needs for broader involvement in other aspects of the society in which she lives. Her family comes first—as it should and must—but it is not exclusive to her personal fulfillment as a mature, Christian adult. She accepts herself for what she is, and manages to maintain a very real independence in an age when conformity is the norm.

The question of identity—personal significance—is a recurring one in these comments. Rose Lucey points it up dramatically in referring to a recent conversation with a missionary nun. She told me that for the first time in her life she was confused about her role as a missionary. There seems to be so much theorizing and confusion about the "role" of the nun and the definition of the missionary. I would guess her personal confusion is pretty general among those women who are reading and thinking in any field.

All the old concepts about women, which we have heard for generations, are being rejected or modified. And it becomes imperative for individual women to sit down and get back to the basic: Who am I?

A few years ago the conflicts and confusions were probably restricted to those women who were more highly educated and who read more widely. Today it is drifting down to the ordinary woman who tends to go along with what she is told. This confusion is one of the biggest problems we will have to face in the next 10 or 20 years. I can see this in trying to talk to my own daughters about their roles. It was so simple just five or six years ago to discuss marriage in terms of giving oneself completely to husband and family, with all the pat answers about the role of father as head of the house and wife as heart.

The fact that woman must also play a part in the outside world in some capacity will need exploring, and it may be years before we get some answers.

Merope Kersten speaks of the pressures bearing down on the "ordinary women" of today: Today's women do not have the leisure their mothers had. Oh, we hear about how much leisure time is available because of the shorter week and the millions of time-saving devices. But with them comes no real leisure. Our life is crowded just keeping events in place. There is no time to reflect on what has happened, for we must begin to think of what is to happen. There is an almost sinful feeling when we do come across the rare day when there's nothing that really must be done.

. . . the obvious problems of emotional breakdowns, scrupulosity, infidelity, and excessive drinking seem more prevalent today . . . some of the Catholic women are confused about their own personal identity. Some are pampered, spoiled, selfish and immature in their refusal to accept responsibility.

The modern priest is not helping this modern problem!

It would seem that not all the women would agree with

the emphasis on an independent activity outside the home.
Mary Houck states: The first three dimensions of a woman
—marriage, motherhood, homemaking—are her basic
commitments. Any other activities should complement
these, not distract or detract from them. . . . A woman
should extend herself to a career, to activities and interests during her young adult and pre-marriage years
. . . they can be built upon, reinforced, but without taking
away from her prime obligations. When a woman chooses
the vocation of marriage, she doesn't lose her identity;
she chooses to lend her identity to the formation of a
family.

In some of her words, Pat Cronin sounds like the comment
of Mary Houck, but her meaning (and her tone) says something quite different:

Maybe one can't mix an awareness of the world and its
problems with "simple life and values." I'm thinking
particularly of Eleanor Roosevelt. Forgetting politics, one
wonders whether a woman should leave behind a great
deal of national and international good, as well as a
mixed-up family. Can one woman really do well by a
family—and by the world? I don't know.

Still, this is the question we face in educating our daughters. I used to think every woman needed time—time to
find herself, time to know herself, time just to *be* herself.
I know I needed it. One reason I don't buckle under the
demands of family living is that I had time to build a career,
to be successful in it, to be a person, to be myself . . . and
most important, time to be bored by a career, to watch
the glamour turn to routine. Now, busy as I am at home,
the outside doesn't look nearly so tempting as it might.

I'm now convinced that some women don't need this in-
terim. But the problem lies with the girl who has "brains"
and talent and interest in what's going on outside her home
—and still is a woman, quite possibly a married woman.
It's *her* education I wish Catholic shools would tackle.
They consider the professional woman, the teacher, the
social worker as spinsters and never as married women
in the community. They don't blend the two.

And this division is extremely serious. If a girl is exposed to a wider world and encouraged to use the mind God gave her, and at the same time is encouraged to produce and raise a family, something has to give . . . and it may well be the girl herself who breaks.

It is the woman in the home who gives, gives, gives; her energy, her time are simply not hers . . . nothing, absolutely nothing, will kill a talent or skill faster than the demands of married and family life. The decision over which to choose — talent or family — seems cruel. But one has to decide: one can be awfully talented and awfully lonesome, too; and that's not much fun. . . . Nothing is so deadly, nothing dries up the spirit faster than constant conversation with children, constant menu-planning, constant picking up, constant domestic routine.

Still on her plea for the married woman with talent and interest in activities outside the home, Mrs. Cronin says: Who downgraded domestic work in the first place? Why — since World War II — is a factory more glamorous than a home? Watching four-year-old Ellen hug our Emma in the kitchen one morning, I couldn't help remark that Emma never got that in the Campbell Soup factory — her first job after coming to Chicago.

And I almost overlooked the most important point about this girl with talent: her husband! Without his support and encouragement, she's through.

Pat Cronin and Virginia Smith would probably come into head-on conflict here. Talking about the Protagonists of the School of Feminine Frustration who lament the years of college education wasted on the woman who stays in the home, Mrs. Smith takes a strong stand:

Down the drain with the bathwater goes not only baby, but mother as well. Poor babe, he should never have been born, for with him comes mother's fixation that she would take care of him. Deny the fundamental nature of woman, unchangeable until a new species be born; deny her role in the creation and nurturing of human beings, and you do away with marriage, childbirth and its attendant respon-

151

sibilities. Then a woman ceases to be woman and becomes that ambiguity, "The Second Sex."

A wise old sheepherder who knew more about biology and the inescapable laws of human nature than many a scientist or philosopher once said to me: "You can commit a crime against nature and God may forgive you, but nature never will!"

Is her education wasted who spends it on those she loves most, flesh of her flesh? Or is it more fulfilling to spend it on others, while her children who are granted to her for so brief years, are given to the impersonal charge of another?

Mrs. Smith quotes Phyllis McGinley: "Learning has a beauty and value of its own. It is part of the richness of life. Its purpose is to enlarge the intellect, enhance the mind, make both work and leisure more self-fulfilling. It is nonsense to say that girls should have to choose between education and the role nature has assigned them (and where lie the true rewards)."

Much space has been given to this discussion of education, use of talents and family because it loomed large in the comments of the panelists, because it represented a sharp disagreement, and because it seemed to bear on many other issues that will come up in this series.

Another major theme that came through these first responses was this: Probably the most distinguishing thing about the New Catholic Woman is her awareness of the world about her, especially the Church, through her education, her reading, her reflection. Some of the panelists referred this awareness to action outside the family; others spoke of it in relation to the full formation of the family. For all of them, such reading and reflection were major characteristics of the woman they were discussing.

. . . In every parish can be found a group (and age is no factor here) of "New Catholic Women" who share, I think, some of the following characteristics: they see their religion as a way of life that must permeate everything they do. They recognize the Mass as their central act of worship . . . and center their lives around it . . . they are aware that they "are the Church." . . . They are convinced that the evils, injustices and social problems tearing the world apart today can only be solved when men begin—no matter how vaguely—to recognize Christ in every other human being.

. . . This woman is educated (if not formally—at least by her own voracious and diversified reading). She's intelligent and articulate, and she READS. I would stress over and over again that this woman reads widely and well in both the Catholic and secular fields.

Another writer: . . . First of all, these women read—avidly. Magazines, books, newspapers—they lend these tools back and forth and they talk about what they read. In every parish I know—scattered throughout this large archdiocese—these women exist.

. . . I sense that if I asked them what was most important in their lives regarding their education they would not say to me that it was a particular school or college, but that it was the result of meeting a person who challenged their traditional thinking about the role of the Catholic woman —and the books and authors with whom they came in contact.

. . . The intellectual who complains of such boredom (routine housework) is by and large only excusing her own sloth. If she is trapped by anything it is by her own inertia. *Dorothy Dohen is quoted:* "The woman who really is intellectually curious will continue to think, and continue to read, come hell or high water." It's wanting to do something badly enough which provides the impetus to conquer obstacles.

. . . once more women began to be educated in the same basic way as men, once their minds were open to the wider world of philosophy and politics and social problems, their interests and enthusiasms approximated men's and the old world of back-yard gossip, church suppers, child care and devotional reading material began to seem a little thin. Whether this is good or bad is really beside the point. It is.

. . . the immediacy of current events has a tremendous effect on our view of the world, and of our place in the world. Such events as the construction of the Berlin wall, the astronauts' flights, and the riots in Harlem . . . have some impact on a woman's life as a Catholic, make her Catholicity more vital and meaningful, a strong and sure foundation in the face of change and uncertainty.

. . . Catholic women have the duty to keep themselves in constant contact . . . the news media of today are fantastic compared to 30 years ago . . . no longer do we have the narrow-minded Catholic school — pulpit — press.

Still another theme which ran through several of the responses was the need of this New Catholic Woman to have answers from the Church which would be meaningful to her . . . She has in many cases been sent back to her own internal truth-testing apparatus to see if a proposition holds up under honest scrutiny . . . She knows that "Father says" is not at all the same thing as "the Pope says," much less "Jesus taught." . . . Now she sees that the competences of any adviser extend only to his own limitations, and that she does him no favor to let him extend them beyond the point at which his Orders end.

She has the problem of autonomy, of conscience, of choices, sometimes painful and muddled, beyond that point. She has the problem of being a woman, a person, a responsible human being.

. . . These new Catholic women are not sanctimonious, pietistic or "holier than thou." Their Catholicism is a reasoned religion, not one based on emotion. . . . The laity no longer have an apologetic attitude toward the Church. When criticism of ecclesiastical policies and practices is justified — and it often is — these Catholics criticize because they love the Church. You don't bother criticizing something or someone unless you are really interested. And in today's Church we are not just criticizing; we are working toward its improvement.

The open questions:
. . . a re-definition of femininity. Does femininity consist in a certain way of life, of thought, of speech, of dress — or is it a deeper, more sacred quality, a unique way of expressing Christ to the world?

. . . Should women be educated differently than men? I don't mean the foolish notions that a woman's education should consist in Creative Cooking I, II, and III—but is there an intuitive faculty more natural to woman than man, and can education train this faculty to the world's advantage?

. . . For the married woman of intelligence and talent, there still remains the problem: Can I carry commitments to my family and to a career and not endanger my marriage and my family?

. . . The crux of the so-called Woman Problem is Woman and Women. There has to be a re-examination of the nature of a woman which IS different from man in the economy of creation and salvation. All the feminist arguments and demands are based on a denial or resentment of this difference, and as such they are immature.

. . . We may be on the verge of an era of completely different family relationships. How we face the coming changes may depend quite a lot on how much we can find out about ourselves personally and how much freedom of life we are willing to allow each other.

. . . Having been relieved of a number of absolutes, the Catholic woman is faced by a number of possibles, subject to the weal of her family. She is not relieved of the conviction that in Love is contained the Law and the Prophets. Her problem now is how and whom to love—wisely and well.

. . . The biggest question about today's woman—Catholic or not—is what now? Where is she going from here?

In summary:
There was a general recognition that there is something "new" in the Catholic woman today—at least a newness in her background, circumstances, pressures and responses.

The panelists agreed that one of the most distinguishing marks of the New Catholic Woman is her awareness of and her reflection on ideas and events outside her home—an awareness fed by wide, regular reading.

There was sharp disagreement on the necessity of outside involvement for the fulfillment of the woman as a person.

In their statements and in their own approach to the questions, these women indicated a new questioning, challenging attitude toward the institutions of the Church. The questions grow not from any disloyalty, but from a greater commitment to the Church, from a greater respect for their own dignity as persons, and from a more mature realization of how their conscience is (and is not) related to ecclesiastical authority.

Conscience and Authority in the Life of the Catholic

ELLIOTT EGAN, O. CARM.

HARDLY AN ISSUE of a Catholic periodical or newspaper reaches the printer without a discussion of the roles conscience and authority play in the life of the Catholic. Perhaps the discussion can be oversimplified in this way:

We are faced with two facts, one theological and one psychological. The theological fact is that Jesus Christ established one true Church to carry on his salvific mission in time and space. He gave a portion of it, under a single vicar, the right and duty to rule, teach and sanctify the faithful by determining, transmitting and proclaiming the truths of revelation in faith and morals. He, in other words, established an authority in the Church.

The second fact concerns man's conscience, which is by definition a judgment of practical reason on the morality of an individual action to be done by us. Conscience is itself also possessed of authority, in fact of sovereign authority. St. Thomas has stated repeatedly that "every conscience, true or false, is binding, in the sense that to act against conscience is always wrong."

What happens when authority and conscience clash?

The examples of this clash are in the headlines:

—What should a man do in civil rights when his prelate dictates one course of action, but his conscience dictates another?

—What is a man to do when his conscience dictates a course of action at loggerheads with the authoritative but not infallible position of the Church?

—Can one's conscience create a moral obligation contrary to an official Church statement on the same matter?

—What freedom does man possess in forming his own conscience?

—Are freedom of conscience and ecclesiastical authority ultimately reconcilable?

To seek answers to these questions, let's look first at authority in the Church, which is monarchical and hierarchical. The Vicar of Christ stands at its summit and the bishops share with him the ruling and teaching functions of the Church. Administratively, the Church is not a classless society, but this fact is not to deny the laity its own proper role in shaping the doctrine or forming the conscience of the People of God.

The Holy Spirit was given to the Church, not just its bishops. The witness of its members may be inspired by the same Holy Spirit. The hierarchy recognizes this witness as a source of and guide to the revelation of God. But by divine institution the hierarchy enjoys the final word as witness to faith and morals; it is the ultimate ratification in determining the revelation of God.

Certainly the authority of the Church embraces more than its infallible decrees, for obviously most of its decrees are not infallible. When the Pope speaks, when the Council speaks, rarely is the Church's infallibility involved. Certainly the assent we owe as members of the Church to her infallible pronouncements differs from the assent we owe to her authoritative pronouncements. When the Church speaks infallibly, in solemn declarations on faith and/or morals, our assent is the assent of faith. We make or give this assent with a certitude of the highest order, the certitude of faith. When the Church speaks authoritatively, we give a different assent, the assent of obedience. This too is characterized by a certitude, the certitude of obedience. This latter assent differs from the assent of faith by the fact that, unlike the former, it is not absolute. The authoritative position of the Church may and can change. But this fact does not make it any less real. The assent of obedience differs from the assent of faith as authoritative teaching differs from infallible teaching. Both or each demands a real assent. The type of assent differs in kind, but both are assent nevertheless.

Fr. Karl Rahner, S.J., remarks in four essays on Freedom in the Church that the Church is a legally established society, with laws, regulations, authorities, and subjects. This will always be so, he notes, so long as the Church is on a pilgrimage towards the final return of Christ. However, her objective nature is not that of a totalitarian system, because the dignity of man is part and parcel of the basic principles that are proclaimed by Her. Furthermore, since the Church is always also a Church made up of sinful men, even affecting those who hold authority, she can also in her individual actions offend against her own principles and against the freedom of the individual both within and without. Because of the authority she possesses and the human element which exercises it, the Church must continually reckon with the real danger of giving scandal of apparent totalitarianism.

However, the Church still possesses the real right and obligation to decide by her teaching and pastoral authority and in a manner binding on the conscience of her children as to what can be objectively reconciled with God's moral law and what cannot.

Fr. Rahner reminds us that the freedom of the Christian is not in effect an emancipation from the teaching and pastoral authority of the Church. He points out that the authority of the Church "applies to the Christian even if in a particular case he can no longer fathom the objective reasons for the binding force of the ecclesiastical norm or understand the application of this norm to life in the concrete, but must simply be satisfied with the fact that, although this is beyond his comprehension, the legitimate authority of the Church has declared this to be incompatible with the moral law."

The fact that the Christian acknowledges the Church's authority by what is itself a free decision, Fr. Rahner continues, does not mean that nothing is left to him but to receive orders and to carry out commands. Even when the Church issues general norms or draws concrete conclusions that are obligatory for the practical conduct of her members she sets limits but does not ascribe to herself the duty of saying in each case what exactly the individual must do. In the concrete, her authoritative function is of a negative kind. When I am faced with a decision in my private life, certain possibilities will be eliminated as being incapable of a Christian or moral realization since they conflict with this or that moral norm promulgated by the Church. But fundamentally all moral decisions must be made by the Christian and they have a concrete and individual dimension which of itself cannot be covered at all by the authority of the Church. There is, in Fr. Rahner's words, "a zone of freedom, but not of freedom to act simply as one chooses." He has noted that there is "nowhere in the Church an absolute monopoly of real power. This "zone of freedom" implies that Church authority leave its members to do as they please as long as the error of their action is not established, rather than prohibit all individual initiative until its legitimacy has been formally proven.

Fr. Rahner brings out in these essays some other very interesting observations. He bids us to recognize that as a matter of fact Christ does not always and necessarily convey His commands to ordinary Christians through the ecclesiastical authorities. The charismatic element in the Church, the inspirational guidance of the Holy Spirit, is not the exclusive privilege of the hierarchical authority. As a matter of fact, the executive authority is not a self-sufficient planner of all that is done in the Church. The Church must recognize the existence of public feeling in the Church. It exists for the same reason that authority exists — by the very fact that the Church is a society of human beings. Within the Church, Fr. Rahner says that this public opinion exists specifically to make plain what people in the Church are really feeling, so that the Church leaders may take account of this fact. With truly scholarly caution he remarks that simply because it is public, the people's opinion does not become correct. There can be no discussion of anything that comes into conflict with the Church's dogma. But it must be remembered, asserts Rahner, that there is always a strong tendency to narrow down far too closely the range of what parts of Faith can legitimately be discussed. We can become victims of what Michael Novak has recently described as a kind of "creeping infallibility."

Perhaps enough has been said on authority to allow us to take up the converse of our question, conscience and its right to freedom. Man is by nature a creature endowed with intellect and will. His claim to fame is that he can both know and love. More important, he can decide to know and to love, for man is also by nature free. The basic question here is whether a Catholic's acceptance of the authority of those who speak in Christ's name can be reconciled with this de facto operational freedom. That man's response to God must be a free act has been emphasized by the Council's insistence that we develop a true sense of individual and personal commitment and responsibility. This has been felt in the sphere of authority by the demand that authority comport itself in a new manner, i.e., more conducive to personal development and growth. It has brought us to a better realization that essentially all of Catholic theology is a movement toward and for complete and endless freedom, freedom "such as belongs to the sons of God." Fr. Haring has thrown new light on the role of the law. It is to be the result of, administered in, and an aid to love. In the thought of St. Paul as seen by Fr. Lyonnet, the law was there to reveal to man his sinful state, for in terms of our non-observance we are brought to an ever-clearer realization that we are not always led by the Spirit. But man's response to the law, to authority, is always basically his own. It is our glory that we do not have to love God, but that we can deliberately and freely choose to do so. Our freedom, therefore, is not something about which we should be apprehensive. However, because the exercise of our freedom falls under the guidance of our conscience, conscience stands out as the highest and most sacred directing principle.

In fact our conscience is both judge and dictator. It judges the rightness or wrongness of acts, and then dictates a choice as it sees it. But conscience is something belonging to a person. It is not conscience which in reality judges and dictates, but the person. You and I, we judge. We know that we are subject to a host of factors in the formation of conscience decisions. Each one of us knows the effect personal involvement in situations has on our conscience decisions, how they can color and shade our judgements. But we also know, no matter how hard we try, we cannot, we would not, strip ourselves of this personal responsibility. We could not do so without denying both our humanity and our dignity.

However, among the immediate results of the exercise of our freedom of conscience is the stark and unsettling fact that our conscience is fallible. It can be wrong. This imposes upon us a most awesome responsibility of personal honesty. By this I mean something more than sincerity. It is one thing to be sincerely wrong. It is quite another to sincerely try to avoid being wrong. Faced with this reality, one who feels impelled to be a critical witness about an authoritative position of the Church must immediately confront himself with the question as to whether he has the necessary certitude to justify his position.

St. Thomas has accurately described conscience as an act, the application of general moral principles to a particular case. Its precision and validity will largely depend on the clarity with which it grasps these moral principles. Having pointed out these facts we can now indicate that St. Thomas himself upheld the absolute authority of conscience. St. Thomas established the absolute obligation of never acting against one's conscience. It is interesting to note that by so espousing the cause of conscience, St. Thomas broke with the common opinion of his predecessors. He capitalized on an innovation of his teacher and friend, St. Albert the Great, an innovation which insisted that any account of conscience must study the subjective factors. But, where the conscience feels certain, it is binding, be it correct or erroneous. St. Thomas rephrased this a bit more strongly saying that "any conscience, true or false is binding, and to act against it is always wrong." To follow conscience is both a right and a duty. If our conscience tells us that we ought to perform a particular act, it is our moral duty to perform it.

Throughout the discussion of the sovereign power of conscience, one proviso is forever met that one has formed one's conscience in good faith. This factor was paramount in the words of Bishop Colombo. He said that the duty belongs to every man to seek the truth with all available means. For the Catholic, he noted, the Church's teaching authority was one of those means.

What we are trying to avoid in asserting the sovereignty of conscience is a kind of "conditioned-reflex" Catholicism. We want thinking Catholics. And I see no reason why this necessarily has to breed radical Catholics, although the element of risk is obvious. We must be true to our convictions. It is no use assuring the layman that his voice counts if there is no way in which it can be heard or no obligation on the part of authority to listen. This observation of Daniel Callahan is endorsed by the recent Constitution on the Church. It states that the laity "should openly reveal their needs and desires with freedom and confidence." It also bids, however, that this always be done "in truth, in courage and in prudence, with reverence and charity."

One question that always arises in regard to freedom of conscience is that of moral relativism. To what degree is the quest for freedom a quest for license? This is to be sure a danger. It points out, I feel, our need for authority and our security when that authority is led by God's spirit.

Maybe we can at this point begin to tie together some loose ends. It is necessary to realize that the democracy, the freedom and the equality of the People of God, is in the Church a democracy of a special kind. It is one thing to be free to, or to be free in, and another to be from. Certainly, freedom does not imply the right to do wrong, but it must at least imply the right to be wrong. Freedom is really the ability to manifest love. But the ultimate object of all love is God, and God is Truth. The exercise of our freedom is then a search after truth. Because truth and God are identified, truth itself cannot be relative. However, man's perception of that truth may be relative. In any conflict between authority and conscience, the principle of charity must prevail; that is, orthodoxy, freedom and good will are taken for granted. We must never deny ourselves the power to love, of that love which allows another to be difficult, even when we do not understand him.

This principle has been applied in practice most recently in the question of religious freedom. "Pacem in Terris" states that "every human being has the right to honor God according to the dictates of an upright conscience." This is demanded by the very nature of the act of faith itself.

Finally, what happens when conscience and Church authority differ on a given issue? Daniel Callahan admits that the key to their reconciliation escapes him. What do people do who are faced with the dilemma of either accepting on authority what they do not accept in their own mind, or of following their own conscience despite an authority they have all their lives respected and obeyed? Perhaps we can draw solace from the words of Fr. Rahner: "The tragic conflict between the objectivity justified and obligatory demand, on the one hand, and the subjective conscience in good faith, on the other hand, is insoluble in practice." To this we can only sigh: Amen!

All this discussion on conscience and authority has produced among us a sense of insecurity, of confusion and of uneasiness. In spite of it all, I think we can make the observation of James Johnson, made in the "National Catholic Reporter," our own: "There is no reason to fear that the situation is as black or as dangerous as the more vociferous alarmists proclaim." Cardinal Suenens assures us that the confusion, though necessary, should prove beneficial. Let us pray that here, as in all things, "His will be done, His kingdom come."

SUPPLEMENTARY READINGS

Greeley, Andrew. THE CHURCH IN THE SUBURBS. *New York: Sheed and Ward, 1959.*

Thomas, John L., S.J. LOOKING TOWARD MARRIAGE. *Notre Dame: Fides, 1964.*

NOTE: There are several fine Catholic magazines in which family-life situations and relationships are frequently the subject of relevant and current articles—*Jubilee, Marriage, Sign, Ave Maria,* etc.

POINTS FOR DISCUSSION

1. A very important point to be considered in detail at this time is the question of the religious formation of children and the parental responsibility necessarily involved here. Particularly during this era of religious freedom and personal independence from authority this can become a sensitive point. The following questions may help to spark pertinent discussion of this important matter:

a. Should Catholic parents show an interest and a concern for their teenage children's religious practice. i.e., reception of the sacraments, attendance at Mass, etc.? If the answer is positive, in what way can parents most prudently and effectively fulfill this responsibility? If negative, explain reasons why.

b. What do you understand to be the relationship of the home, school, and parish in the religious formation of Catholic children? To what extent should parents be concerned with the formation given in school and parish? Are parents justified in saying that they leave the religious formation of their children to the "experts," i.e., the priests and teachers in school and parish? Explain.

c. What is your opinion of family religious practices, i.e., family prayers, common attendance at Mass? Give reasons for positive or negative opinions.

d. What is your opinion of a parental view that parents should not influence in any way the religious dimension of their children's lives, because this is a purely personal matter between themselves and God, and they should be totally free from any outside influence in forming their value judgments and decisions in this area of life?

2. A general discussion of the entire area of family relationships can be centered around questions such as the following:

a. A 17-year-old is a different person from a 13-year-old, and boys are different from girls. In what ways should parents show that they acknowledge this difference?

b. What is the most typical mistake, in your opinion, that parents make with regard to their teenage sons and daughters?

c. What, in your opinion, is the most typical mistake that teenage boys and girls make with regard to their parents and also with regard to their brothers and sisters, younger and older?

d. Why do parents and teenagers find it so difficult to communicate with each other? Do you have any concrete suggestions to facilitate this exchange?

e. There will always be a certain conflict and tension between parental authority and obligations on the one hand, and teenagers' rights and their personal individuality on the other hand. If in the future it is your privilege to become the parents of teenage sons and daughters, how are you going to try to live with and resolve this inevitable problem?

3. Do you agree or disagree with Mr. Willock's analysis of the husband-wife, father-family relationship as it exists in American society? Has there been a substantial change in either direction during the 20 years since this article was written? Explain your point of view.

4. How does the image of the modern American woman which emerges from the panel discussion reported in AVE MARIA magazine compare with the image described in the former article? Do you agree or disagree with the views expressed in this editorial? Explain.

5. What is YOUR understanding of the relationship between conscience and authority in the life of a Catholic today? What analogous application do you make in the parent-child relationship? Can a Catholic ever be justifiably disobedient to Church authority? A child disobedient to its parents? Explain your answer fully.

UNIT II

CHRISTIAN PERSPECTIVES IN PUBLIC LIFE

The primary emphasis of the problems and subjects considered thus far during second term has been focused on the individual student himself and on his personal response to circumstances and people as they affect his private life. The aim was to bring you to grips with concrete situations which you now face and will face as you struggle towards mature Christian witness as a person and as a Christian.

Being a good person and a good Christian, however, involves much more than being "good" in one's private little world. It is not only a question of personally assimilating Christian points of view and actualizing Christian virtues and habits in one's private life. Man is social by nature. He does not live in isolation. He is constantly in contact with others (indeed, even during the consideration of the earlier questions there was always a social dimension involved). For the remainder of the course, however, our concern will be more primarily directed to the individual's relatiors with others and with the community, and to the righ's and responsibilities which are his because of his community relationship and identity.

SOME PRELIMINARY CONSIDERATIONS
I. The Human and Divine Virtue of Justice. As we begin the study of the individual in his relationships to others in the non-political and political areas of real life, it is evident that a solid knowledge of the meaning of justice be achieved and, even more importantly, that this virtue be valued on a human and on a divine level. It is not our concern, however, to launch into a complete study of this virtue. Neither is it wise to spend a lot of time analyzing the concept of justice in the abstract. It will be far more effective to see justice (and injustice!) in action in man's dealings with his brothers. At the same time an introduction to the whole question of justice seems to be in order at this time, if only to clarify terminology and to serve as a general introduction to this part of the course. One possible approach might helpfully be outlined here.

Man has been defined as a social being, a rational animal.

He has many personal relationships in life.

168

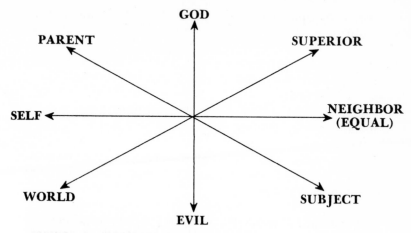

In these relationships, as we will see and as you have experienced, man has certain rights and corresponding responsibilities towards the rights of others.

Some of these rights he has by virtue of being a man, a person. Others he has by reason of his status in a community, his position, etc.

The former rights are more basic and they are universal. They are called "human rights" and they are personal, inalienable, inviolable, and moral. (These terms will become clear in concrete cases described later.)

Other men are forbidden, because they are men, to abolish, infringe, or hinder and render impossible the possession or exercise of these basic human rights.

The State is made up for and by the people, to promote and perpetuate the common and individual welfare of the community and of each member of the community.

The State, therefore, is primarily intended for the good of the people and people are not primarily for the good of the State.

NOTE: Concrete examples of all this will be seen in detail later.

The rights of man, therefore, are to be respected and protected by other men and by the State (the community of men).

Justice is the virtue which is involved in this respect and protection of the rights of men.

—justice is, of course, an analogous term. It has several meanings with different nuances.

—basic notion common to all nuances: a moral virtue inclining and supporting man's will to give unto others what is their rightful due.

—it is a natural virtue which needs practice to develop.

—it is also a supernatural virtue which is infused with the gift of baptism, but which likewise must be practiced. Christians receive the capacity (potential) to act justly as Christians but for this capacity to become an active habit there is need for its Christian exercise.

II. General Divisions of Justice According to Different Relationships.

1. Legal Justice. Responsibility of citizens to respect and fulfill duties toward the State (to give State its due).

2. Distributive Justice. Responsibility of State to citizens as a group and as individuals (to give citizens their due corporately and personally).

3. Commutative Justice. Responsibility of a person to person (moral person, i.e., a business corporation, is included here); to give another person his due.

4. Social Justice. This aspect of justice has been given prominence in recent years. It has never been too sharply defined. It includes elements from the other divisions mentioned above. The reality is the important thing and not a perfect definition. For the present purposes the following definition is given: *Social justice is that virtue by which members of a given society perform whatever acts, etc., are necessary for attaining or for maintaining the common good of that society, and regulates their conduct in right relation to that common good.*

NOTE. When the term *justice in the strict sense* is used, reference is being made to commutative justice. It is in questions of commutative justice that the obligation of restitution is of special importance.

The object of social justice, therefore, is the general welfare of all men and it pertains to all the areas of human relations, i.e., relations among men. A logical process would consist in making a study first of the general social doctrine of the Church as it has been expounded very clearly in the great encyclicals of social justice, beginning with Rerum Novarum of Pope Leo XIII and culminating in Pope John's masterpieces, *Mater et Magistra* and *Pacem in Terris.* However, in practice it does seem that the social encyclicals in themselves are too abstract and too dull to hold the attention of young people generally. Thus, a traditional "ethics" approach to studying the Natural Law, human rights, role of the State, etc., is not "relevant" today. Still, it will be necessary for all to be aware of this development of logical thought. Toward this objective some ideas in outline form have been presented earlier which will suggest some of the key ideas to be stressed. Such concepts come up quite naturally within the context of an investigation of some particular social situation or case. Others will be found in the paper which follows. The better method would seem to be to begin with a concrete problem, which is either personally known to the class or else is currently in the public eye through the newspapers and T.V., e.g., the airlines' strike in the summer of 1966, the steel strike which so affected the national economy a few years back, the transit system strike in New York City in early 1966. After the students have investigated and researched the facts of the situation, the corporate search for helpful insights towards solution can be sought in the encyclicals, in the entire work by those especially interested, or in short synopses of *Mater et Magistra* by the rest of the class. It will not be difficult to show how very often Catholic Social Teaching, as contained in these sources, touches the very heart of the problem.

III. Justice Seen in the Light of the Ten Commandments.
We can look upon the commandments as norms of justice in man's personal relationships to God, to himself, and to others.

I ⎫ II ⎬ III ⎭	JUSTICE AS VIRTUE OF RELIGION GIVING TO GOD HIS DUE	⎧ PERSON ⎨ NAME ⎩ WORSHIP

NOTE. In a real sense, however, man's relationship with God is something unique and outside total implications of justice because man can never really give to God His full due. Man can never "repay" God. Neither can there be any mutual obligation arising on God's part in relation to man unless freely willed to exist by God. Man has "no rights" in the absolute sense in his relationship to God. What he has and is, God has freely given him and freely bound Himself to respect and protect.

IV	JUSTICE AS FILIAL PIETY AND PARENTAL RESPONSIBILITY	⎧ towards ⎨ parents ⎬ towards ⎩ children
V to X	JUSTICE IN MAN'S RELATIONSHIPS TO SELF AND ALL OTHERS	

NOTE. Although the virtue of justice is intrinsic to all the commandments, it is ordinarily most frequently related to the seventh, eighth, and tenth commandments. Since a full treatment of the other commandments was given in the previous three years of the course, it is only the seventh and the tenth commandments which will be given special consideration during this term. This can be done at various opportunities within the discussion program, i.e., when considering property rights, poverty, labor-management relations, etc.

IV. Justice and Charity.
Throughout the consideration of justice in the different discussions of concrete situations

you must be careful to distinguish it from charity but not to divorce it from charity. One's motivation should not become: what must I do out of obligation in justice. At the same time a man should realize that in the fulfillment of some duty towards another person he is not always free to fulfill or not to fulfill it according to his personal whim. Neither should he esteem himself as being especially charitable when he fulfills a duty of justice. On the other hand this duty of justice should be performed with charity. This seems to me to be an important point to be stressed and emphasized regularly during the consideration of the different social problems of today, for example, race relations, just wage, and peace.

One axiomatic way of summing up the difference between justice and charity is to say that charity goes beyond justice, giving more than is one's due; another catchy slogan says justice gives another what is rightfully his while charity gives another what is rightfully mine but what I give to him as his out of love.

The intimate connection between justice and charity, therefore, is readily apparent in the relationship between persons, in the "His/Mine" polarity. It may be helpful here to speak somewhat on the "I-Thou" ideas of modern thinkers like Martin Buber and the "I-You" addition of Harvey Cox. In both justice and charity a self-centered and selfish orientation is destructive. It is often the uncontrolled desire for self-aggrandizement and for the accumulation of earthly goods which fosters acts of injustice and uncharity. Again, this will become very clear as we discuss different cases.

V. Some General Ideas on the Social Teaching of the Church.

1. The general aim of this section of the course is to impart a social consciousness and a sense of social responsibility. A genuine concern for others is the object of our teaching and discussion, a concern for others as members of the People of God and of the World Community, all brothers under a common Father and Creator. Motivation should be supernatural love as well as natural love, spiritual and

human brotherhood. Note the devotion of the Peace Corps volunteers to the noble humanitarian ideals of freedom, justice, kindness, peace, and charity for all men of the world. Christians should add the supernatural dimension to these same virtues for the love of God, "Whoever receives one such little child for my sake, receives me" (Mark 9:36).

2. The Christian dimension to the social question, i.e., specifically religious points which should be impressed upon all Catholics, has been expressed very well in Article 26 of the Roman Synod's document on the laity as excerpted from an article by Father John Reed, S.J.:

> "In the matter of social theory, Catholics should be instructed in the following principles: that all are to contribute, according to their opportunity, to the solution of the social question, mindful that it cannot be solved without dependence on religion and Christian morality; that Catholics cannot accept or lend favor to social systems condemned by the Church; that the goods created by God for all men should be distributed equally, according to the laws of justice and charity; that there is an obligation to give of one's superfluities to the needy in acknowledgment of the notion that the rich are dispensers and administrators of the things of God; and that the best possible effort must be made to assure all, even of the most humble condition, the opportunity of work, with a view to procuring the necessities of life and providing, honestly and securely, for their own future and that of their loved ones."[1]

3. It is a point worth noting that not infrequently students will become scandalized by social injustice in a general

[1] John Reed, S.J., *Theological Studies* (December, 1963).

way. You may become absorbed in some vast international and social problem outside your immediate experience, yet remain quite insensitive to very real social problems right on your doorstep. Another rather frequent occurrence with youth on the social question is that through experience they will often underestimate the real difficulty of social reform and become easily deceived by hopeful (wishful) panaceas of different types.

VI. The Importance of Social Studies in a Religion Program. The importance and the relevance of serious study, reflection, and discussion of the social teachings of the Church within the school program of religious education has been well and forcefully expressed by Father Louis Twomey, S.J., director of the Loyola Institute of Social Order in New Orleans. In answer to the question "Why the Irrelevance of Catholic Education in the Modern World?" he said:

"Many times in the past we have suggested that the reason why Catholic education faces the great danger of 'irrelevance' in the modern world, and why the clergy has felt the repelling aversion of society in the midst of the new needs of the century lies in the failure to recognize that although the substance of Catholic education never changes, the forms into which it is cast must vary according to the changing demands of changing times. Too often it is true that we are still trying to do new jobs with old tools. No wonder, then, that the Church is made to appear as though it were the ally of selfish conservatism; no wonder that the priest often is regarded as the high priest of a silenced litany, as a stranger to modern man.

"This failure in updating can be traced chiefly to the neglect to incorporate the social teachings of the Church into curricula on every level of our educational system and thus to fall considerably short of teaching integral Catholicism, of presenting Catholicism in its fulness.

"It is scarcely an exaggeration to state that the large majority of graduates from Catholic high schools, colleges and seminaries simply are not equipped with any meaningful sense of social responsibility. If this were not true, the scandal of Catholics going off in all directions in political, economic and social life would not exist at least not in the dimensions that it does today.

"These Catholics lacking any firm grounding in social principles and practices can hardly be expected to make any significant contributions toward the Christian reshaping of the overall objective of the papal social encyclicals. But without knowledge of these encyclicals, most Catholics in their post school years do not enter into the apostolate of social thought and action as prescribed by the encyclicals. On the contrary, whatever social philosophy they may have is absorbed from the 'mores' of their secular environment, which, in many instances, go directly counter to the social directives of the Church.

"The Key to Relevance
"The point we are striving to make here is that the extent to which the teachings of the Church will be regarded by the average man as irrelevant and impertinent to his dilemma can be gauged by the degree in which graduates are coming out of our schools and seminaries with neither intellectual commitment to the social teachings of the Church nor practical skills to implement them. In other words, if Catholic graduates take their place in the occupational hierarchy without knowledge of and hence without commitment to and involvement in the social directives of the Church there can be little hope of their acting as leaven in the mass to promote the observance of social justice and social charity.

"In this connection it may not be out of place to cite from Dr. Martin Luther King, the founder of the Southern Christian Leadership Conference and one of the most distinguished religious leaders in this country today:

'Any religion which professes to be concerned about the souls of men and is not concerned about the social and economic conditions that scar the soul, is a spiritually moribund religion only waiting for the day to be buried.'

"To identify Catholicism with the 'any religion' of the quotation is to do violence to the Faith. And yet in the minds of many outside the Church Catholicism is so being identified. This is so because too many Catholics both in the clergy and laity, are unmindful of their social obligations or unwilling to assume the risks necessarily involved in applying the Church's social doctrine to the concrete circumstances of given social evils, the evils, for instance, of racial segregation. For Catholics to stand aloof even in the face of obvious and serious violations of justice and charity which undercut human dignity is to project the Church in the image of an irrelevant institution outside the main stream of life in today's world.

"People do not meet the Church; they meet Catholics. Hence, the nature of the Church and its relevance to the problems of our times are most often judged by the conduct of Catholics. And when Catholics are delinquent in their social responsibilities, the Church itself, however illogically, is reckoned callous toward or indifferent to human sufferings.

"The key to relevance in the Church's modern apostolate, therefore, is an educational system geared to the development of a select corps of priests and laity with sound knowledge of the social teachings of the Church and with a determination to find through research and practical experience effective means of translating the general principles of social justice and social charity into realistic instruments of remedy and reform in the existential world of men and their problems.

"As Father Yves de Montcheuil, a French Jesuit who was murdered, probably martyred, in 1943 by the Nazis for his chaplaincy among the young Catholic militants of France has said:

'The all-out struggle against injustice should be inculcated in all Christians. In short, the fight against the institutions which isolate and divide should seem as intimately connected with the Christian life as the fight against capital sins, because the Kingdom of God not only requires that man establish right order in himself, but also that he initiate and promote it among all men. If we sufficiently understood this, our Christianity would be different!' (FOR MEN OF ACTION, CHICAGO: FIDES) 142–43.

"Father de Montcheuil puts it strongly in saying that those who are concerned in their relations with their fellow men only with individual justice and charity are 'regretably misguided.' But in the light of so much of this type of individualism in the spiritual lives even of very many good people, it can hardly be said that he overstates the case.

"The relevancy, therefore, of our Catholic Faith to the whole gamut of human living and not merely to its individualistic expression will become evident only when graduates of the Catholic educational system go out into society trained to function as 'transmission belts' of Christ's glad tidings to their fellow men in every walk of life.

"But this happy result can be hoped for only if the products of our schools are made to understand the practical pertinence of theological and philosophical truth to the down-to-earth problems besetting modern man, such as, materialism, Communism, secularism, thermo-nuclear weapons, national and domestic scandal of racial discrimination, the human and economic effects of automation, the paradox of poverty in the midst of the 'affluent society,' of chronic unemployment, of substandard housing, of the decaying central city within this same society, etc.

"The admittedly difficult assignment to get young men and women ready to meet these problems with the Christian ethic is the overriding challenge to Catholic educators. But the challenge will go unheeded and the greatest opportunity perhaps in all history will be lost to the Church unless 'the social teachings proclaimed by the Catholic Church is made a vital component of her traditional teaching regarding man's life.' For only through the principles and practices of her social doctrine can the bridge be built between the sanctuary and the vast arena of man's temporal life. Otherwise, society will set its course outside the influence of the Church's redemptive mission and the danger of her irrelevance to the modern world will be realized."[1]

---

[1] EXCERPTS FROM UNPUBLISHED MATERIAL WRITTEN BY FATHER LOUIS J. TWOMEY, s.j., DIRECTOR OF THE LOYOLA INSTITUTE OF SOCIAL ORDER IN NEW ORLEANS. WE ARE GRATEFUL FOR HIS KIND PERMISSION TO INCLUDE IT HERE.

POINTS FOR DISCUSSION

NOTE. These basic concepts of social justice should be discussed rather in the concrete circumstances of human events and actions involving social justice than in merely the abstract order of ideas. For review purposes, however, the following points are suggested for reflection and critical judgment.

1. In what precise ways is it true that every human right of one person involves a cooresponding human responsibility on the part of another person? How does this principle apply in the supernatural order?

2. Explain the distinction between, and yet the mutual interrelation of, justice and charity. Why is it important not to look upon these two virtues in isolation from each other?

3. Is social justice really totally distinguishable from the other three forms of justice? Explain their interconnection if you feel such exists. What important point is involved if there is a connection with commutative justice? Explain.

4. Does the fact that man can never really "render to God His due" mean that man is not bound by the virtue of justice in his dealings with God? Explain your answer.

5. In Father Twomey's eyes what is the key to the relevance of Christianity in the modern world? Explain. Do you agree with Father Twomey? Disagree? Why?

chapter 6
LABOR-MANAGEMENT RELATIONS

There are many areas of human life and activity in which the social doctrine of the Church, as put forward in the great social encyclicals of the past 70 years, have particular relevance. It will not be possible to cover all or even many of them within the time allotted for religion class during second term, but most of the important social problems will be developed at least to some degree. General principles, seen in application to one aspect of the social problem, can often be judged to be analogously relevant to other situations and understood as such even without any special study.

One very important subject which vitally affects the economy of any country — and hence the temporal and spiritual lives of all of its citizens — is the question of labor-management relations. There are many specialized problems involved in this general subject area, i.e., just family wage, unions and strikes, automation and unemployment, business ethics, dignity of work, leisure-time activity, urban-rural problems, link between industrialization and de-Christianization, etc. It is possible to open up the scope of many of these difficult problem areas in class, but clearly it is impossible to handle them with any kind of detailed consideration. Keep in mind, however, that *a general social awareness and proper social attitudes* are the primary objectives of these studies and discussions. It is not necessary for you to become informed or competent in all of these areas in order to achieve this desired result. The article which follows will serve to open up several of the afore-mentioned problems and provide fine material for your understanding and discussion of this topic. It is the work of two students from Fordham Preparatory School, class of 1965, who presented these ideas to their classmates in a lively joint presentation and submitted this paper as a report of their research. It is included here both because of its fine content and because it serves as an indication of the high calibre of work of which competent and interested senior students are capable.

Labor-Management Relations
The Christian Economics
of Free Enterprise

MICHAEL HAYES AND TERENCE LENAHAN

I – Introduction

LABOR-MANAGEMENT relations play an increasingly important role in the economy of the United States. Various business activities have become so interdependent that the decisions of labor or management in any one sector of the economy often affect many other areas. In such a situation, the application of Christian justice to modern labor-management disputes becomes more essential than ever before. For, even aside from moral considerations, the maintenance of a sound economy is vitally dependent upon the administration of such justice. Perhaps nowhere else is the relationship between Christian doctrine stemming directly from supernatural inspiration, and order on the natural level as readily apparent as in the economics of labor-management relations.

The purpose of this paper is twofold: to examine the essentials of Christian justice for labor-management relations, establishing the link between the application of these principles and a sound economy, and to apply these principles to several contemporary problems facing labor and management.

II – The Principles of Christian Justice
The relation between labor and management becomes more crucial and correspondingly more complex as the years progress. The fact that our economy has just roared through its forty-ninth straight month of expansion[1] constitutes clear evidence that the two have largely fulfilled their individual roles in the free enterprise system. Yet there remain unsolved problems and frictions between labor and management upon whose solution will rest the

SUBMITTED AS A CLASS REPORT AT FORDHAM PREPARATORY SCHOOL, NEW YORK. REPRINTED WITH PERMISSION.

[1] *New York Times*, April 4, 1966.

future of our economic system. For, as Pope John XXIII expressed it:

> "Any human society if it is to be well ordered and productive, must lay down as a foundation this principle: that every human being is a person, his nature is endowed with intelligence and free will."[2]

This implies that a productive society depends on human justice and charity in its economy as well as in the areas of civil, social, and educational rights. Christian justice implies definite standards for both management and labor which must be established before the contemporary problems facing them can be resolved.

The purpose of management is to operate business at maximal efficiency and thus at maximal profit. But in so doing, it is obliged to give just compensation to all its employees. The term, a "just wage," is often used but seldom defined. Even during the nineteenth century, when the injustice of management gave rise to organized labor, employers agreed that they should pay a "just wage." But there is seldom agreement, even today, between employer and employee on the definition of a "just wage." In 1931, Pope Pius XI in *Quadragesimo Anno* outlined three considerations in calculating the just wage. These guidelines are summarized in *Christianity and Economics*:

> "It (the just wage) is to be considered what is necessary to support the working man and his family. Catholic teaching cannot approve of a system which, in order that the family may have a sufficiency, compels the mother and young children to go out to work. Secondly, the state of business must be considered. It is idle to require business to pay such wages . . . that it is

[2] Pope John XXIII, *Pacem in Terris*.

unable to sell its product. Thirdly, what the
Pope calls 'the exigencies of the common
good' must be considered. By this he
means principally that wages should be
such as to maintain a general full employment."[3]

The Pope's calculation of the just wage is a clear statement of justice for the working man. Perhaps less clear,
however, is the fact that his last consideration, "the common good," equates this justice with sound economics.
There are really two ways that wages can cause unemployment and the Pope is dealing with both. If the wages paid
are too low, there is a general insufficiency of purchasing
power with a corresponding deflationary effect and unemployment. On the other hand, if the employer pays wages
that are too high, the product is unsalable and the firm
is driven into bankruptcy with corresponding unemployment. Thus, justice for the working man is necessary for
a sound economy. Further, this idea may be extended to
condemn the situation in the United States during the
1890's when capital was concentrated in the hands of a
few. For if incomes are so distributed that a few have a
great deal and the majority very little, it must inevitably
follow that the goods which the society produces will be
unsalable. Pope Pius XI advised in *Quadragesimo Anno*
that "we deem it advisable that the wage control should,
when possible, be modified somewhat by a contract of
partnership." While partnership is seldom possible in the
modern economy, equitable distribution of property in the
form of capital remains an obligation of management.

If justice demands this standard of management, there
must be corresponding demands upon labor. Pope John
summed up this relationship of rights and duties by de-
claring that:

"If a man becomes conscious of his rights,
he must become equally aware of his du-

[3] Christopher Hollis, *Christianity and Economics* (1961: Hawthorne, New York).

184

> ties. He who possesses certain rights like-
> wise has the duty to claim those rights as
> marks of his dignity, just as all others
> have the duty to acknowledge and respect
> them."[4]

While labor has the duty to press for its rights, it also has the obligation to limit its demands in accord with the same "common good" as management. Indeed, justice binds labor to all the duties corresponding to the obligations of management. If employers must pay a just wage, then employees are obliged to return a just day's work. Yet the term "just day's work" is as hard to define as the term "just wage." While conservative management tends to argue for stabilization of present wages, labor demands more wages for the same work. Christian justice demands that the worker give the employer the full value of his wage, to which management has a right. The same economic principles apply to employee as to employer. If the worker refuses to do the work he is paid for, the product must be finished at such a great cost that it becomes unsalable and the employer is bankrupt. If, on the other hand, as happened in the late nineteenth century, labor does more work than it is actually paid for, the supply far exceeds the demand. In this case, as Lenin argued with a good deal of truth, foreign or colonial markets must be developed to support the economy or deflation results. Thus, our economic system also depends on the justice of labor. Since labor has become organized into unions of considerable size and influence, justice in labor policies has taken on additional social meaning. The "common good" with which labor must be concerned includes both management and consumer. Large unions today hold the power to severely damage or bankrupt business by striking. As a current example, if the Printers' Union of New York City had recently attempted a long newspaper strike, they might well have forced the New York Herald-Tribune into bankruptcy in the process of trying to make it increase wages. Labor has the responsibility of weighing the results of its actions and of abandoning policies whose harmful consequences outweigh their good results. Like-

[4] Pope John XXIII, *Pacem in Terris*.

wise, labor must consider the effect of its actions on the general public. For this reason, the government forbids many vital workers, such as teachers, from striking in order to protect society. Thus, for each of the rights it can demand from management, labor must recognize its corresponding duty.

The general economic welfare of the nation, therefore, does depend greatly on the justice of both labor and management. The fact that we are experiencing unparalleled economic prosperity speaks well for the efforts of the two to reach equitable settlements in the past. Conflict between labor and management is not a necessity, as Leo XIII pointed out:

"The great mistake made in regard to the matter now under consideration is to take up the notion that class is naturally hostile to class, and that wealthy and workingman are intended by nature to live in mutual conflict. So irrational and so false is this view, that the direct contrary is the truth . . . Each needs the other: Capital cannot do without Labor, nor Labor without Capital."[5]

However, while the doctrine of the Church on labor-management relations is clear, often its application to actual situations is not. Even men of the best intention find it impossible to apply Christian justice to modern problems and arrive at the same solutions. Since the nineteenth century, most of the issues between labor and management involving clear violations of justices have been resolved. The unsolved problems which remain often demand subjective interpretation and, thus far, no consensus of opinion about them has been reached. Yet it is interesting to note that while the solution to contemporary labor-management problems often seems clouded, our present policies, many of which today seem so ob-

[5] Pope Leo XIII, *Rerum Novarum*, May 15, 1891.

vious and just, were just as contested a few years ago. For example, the right of labor to strike, which today is granted by all, was once denied as an abuse of power by management and the law alike. In the same section, some of the contemporary problems facing labor and management will be discussed and the relevance of Christian justice to each case explored.

III — Contemporary Labor-Management Problems

The contemporary problems facing labor and management are both diverse and complex. Perhaps in a quarter-century, their solution in accord with the principles of Christian justice will seem obvious. But today there is no obvious method to effect an equitable settlement of many issues. In the present system, organized labor has taken the initiative in demanding change. Management often finds itself conservatively defending the *status quo*. Yet management also has definite rights upon which labor must not infringe. Most of the contemporary friction between labor and management stems from two basic areas: the precise definition of the role of management, and labor's demand for total job security. In each, the problem is to determine the exact rights of each party and to establish a working agreement of control in the undefined areas to which neither side has an established right. Each of these problem areas deserves separate analysis, for one is primarily concerned with management and the other with labor.

One key contemporary problem is the definition of the role of management. Management has both the legal and moral right to control the property it owns. On the other hand, the right of management to control labor is primarily based upon economic power. Both Church and civil law give the worker equal right to withhold his efforts unless paid a fair wage and to refuse assignments he feels are unjust. In the modern economy, the worker, through collective bargaining, has become powerful enough to balance the economic power of management. The result has been a situation in which labor has gained more and more control over the property which is owned by management. This power is certainly just because the worker has the right to regulate property for the general welfare if the employer will not. However, there is question as to how much control labor can exercise over the property of the employer before it is usurping the latter's just right to manage. The opposing views on the role of management were expressed as early as 1945. Management included the following items as "clearly the functions of management":

"The determination of job content (not wages but the duties required in the performance of any job); the determination of the size of the work force; the allocation and assignment of work to workers; determination of the policies affecting the selection of employees; establishment of quality standards and judgment of workmanship required; the maintenance of discipline and control and use of the plant property; the scheduling of operations and the number of shifts; the determination of safety, health, and property protection measures, where legal responsibility of the employer is involved."[6]

Obviously, some of the functions that management listed have already become matters of arbitration with labor. However, labor has refused to categorize which management functions it feels are open to arbitration. Labor's only statement is:

"It would be extremely unwise to build a fence around the rights and responsibilities of management on the one hand and the unions on the other. The experience of many years shows that with the growth of mutual understanding the responsibilities of one of the parties today may

[6] *The President's National Labor Management Conference* Nov. 5–30, 1945 (U.S. Dept. of Labor, Div. of Labor Standards. Bull. No. 77, 1946).

well become the joint responsibility of
both parties tomorrow."[7]

Yet somewhere, management insists, a line must be
drawn. If labor can exercise complete control over the
property of management, then free enterprise loses its
meaning. The Christian solution must lie somewhere between management's extreme theory of "residual rights"
and the extreme labor theory of "implied limitations." The
theory of residual rights simply states that the employer
has absolute power to do anything which is not forbidden
by law or union contract. On the contrary, the theory of
implied limitations holds that every labor contract com-
mits the employer to maintain the *status quo* in every area
not specifically mentioned. While neither management nor
labor holds strictly to either of these views, the friction between them on the role of management often stems from
the tendency of each to drift toward such extremes. The
definition of management's role must include provisions
for labor's welfare, but the owner's control of his property
must also be retained. As labor proposes further regulation
of the employers' property, each new suggestion must be
considered from the dual perspective of the protection of
management's property as well as labor's rights.

Another key question in labor management relations is
labor's demand for "total job security." More strikes
occur today over the inability of labor and management
to reach agreement on fringe benefits than are caused by
disagreement over actual wages. While workers are, by
and large, content with present wage levels, few express
satisfaction about their over-all security. The demand for
"total job security" includes the demand for guaranteed
employment, guaranteed annual wage, more paid vacation,
higher pensions, and protection against automation.
The basic conflict is to determine the extent to which the
employer "owes a living" to the employee and the point
after which the worker is on his own. By law, the employer
is now forced to bargain about job security as well as
wages. The area in which he must bargain, by laws such

[7] Ibid.

as the Wagner and Taft-Hartley Acts, is steadily widen-ing. These areas include:

"Health and accident insurance. Christmas bonuses, holidays, vacations, profit-shar-ing plans, stock purchases, sick leave, severance pay, and other guarantees of job security which were once thought to be voluntary gratuities were declared to be intitled to the same consideration as wages."[8]

Modern management agrees that these benefits are the right of labor and often offers more job security in place of increased wages. The increasing and insistent demands of labor, however, for absolute security from economic worry at the employer's expense, may be asking for a bit too much. Management has no obligation to provide the employee of a concern with more economic security than the concern itself experiences. Economists predict that if labor's demands for more security at the expense of sound economic practice persist, the result could well be harmful:

"The guaranteed annual wage does not necessarily go hand in hand with maxi-mum production. In fact, it may be incon-sistent with both. For regularization of production may require sacrificing the interests of maximum employment and maximum production. Complete job se-curity in a given plant or industry may harm the interests of workers and busi-ness prosperity in other industries for a variety of reasons. If employment is guaranteed year-round in a business with

---

[8] Morris Stone, *Managerial Freedom and Job Security* (1964: Harper and Row, New York), p. 3.

seasonal fluctuations, the cost of maintaining the work force at the level required during the time of maximum demand will prove harmful to the business, and, if it occurs on a wide scale, to the economy. As the United States Bureau of Labor stated, 'The most stable economy is the economy which has the most effective and efficient use of its material, and particularly its human resources. It is perfectly conceivable that stability as thus defined can best be achieved by having a substantial group of employees work for several employers during the year.' "[9]

Thus, the total job security demanded by individual unions is not always beneficial either to their own employers or to the economy as a whole. Christian justice demands that even as the employer must sacrifice his absolute control of property for the common good, so must the employee be willing to accept the same economic insecurity as management.

Perhaps the most striking conclusion of any such analysis is the impossibility of resolving all labor-management disputes. Even when both sides honestly attempt to do justice to the other, no satisfactory solution is immediately assured. Yet this friction in itself is not a drawback, but an advantage of our economic system, as the conclusion of *Managerial Freedom and Job Security* points out:

"It is pointless to hope for a perfect reconciliation of labor and managerial viewpoints. Job security depends, in the final analysis, on the ability of American industry to provide profitable jobs. From

[9] Ludwig Teller, *Management Functions under Collective Bargaining* (1958: Baker, Voorhis, New York).

this point of view, companies and unions have identical interests. But each side has its own interests, its own special pre-occupations. If each side is also aware of the other's problems in a secondary way, the clash of viewpoints can be kept short of the point impasse. But it is doubtful whether any beneficial result would follow if either partner in labor-management relations became so 'understanding' of the other as to neglect the contribution which it uniquely makes to the economy. Fortunately, under the American system of industrial relations, and in our pluralistic society, no such abdication of function is likely to occur."[10]

---

[10] Morris Stone, *Managerial Freedom and Job Security* (op. cit.), p. 246.

SUPPLEMENTARY READINGS

Haupt, Mother Maria Carl, o.s.u. THE SOCIAL ASPECTS OF THE CHRISTIAN FAITH CONTAINED IN MATER ET MAGISTRA AND PACEM IN TERRIS. *Glen Rock, N.J.: Paulist Press (Deus Books), 1965. This booklet is divided into 15 chapters, corresponding to class sessions, with outlines for class consideration and passages selected for study and discussion.*

Morgan, Everett J., s.j., *and Twomey, Louis J.,* s.j., THE SOCIAL CONSCIENCE OF A CATHOLIC: THE SOCIAL DOCTRINE OF THE CHURCH APPLIED TO PROBLEMS OF OUR CONTEMPORARY SOCIETY. *Berkeley: McCutchan Publishing Company, 1964. Distributed by Marquette University Bookstore.*

POINTS FOR DISCUSSION

1. How did Pius XI define a "just wage"? What important factors must be considered in order to make a valid judgment regarding this just wage? What effect do wages have on the economy of a country? Discuss their effect on family life, especially on families in the lower income brackets. What is the responsibility of government in this matter? Of the Church? Of individual Christians?

2. Comment upon the following statement and give some concrete examples of its application in daily life: "Thus, for each of the rights it can demand from management, labor must recognize its corresponding duty."

3. What do the authors of this article feel to be the two basic causes of the contemporary friction existing between labor and management? What are their reasons for this point of view? Do you agree? Disagree? Explain.

4. What conditions must be verified for a strike to be considered "just" according to Christian principles? Apply this criterion to a current or recent local strike situation.

5. What positive statements regarding the dignity of work and of the person of the worker were made by recent popes in the several social encyclicals? In what concrete ways can this positive point of view towards work and the worker be implemented in society today? How does this approach tie in with the theme of vocation and with the modern ideas on man and his place in the universe found in the writings of Father Teilhard de Chardin?

6. Discuss the effects of automation on our modern society generally and, more particularly, on the person of the individual worker.

7. Why is the subject of leisure-time activity assuming a greater importance in modern living? Why is it sometimes considered to be a problem? A problem for whom? Why?

8. The observation has been made that the more a country or a city becomes industrialized the more it becomes de-Christianized. Do you agree or disagree with this statement? What are your reasons? What is the sociological fact? What are the basic reasons behind the fact?

9. Is the Church opposed to technological progress? In favor of it? Neutral? Give your reasons.

10. Do religion and religious values really have any place in business dealings and the workings of industry? Can you be religious and still "get ahead in the world"? Is there anything really wrong in getting ahead at the expense of others? Discuss concrete cases in which there is often a conflict between religious values and business practices. How does one form his conscience with regard to a course of action in such circumstances?

chapter 7
COMMUNICATION ARTS

It may come as a surprise to some that the subject of communication arts should be suggested for consideration within the religion program. The scope of this field, which embraces the film, television, radio, and the recording industry may not, upon first glance, appear to be integral to the study of religion. Some might see its relevance, but only with regard to the formation of a morally critical approach to the media of entertainment. Thus, the aim of the religion course would be to help form consciences as to what is wholesome or morally dangerous, in part or in its totality, in films, TV programs, and music.

Although it *is* important to make a careful study of the purpose, accomplishments, and present function of groups such as the National Office for Motion Pictures (formerly called The Legion of Decency) within the religion program, *it is by no means the sole or primary purpose* of considering communication arts at this time. The objectives we have in mind are far broader than that.

One competent authority in the field has said that the present generation will be known not only as a literate but also as a cinemate people. The influence of the film in movies and television upon people's ideas, ideals, and daily practices is at present very substantial, and it shows every sign of growing in importance with the passing years. It is most urgent, therefore, that you gain a critical knowledge and habit of mind toward these media of communication and carefully weigh and evaluate their effect upon your intellectual, emotional, and religious development.

Thus, the more explicit aim of our considerations in class will be directed toward the cultivation of a maturely critical approach to these media, both positively and negatively. Understanding and making use of these media can help us to grow and to develop into mature persons with valid human and religious attitudes and values. When we consider the content of our senior religion course—vocation, careers, love, marriage, family, social problems, human relations, politics, and world problems of war and peace—and when we consider the usual content of significant films playing upon the same themes, it becomes obvious how relevant to religious education, especially on the senior level, is the communication arts field in general and the film in particular.

As an instrument for exploring and for communicating basic human and religious truths about life and its meaning, there are few more effective means than through the presentation of a pertinent and well-done film which is followed by student-centered discussion under the permissive guidance of an experienced and knowledgeable teacher.

The main basis for the study of this subject should be realized in the experience of a thoughtful viewing and provocative discussion of stimulating films. The two articles included here are intended to give some insight and understanding of the educational potential of film-viewing and to present a balanced picture of the important contribution made by the National Catholic Office for Motion Pictures.

I Was a Teenage Movie Teacher

JOHN M. CULKIN, s.j.

TEENAGE MOVIE TEACHERS teach two things: teenagers and movies. Both are fun to work with. Both need working with. Some TMTs put the stress on teaching *teenagers* and some on teaching *movies*. The former use films as a way of helping the student to illumine his own experience and to develop a personal point of view. The latter use the student as the audience for a course emphasizing the history and aesthetics of film. There is a middle ground to be discovered and defended. And, like all teachers, TMTs teach themselves — their own attitudes, prejudices, likes and dislikes.

There aren't too many TMTs in captivity, but the number of interested candidates is increasing rapidly. Some teach courses; some teach film units within courses; some organize film clubs. Their work is variously described as "motion picture appreciation" (deadly!), "film study," or, when television is included, "screen education." They are constantly confused with audio-visual specialists, whose films deal with the dissection of frogs, or with English teachers, who occasionally use a feature film like *Pride and Prejudice* to seduce students into reading the book.

TMTs want their students to see as many fine films as possible, in much the same way that teachers have always wanted their students to read great books and experience great art. They want to free students from the narrow confines of their own "I, my, me" world by showing them films which widen and deepen their understanding of what it means to be human. They want to equip the student with ways of analyzing and reflecting upon the constant flow of moving images which flood his world. They want to produce an enthusiastic, intelligent, selective, and mature film and television viewer.

The balance between what Whitehead calls the "stage of romance" and the "stage of precision" is crucial. TMTs

FROM *SATURDAY REVIEW*, REPRINTED WITH PERMISSION.

want students with all the intuitive values associated with the left hand and all the analytical powers of the right hand. Knowledge doesn't have to mark the end of innocence or enthusiasm. The goal is innocence after knowledge.

What kinds of films are involved? All kinds. In-school screenings might include titles like *Hud; The Loneliness of the Long Distance Runner; Singin' in the Rain; Bicycle Thief; Henry V; The Hustler; To Kill a Mockingbird; On the Waterfront; The Golden Age of Comedy; La Strada; David and Lisa; Twelve Angry Men; High Noon; Citizen Kane; Ballad of a Soldier; Requiem for a Heavyweight; Raisin in the Sun; The 400 Blows; Shane; Paths of Glory; Nobody Waved Goodbye.*

Everyone has his own list of favorites. Classroom discussions also focus on currently popular films and TV programs like the Bond cycle, *Batman, The Fugitive, Bonanza,* and *The Man from U.N.C.L.E.* Better to help them analyze what they are seeing than to develop critical standards for films or books they may never see or read.

The schools had a go at the movies once before back in the '30's. The crusade started fast and faded fast since it was built on a negative approach to film. The second spring of the movement is based on a respect for film rather than on a fear of film. It regards film as one of the humanities, as one of the liberating arts, and it strives to produce the largest possible audiences for the best possible films. Its methodology is built around the screening, discussion, and analysis of well-made, relevant films. It believes that a lively art demands lively teaching and it is, therefore, opposed to a pedanticism which would stifle the spontaneity and enthusiasm which most of us bring to films. It maintains that in an image-saturated culture *all* students should become their own TV and movie critics.

The views here presented are those not of a theoretician but of a practicing fanatic. They have been worked out through personal involvement with more than 10,000 high school students in a variety of situations ranging from the blue-chip college prep schools to Harlem and a dozen Job

Corps camps. The article also profits from the practical experience of teachers both in this country and in Europe where the movement has been active for more than fifteen years. There is no one way to play the game and it will be a lovely moment in education if we can create one little island in the curriculum which will be free from texts and machine-scored tests and free for approaches as varied as the people in the seats and in front of the classroom.

At present the movement is but a cloud on the horizon, no larger than a man's hand, but it will inevitably grow because it is both wanted and needed. To speak in cinematic terms, we can consider the film study movement at three focal lengths: a *long shot* on its cultural context, a *medium shot* on the changing student, and a *closeup* on the role of the schools.

a) Long Shot—A Changing Culture

Marshall McLuhan, who has emerged as the oracle of mass culture and the darling of the magazine writers, has been telling us, for a long while and in his own obscure fashion, that we live in a post-literate world. Not *illiterate*, although that has often been suggested too, but *post-literate*—a world in which print no longer has a monopoly of communication either within the culture or within the schools. The new environment created by the electronic media has formed a free-flow, total information ecology within which people receive their communication through a great variety of media and at a pace not within the control of the established and traditional mediators of culture —the family, the church, and the school. We can get some idea of both the extent and rapidity of this change by imagining the effects of a month-long national experiment in which we would be deprived of all the communications media developed and mass-produced within our own century. Goodbye TV, movies, telephones, record-players, radios, and a whole way of life stitched together by the new media.

McLuhan holds that the introduction of any new medium into a culture inevitably produces two effects: an apparent threat to established patterns and a change in the perceptual habits of the people. Thus it was with the phonetic alphabet and the printing press. Thus it is with films and television. He suggests that we bypass the tiresome and predictable clashes of the transition by arriving at an early and reasonable synthesis.

> *"If these 'mass media' should serve only to weaken or corrupt previously achieved levels of verbal and pictorial culture, it won't be because there's anything inherently wrong with them. It will be because we've failed to master them as new languages in time to assimilate them to our total cultural heritage.*

The ability to lament vice is no sure proof of virtue. In this period of transition, therefore, we can really do without the tedious replay of the glib generalities about the quality and effect of the mass media, the exhortations to bury our TV sets, the unfair comparisons between the best of one medium and the worst of another, and the either-or fallacies which only dig ditches when we need to build bridges. It's a time for *doing* things.

The brief for some kind of media study within the schools normally follows either of two lines of argument: a) make the media seem so *respectable* that the schools have to recognize them as worthy of inclusion within the curriculum; or b) make their impact seem so *lethal* that the schools feel forced to deal with them as a tactic of survival. *In medio stat virtus,* as the old Romans used to say—infrequently.

Film as Art
The man in *Time* said it: "In the decade since Hollywood became unstuck and television became the reigning medium of mass entertainment, the movies have suddenly and powerfully emerged as a new and brilliant international art, indeed as perhaps the central and characteristic art of the age." He then suggests that the logical response to this

new cultural fact is the creation of a generation which is "cinemate as well as literate."

Walt Whitman said it: "To have great poets there must be a great audience." Great audiences for any art form are not born; they are made. They are created by an exposure to and an analysis of excellence within the medium. Some people are distracted because the movies are "mere entertainment" (as though that were a bad thing in itself). The same tag once kept Elizabethan drama, the novel, and vernacular literature out of the schools. Others stress the number of worthless or tasteless films. The piffle index, however, is high for any medium, and the percentage of poor films is probably about the same as the percentage of poor work in print, paint, and other media. The best within the film medium deserves the same attention to content and style that we accord to the traditional arts.

Although the fancy talk about film as an art form is true enough and suasive enough, it is not without its dangers. There is a Steinbeck quote which is to the point: "Culture is a lousy word to describe what mankind is all about." Too often we let talk *about* art substitute for the experience *of* art. Once a false mystique about art gets into the air, people begin to become insecure about their own instincts and to react to the expectations of the high priests of art rather than to their own honest reactions. This is especially lamentable in a nice friendly field like the movies where everyone has for so long presumed that he is an expert. Film critic Pauline Kael voices this same warning; "It's only a movie. What beautiful words. At the movies you are left gloriously alone. You can say it stinks and nobody's shocked. That's something you can't do with a Dickens novel or a Beethoven symphony or even a poen by Browning, and because you can't, because they're all pre-selected and pre-judged and graded for greatness, you don't talk about them with the other kids the way you do about movies . . . Respectable is what the movies are not, and that's what we love about them." The experience of art is more important than its definition or any roll call of critical opinion.

If Whitman's thesis about the relation of art and audience is true for poems which can be written on the backs of old envelopes by a production staff of one, it holds with multiplied validity for the motion picture and television which are wild combinations of art, technology, and commerce. The traditional interplay of artist and patron has to be rethought for each of the new media. Numbers have a great deal to do with what can be communicated through any of the media which involve large financial investments. Both risk and success are measured by increasingly larger numbers as one moves from print to stage to film and to television. A hardbound book hits the best-seller lists when it sells 20,000 copies; a Broadway play starts making money after the first 100,000 tickets; a commercial film has to have roughly 2½ patrons for every dollar invested before it breaks even with the result that a million dollar movie needs two and a half million patrons; and in television, which is the massest of mass media, a series in prime time needs a continuing audience of approximately 25 million viewers to stay on the air. Last season, for instance, *East Side/West Side* went off the air with a sustaining audience of 14 million regular viewers — an audience which would be astronomical for any of the other media but which is too esoteric to be served by television.

In the commercial media the name of the game is numbers. The one-to-one relationship between De Medici and Michelangelo has given way to a complicated feedback system between the public and the network or the studio. The public is the patron and, distasteful as this may be to the elitists, this numerical approach to taste is the fact of media life. It has its obvious problems. What most want is not what all should get. And just because people take what they get doesn't necessarily mean that they are getting what they want. The public doesn't know what it wants until it gets it and then they may only be accepting what they appear to want. What we need are more choices and more people qualified to make wise choices. Since the quality of films and television depends on the quality of the audience, we should be at pains to improve the quality of that audience. That is what film study is all about.

b) Medium Shot — A Changing Student
It has been said that if Booth Tarkington were writing

Seventeen today he would have to call it *Twelve.* The mass media have something to do with those five years which we have lost or gained, depending on your point of view. By the time the average American student graduates from high school today, he has watched more than 15,000 hours of television and seen more than 500 films. The TV figure the result of an average of twenty hours of weekly viewing for fifteen years; it adds up to two full years of twenty-four-hour-a-day viewing. During this same period, this average student has attended school five hours a day, 180 days a year, for twelve years, to produce a total of 10,800 hours of school time. School loses, in more ways than one.

All this arithmetic adds up to a challenge of relevance. The schools are no longer dealing with the student of 1900 whose sources of information were limited to the home, church, school, and neighborhood gang. Today's student comes equipped with a vast reservoir of facts and vicarious experiences gleaned from the new media. All the analogies comparing the mind to a blank page or an empty bucket died with Edison. The teacher is now in competition with a host of rival communicators, most of whom are smarter, richer, and considerably more efficient. Relevance and competence are educational tactics against which students have not devised a defense.

It is almost sacrilegious to find fault with Bel Kaufman's *Up the Down Staircase* because it is so human and so in sympathy with our own loves and hates. But the lady made me sad on page 198. "I don't think I got through to them, in spite of all my careful paper-plans . . . The trouble is their utter lack of background. 'I never read a book in my life, and I ain't starting now', a boy informed me."

Honest, Bel, they've got a background; it's the one thing we're sure they do have. It may not look much like your background and my background and it isn't spangled with titles from the great books of the Western world. But it's there. We know for sure that it is well-stocked with plenty of TV material just waiting to be tapped with probing questions about phoniness and realness, winners and losers, style and *schmaltz*—all the new ways of talking about the old ideas of the true, the good, and the beautiful. If the school is in business to communicate with these students, it is up to the school to get plugged in to their background. Whatever the eventual goal may be, there is only one place to start and that is—where they *are.*

A digression on classroom communication. It was a beautiful speech. Logical. Witty. Relevant. Delivered flawlessly and with elan. The audience didn't understand English. It was a terrible speech. Communication happens when the receiver gets the sender's message. How simple. If the message doesn't get through, it's the sender's fault. He started the whole thing. It's up to him to find out what language the audience understands. It is up to him to find out the prejudices, values, fears, blocks, vocabulary, and attitudes of the audience. It's up to him to get through to the audience. Saying true things has little to do with communicating. Having true things heard has everything to do with it.

The *whom* and not the *who* is the focal point of good communication. The language of good communication is *whom-ese,* the language of the receiver, the *whom.* There's a lot of good *whom-ese* being spoken in the TV commercials. The audience is researched, the message prepared, the results tabulated, and if the message doesn't get through they bounce the teacher. The schools have a nasty habit of bouncing the audience. The ads for teachers should read: "Wanted: Speakers of *Whom-ese.*" All the great teachers speak it fluently.

Meanwhile, back at the movies. The speech on *Whom-ese* is not unrelated to teenage movie teaching. Teachers have seldom felt more alienated from the kids; yet it has seldom been easier to make contact with their world. We communicate with people by having something in common with them. One thing we can all have in common is the mass media. TV and film help to shape the dreams of today's students. Students often have a kind of defenseless direct, but interested, approach to the media. They love to talk about TV programs and movies. They don't realize how much they're talking about themselves in the process. If the teacher doesn't watch these programs and if he never discusses them with the kids, he's missing the easiest way to wiretap their private world. He's missing a great way to communicate with the kids. This is why all this elite versus popular culture business is so important. The snobs pride themselves on not watching television. Too bad. Pity. What happens when this culturally deprived teacher starts waxing lyrical about Elizabethan poetry? Not much. The kids have some polite teacher-talk which they dish out dutifully so that the teacher thinks something is going on in the class. If they like the teacher, they are very generous in keeping the truth from him. If they don't like him they still have enough fear for the sanction of the report card to go along with the game. They seldom say what they really think. Nobody wants to hear it, except, of course, the great teacher, who is by definition the relevant person, the one who understands, communicates, gets through.

Whitehead called "inert ideas" the curse of education. They are ideas which are not relevant or are not made relevant for students. And relevance is a subjective judgment, determined by the student. This doesn't mean that the schools should sell out to the student. Those who do so render themselves useless to the student. It does mean, however, that the schools must begin where the student is and not where they would like him to be. And to do this the school must constantly check out the relevance of its program.

c) Closeup — A Changing Education
Stanley Kauffman said it: "The film in this country is possibly the one art form that is *wanted*." Television may or may not be an art form, but it is wanted too. Why not start where the action is?

Teenage movie teachers have all kinds of options in their approach to film. My own prejudice at the high school level is for keeping as close as possible to what Robert Warshow has called "the immediate experience." For me this means the vertical interaction between the student and the screen and the horizontal interaction between students who have seen and discussed the same film. Ancillary knowledge *about* film is less relevant here and is perhaps more appropriate for the specialist or for more advanced film courses. A great deal of snobbery takes over once some people learn how to pronounce the names of all the foreign film directors and can recite in chronological order the titles of all 9½ of Fellini's films.

If I had my "druthers" in the schools, I would like to have each student go through a unit on film and television for about 30 hours in his freshman year and then see and discuss one feature film each month during his four years of high school. A modest amount of time compared to the actual viewing hours which he is clocking. The whole process can be broken down into four approaches to films: show them, discuss them, teach about them, and make them. A few words on each.

a) SHOW THEM. The success of literature teachers can be legitimately measured by the number of books which their students read. Same for the TMT. A film per month for four years would add up to 40 films. The celluloid syllabus should include both American and foreign films, 16mm in-school screenings and 35mm theater screenings, and a generous blend of feature, documentary, and animated films. From time to time it should include a dishonest or pretentious film and occasionally there might be a second screening of a film to check out insights or arguments which arose in the discussion of the film. What is important is that the films be well-made, relevant, and representative. Although most of the films should have the texture of reality about them, a steady diet of grim film gets depressing. Musicals and comedies belong in the series.

b) DISCUSS THEM. When a TMT is asked whether he is just sitting around showing films and talking about them with the kids, the prescribed answer is: "Yup." This is where the fun begins. When students are given a free forum to discuss films, they are also invited to discuss themselves. This type of viewer-centered, free-flow discussion is built into the nature of the film medium. Film is literally an other-directed medium. Both the sequence and the pace of the communication are determined by the director. There is no chance to pause, reflect, and relate as there is with a book. In the darkness of the theater the viewer's attention is rivetted on the screen and he is swept along by the succession of sights and sounds which impinge on his eye and ear. This primarily sensory experience leaves the viewer with a stack of unsorted images which has piled up within him during the course of the film. A group discussion is a great way to sort out these images, to interpret and relate them, and to discover the structure which links them together into a fully human experience.

This physical and psychological context explains why the same film can affect different individuals in different ways. Each person sees his own film. This paradox is merely the reaffirmation in a new context of the thesis of individual differences, and selective perception. The same film on the screen washes over each viewer as an individual, with individual past experiences, hopes, loves, fears, needs, and intelligence. The psychological mechanisms of identification and projection come into play and further individualize the experience. We empathize with some character on the screen. For a while we become who he is, and we will fill out the experience by reading our own emotions into the character. The result is a variety of responses to the same stimulus. It is normally not a solipsistic kind of irresponsible and indeterminate variety, but usually a range of responses hovering around the central theme of the film.

If the teacher can resist the temptation to reward and punish "correct" answers (this usually means his own subjective interpretation) and can create a climate in which all opinions are respected, these free-winging sessions can dredge up some memorable moments. My winters are warmed by memories of some Job Corpsmen debating the meaning of what it meant to be a winner or a loser in *The Hustler*, of the understanding that resulted from a group of parents and students who had seen and separately discussed the rebellion of Colin Smith in *The Loneliness of the Long Distance Runner*, of ten minutes of sheer poetry in a Harlem basement by a teacher commenting on Terry Molloy's care for his pigeons in *On the Waterfront*, of 200 girls discussing the loneliness and purpose of Zampano and Gelsomina in *La Strada*, of the ten year old girl in New York whose favorite scene in *Raisin in the Sun* was "when the movin' man came, 'cause that meant they were gettin' out." Nice things happen in film discussions. Some teachers find that they are talking less and that the kids are learning more.

As the students build up a background of shared experiences, they can then use these films and discussions as reference points for making some sense out of their own lives or for communicating with each other. The phrase, "He's a real loser," says everything to someone who has seen and discussed *The Hustler*. The better we know each other, the shorter the sentences we can use.

c) TEACH ABOUT THEM. Not everything that *can* be known about film and television *should* be known about them. Each TMT has to make his own way in deciding how much the student should know about film history, techniques, production, and economics. The best advice is to play it loose and to start with the film-as-experienced.By some people's standards this will be a sloppy and subjective approach, but it is better to recognize and work with the subjectivity than to impose an arbitrary set of objective standards. The approach should be inductive. The standards should grow out of the experience and not be imposed on the experience. We can do without abstract lists of criteria which begin: "A great movie is one which fulfills the following requirements . . ." People know what they like. Those who spend their time telling people that they *shouldn't* like what they *do* like have discovered a first-class way of getting tuned out. Pulling rank won't change taste. Lively analysis in a fair game may do it.

d) MAKE THEM. The study of film inevitably leads students to a desire to try their hand at making a film. The results are wondrous to behold. In England films are now being made by eight- and nine-year olds. There are tentative beginnings of such a development in this country under pioneering teachers like George Bouwman of Horace Mann in New York, Zane Rodriguez of Fordham Prep, Sister Bede Sullivan of Lillis High in Kansas City, and Roger

Larson who has been working with the Neighborhood Youth Corps in Harlem.

There isn't room to go into some of the varied film projects which are just beginning around the country. But all kinds of respectable organizations and teachers are getting into the act. Within ten years we will wonder what all the fuss was about and will have transcended the need for developing a rationale colored by the hortatory tone of the piece you are reading.

Expensive media like films and television cannot get too far ahead of their audience. They have to rely on public acceptance. John Frankenheimer (director of *Seven Days in May; The Train*) challenged film critics in words which are just as applicable to film teachers:

There is, however, another field in which I feel the critic has a vital job to do. This is in helping to create, not only an informed public opinion, but a public love of the cinema; to help form a generation of movie-goers who love the film not only as entertainment but as a unique art form. . . . I believe that our greatest art form is the film. It belongs to our century and to our time. It is the only art form that so totally involves the onlooker, where in fact he cannot escape being involved.

If the critic could influence the youth—that group which seems most to influence the taste of the nation—to want to see better movies, I am quite sure that more good movies would be made. As creators in this field, we are dependent on the public and need a true climate of acceptance for our best efforts. . . . A good critic should stimulate them to discuss films, to argue about them, to become excited about them.

Americans have spent a lot of time and energy in the past thirty years complaining about the producers of films and television. Much of the energy would have been better utilized in working with the audience. It's not too late to begin.

The final quote is from someone active in the field: "I think that film education is a very good thing to have on the school timetable and it is a great pity that all schools do not have it." — Wendy Puddle, Age 12, Dunraven School, London.

The Modern Legion
and its Modern Outlook

MSGR. THOMAS F. LITTLE

"CHANGE," "AGGIORNAMENTO," "RENEWAL," "UPDATING" —
these have become key words in every phase of Catholic
life today. All, of course, in the spirit of the Second Vatican
Council. This being so, an interesting question may be
coming up with regard to the National Legion of Decency.
For there are those who see this ecclesiastical office as
the very antithesis of the aggiornamento. To them it appears no more than a stubborn, antiquarian, unrealistic
defender of Catholic moviegoers against moral corrup-
tion — a group of censors who pass moral judgment on
films they cannot begin to understand, and operate by
arbitrary rules of thumb that are insulting to intelligent
Catholics. And so it may very well be asked: what is to
become of the Legion of Decency?

Those who still think of the Legion in these terms are themselves in need of an "updating." Long before the Council
was convoked by Pope John, renewal and aggiornamento
were sweeping through this organization.

Our "little aggiornamento" began in the mid-1950's. With
the publication in 1955 of Pius XII's allocutions on the ideal
film, the Legion began to open its windows. They were
thrown wide open in 1957 with the appearance of Pope
Pius' encyclical on the mass media, *Miranda Prorsus* ("Remarkable Inventions"). It was a plea to Catholics throughout the world to accept motion pictures as something good
and useful for the cultural and spiritual progress of man,
rather than simply as possible occasions of sin.

From the time of its establishment in 1934, the Legion's
primary attitude toward the motion picture medium had
been largely one of defensiveness, of caution, of treating
films as merely a form of escapist entertainment that must
never shock or upset or confuse the average moviegoer.
Many friendly voices were already advising the Legion that

FROM *AMERICA*, DECEMBER 11, 1965. REPRINTED WITH PERMISSION FROM *AMERICA*,
THE NATIONAL CATHOLIC WEEKLY REVIEW, 106 W. 56th STREET, NEW YORK, N.Y. 10019.

change was necessary. The teaching of Pius XII encouraged it to give these voices even fuller attention.

In response to this constructive criticism, the Legion undertook a study of its place in our changing world. Among other things, it learned that it faced a new generation of Catholics. Because of their higher level of education, these Catholics were much better fitted to cope with the content of films than their parents were. Hence they were dissatisfied with what they considered an oversimplified and censorious approach to the film medium. Such an approach, they felt, gave the American Church the un-Catholic reputation of being a repressive policeman of the film art rather than its patron.

Secondly, the Legion's investigations revealed that the film industry, in its commercial competition with television, was rapidly moving away from its once exclusive position as the mass medium of purely escapist entertainment and becoming a most important medium for the communication of ideas and for serious artistic expression. This development in motion pictures, moreover, was being recognized and supported by the young — in high schools, colleges and seminaries. Students had begun to expect that the Church's film apostolate should broaden its horizons to include serious study of the cinema and positive support of the best that this developing art had to offer.

The annual pledge of the Legion, with its negative "I condemn" approach, was now found to be in conflict with this emerging public opinion within the American Church concerning motion pictures. Besides, many Catholics resented what they felt habitually attended the annual administration of the pledge in too many parishes: an arrogant disregard of conscience and of a poorly motivated commitment. Theologians began to be concerned about the false consciences and the moral confusion that were being created by a widespread lack of intelligent pastoral instruction. Indeed, some preachers were elevating the Legion's classifications, without warrant, from the status of moral guides to that of ecclesiastical laws seriously binding in conscience.

The Legion's study called for renewal. The precise year for the beginning of this renewal was 1957; it is altogether proper to refer to a pre-1957 Legion of Decency and a post-1957 Legion, just as it is fitting now to refer to a pre-conciliar and post-conciliar Church. For it was in late 1957 that this office instituted the first of many major changes in its now eight-year-old aggiornamento.

The first major change was the creation of a new film category, representing our response to the fact that the film medium was indeed beginning to mature. This was the "adult" film category, our present A-III classification: "morally unobjectionable for adults."

Prior to this time, the Legion operated with only two approved categories: A-I, "morally unobjectionable for general patronage," and A-II. Although the latter was defined prior to 1957 as "morally unobjectionable for adults," in actual application it meant, like our current A-II category, that a film was "morally unobjectionable for adults *and adolescents.*" If a film was deemed unsuitable for adolescents, the Legion found itself forced to give it a B classification: "morally objectionable in part for all." Thus finding ourselves without an approved category for legitimate mature films, we adopted the obvious solution of introducing a truly adult classification.

In time, this one adult classification itself proved insufficient. More and more films were being made that, although morally unobjectionable, contained subject matter and treatment likely to confuse the sensitive or casual adult moviegoer. To meet this problem, the Legion began to apply more frequently an old but little used category known as the "Separate Classification," a misleading label altered in 1963 to A-IV: "morally unobjectionable for adults, with reservations."

These changes were not received without opposition— opposition that finds an occasional echo even today. We appreciate the fact that there are some moviegoers who are easily offended and shocked by certain films that have been placed in the A-III and A-IV classifications. They argue that these films will be seen by adolescents and should not therefore be approved. Such an argument, however, is uninformed. The Legion's proper function is to guide the conscience of the individual and not to pre-empt the role of parents. The argument is also unfair, because it expects the Church to discourage serious film-making and to deprive mature viewers of legitimate fare.

Certain well-intentioned people find it difficult to accept the Church's aggiornamento with respect to the film medium. For them, the portrayal of evil in movies is a particular stumbling block. The Second Vatican Council's decree On the Media of Social Communication leaves little doubt what the authentic Catholic attitude on this matter should be:

> "The narration, description or portrayal of moral evil, even though the media of social communication, can indeed serve to bring about a deeper knowledge and study of humanity and, with the aid of appropriately heightened dramatic effects, can reveal and glorify the grand dimensions of truth and goodness."

On the 30th anniversary of the Legion, this view was strongly supported by the Episcopal Committee for Motion Pictures, Radio and Television:

> "The fact that moral evil may, with due restraints, be treated in films, is an aspect of Church teaching which may confuse delicate consciences. For their sake, we think it prudent to recall that the view here expressed by the Council represents no startling innovation but rather applies to the new arts of communication the traditional criteria of Christian humanism. These criteria are as ancient as the sacred books of the Old and New Testaments."

In his treatise "The Ideal Film," discussing the treatment of evil in motion pictures against the backdrop of the biblical presentation of evil, Pius XII wrote:

> "Wrongdoing and guilt are not masked by deceitful veils, but told as they really happened. . . . The crude truth does not arouse disordered passions or impulses, at least in mature persons. On the contrary, the serious reader becomes more reflective, more clear-sighted; his mind, turning inward, is led to say: 'Take heed lest you too be led into temptation' (GAL. 5:1)."

These are the principles that have been incorporated into the Legion's over-all renewal. A-III and A-IV classifications are thus given to some films today that certainly would have been declared morally objectionable prior to 1957. As film artists attempt more and more to grapple with serious themes, it is reasonable to expect that these categories will be used more frequently.

This is not to say that the Legion wishes to discourage quality films for the family and the young. On the contrary, the Legion commends the film industry's recent efforts to increase production of family films. Nor is it to say that we will approve films that preach a philosophy of life opposed to the Judeo-Christian view of man. The key word here is *preach*. There is a world of difference between a film that holds up to view a situation that is obviously reprehensible morally and a film that says such a situation is desirable and worthy of emulation. Moviegoers must learn to tell the difference.

Here it must be strongly emphasized that we have no intention of ignoring the moral dimension of films in favor of the artistic. In the work of classifying movies, the Legion will continue to speak out against morally harmful trends in film production and against singular instances of films that are threats to private or public morality.

To cite one current example, we have made a firm stand against any and all forms of nudity in motion pictures. The Legion has condemned films for the sole reason that they have employed nudity—even films that were otherwise worthy of acceptance by filmgoers. It is not our opinion that nudity in itself is obscene. Nor would we deny that nudity *can* serve an artistic function in a serious film. But however *useful* nudity may be as a device, it is never a *necessary* device to achieve an artistic effect. Once the Legion approved nudity in films, for any reason, a dangerous and irreversible precedent would have been set. Before long, the competitive pressures on the average producer would most certainly result in a transfer of newsstand pornography to the screen. We know what we are speaking of, because in the last two years 34 films, of which 20 were major American productions, would have been released with scenes employing nudity had not the producers realized that they would then have been condemned.

But to accomplish our aggiornamento, much more was needed than the mere updating of our classification system. The encyclical *Miranda Prorsus* gave a clear mandate to launch a far-reaching positive program that would give the Church's film apostolate new vitality. That mandate, raised to the level of conciliar teaching in the decree On the Media of Social Communication, calls on us to realize that these media, if properly utilized, "can be of great service to mankind, since they greatly contribute to men's entertainment and instruction as well as to the spread and support of the Kingdom of God."

Accordingly, during the past eight years this office has taken specific steps to implement the mandate. The first step was to begin giving positive backing to films of superior artistic and spiritual value. To date, we have cited more than forty such films.

Next, beginning in 1958 the Legion began to promote the cause of film education in the belief that great films are not possible without a great audience. In the summer of 1964, our efforts culminated in the establishment of an educational affiliate for the Legion. This "National Center for Film Study" (a division of the Adult Education Center of the Archdiocese of Chicago), in addition to assisting the Legion in promoting better films, is charged with developing and servicing the film education movement in schools, colleges, seminaries and parishes.

Last December, with the collaboration of the Chicago office, the Legion launched the *Catholic Film Newsletter*, a monthly publication that provides full analysis and commentary on major current films and offers guidance to groups interested in film study. And the National Center itself, in its first year of operation, has prepared various materials for film study, has conducted workshops for educators and has assisted over 700 groups with programs.

With this coming January, the Legion and its educational affiliate will begin to award prizes each year to films of outstanding merit in each of several categories. This public recognition of achievement, perhaps long overdue, is intended to assure film-makers that their efforts are genuinely appreciated by the Church.

At the heart of the Legion's film apostolate in the aggiornamento remains the generous cooperation of Catholic moviegoers. Whereas in the past that cooperation was overly focused on the negative, now the emphasis is decidedly on the positive. Nowhere is this more evident than in one of our most significant changes: the introduction of an entirely new pledge accompanied by proper pastoral instruction when it is administered.

The text of this pledge incorporates in capsule form the principal points of the Church's teaching concerning films as found in Pius XII's *Miranda Prorsus* and in the Vatican Council's decree on the mass media. The pastoral instruction aims at eliminating the confusion of the past and at imparting what should be the main motivating force: Christian witness.

The pledge does not add any new obligations in conscience. Much less does it change the Legion's classifications from the status of moral guides to binding ecclesiastical laws. The content of the pledge is no more than a summary statement of already existing obligations from the natural moral law and the Christian imperative of charity. In other words, the individual promises not to support films that are classified as objectionable, not so much because they will necessarily harm him personally, but because such films may be dangerous to others—to whom he has an obligation by virtue of having received the sacrament of confirmation.

In this matter of the pledge, the Episcopal Committee for Motion Pictures, Radio and Television has well summarized the spirit that should not only motivate the taking of the pledge but also animate the cooperation of Catholics with the Legion in this age of renewal. Its statement of April 15, 1964, "The National Legion of Decency, Thirty Years of Christian Witness," declares:

"The purpose of the pledge is to provide Catholics with the annual opportunity of making a corporate witness to their faith to those matters which pertain to a mature and Christian choice of film entertainment. By their pledge they freely commit themselves to a support of the Legion's apostolate.

"The pledge is taken in the solemn context of the celebration of the liturgy. This context is spiritually appropriate because by the sacrament of confirmation every Christian has been forever consecrated to the vocation of giving witness to Christ in his daily life. The seal of the Holy Spirit which he has received at his confirmation impels a Christian to give witness to his Lord in his choice of films.

"During the celebration of the paschal liturgy, we solemnly renew our baptismal promises as a sign of the new life which we have received in and through the risen Christ. During the celebration of the Advent liturgy, which prepares us for the coming again of the Word of God, we renew these promises of the pledge as a sign of the mature witness to which those confirmed in the Lord have been consecrated by His Spirit."

Christian witness in the film apostolate will be meaningful only to the extent that all the People of God open their minds and hearts to the spirit that has animated and will continue to animate the Legion's aggiornamento.

SUPPLEMENTARY READINGS

Culkin, John, S.J. FILM STUDY IN THE HIGH SCHOOL. *A bro-chure available from the Communication Arts Department, Fordham University, New York, New York, for $1.00. Originally published in the* NCEA BULLETIN *XXIII, 3 (October 1965) under the title* "THE MOTION PICTURE AS AN ART FORM."

——————. "MASS MEDIA STUDY IN THE SCHOOLS," NCEA BULLETIN *(February 1963), 12-28.*

McAnamy, E. G., S.J. and Williams, R., S.J. THE FILMVIEWER'S HANDBOOK. *Glen Rock, N.J.: Paulist Press, 1965. 208 pages.*

POINTS FOR DISCUSSION

The main burden of discussion within class should be focused upon the films themselves rather than upon an abstract study of the film as a medium of insight and education. There is no one mold for such discussions, not even for the same film, in every circumstance. The flow of dialogue should come from the spontaneous reaction of the class and of the teacher with no clearly preordained focus of attention. It should be noted here that one of the cardinal rules of all film discussion is that its development should be sequential, i.e., each comment should follow upon the previous one rather than moving off each time into a totally new direction. This is the one area in which the teacher or a student-moderator should exert some influence in preventing the discussion from becoming dissipated by the con-tinual change of focus.

Granted the primary orientation for class discussion, as explained in the Introduction to this chapter, the following questions are suggested in order to highlight some of the important points made in the two articles included here.

1. What is the significance of Marshall McLuhan's remark that we now live "in a post-literate world"? Is this fact an advance or a retrogression educationally? Why? What do you feel to be the important contribution that films can make to the educational enterprise?

2. In his article Father Culkin has coined the expression "whom-ese." What is your understanding of this idea? Why is it so important? How does one develop his own sense of the "whom-ese"?

3. Do you think that films really contribute to a fuller under-standing of human and spiritual values and, hence, have an important place within the senior religion program, or do you feel that they are merely entertainment and a waste of time? Explain your point of view. Give concrete examples to illustrate your point.

4. What were the main reasons why the name of the Legion of Decency was changed to that of the National Catholic Office for Motion Pictures?

5. How does the National Office arrive at the final classification of a particular film? What significance does this classification have for the individual Catholic? What should it have? Under what circumstances can individuals, in good conscience, see pictures which have been rated as objectionable either in part or totally? What basic Catholic principles of sound moral the-ology are at the root of such decisions regarding the viewing of films in the different classifications? In this connection explain the significance and binding power of the pledge made annually in our Churches with regard to the viewing of motion pictures.

chapter 8
RACE RELATIONS

The problem of race relations has been termed by some experts the most critical problem facing America today. The troubles at Selma and Montgomery, the riots in Los Angeles, the disturbances in New York, Chicago, Rochester, and other cities, all have received national and international coverage in the communications media so that this problem is very much in the forefront of people's thinking. All men are realizing more and more that *it is their problem* no matter where they live. Any problem affecting members of the human family should be of concern to the whole family. Christians have the added dimension of spiritual brotherhood within the People of God as a motive for active concern in this area of life today.

To be concerned we must know the facts of the situation and we must see ourselves in relation to these facts, both from the standpoint of our reaction to the situation and of our contribution to its existence. For this reason it is very important that a careful study and an honest observation of the basic circumstances of the life of the Negro in America today, and in your particular section of America, should be made. This objective study is, perhaps, more properly the function of a social studies course. If it has been accomplished, then its findings can be presented more quickly in class and the time better spent on the more difficult question of proper attitudes, judgments, and actions which are integral to the life of any true Christian at this particular time. One of the tests of our Christian spirit is found right here in the practice, and not only in the acceptance, of the principles and rights involved in this question of race relations.

The main purpose of the articles which follow is to point out in vivid terms the injustice of the lived experience of many Negro people, citizens of our country, as described by both white and Negro Americans. Each article should be read thoughtfully and reflected upon.

Racist Sins of Christians

JOHN HOWARD GRIFFIN
(AUTHOR OF BLACK LIKE ME)

TWO GROUPS of American citizens are hurtling toward one another in a conflict that can result in the worst bloodshed since the Indian wars. I have toured the entire country this year—with an additional two survey trips through the Deep South—and I am convinced that a Negro-white clash is inevitable. While the North and South have wasted time bickering about which is worse, Negroes, particularly young Negroes, have lost their illusions about "good whites." They have seen us equivocate endlessly and finally grow silent in times of crisis, when issues were clear and words of protest or sanity would have sounded with clarion clarity.

Racism—discrimination based on skin color—has grown strong, hard, and bitter throughout the length and breadth of America. Racists who claim to be anti-Communists are doing the Communists' work magnificently well by showing the world our racist abuses and thereby turning the world from us in disgust.

Recent murders of William Moore in Alabama and Medgar Evers in Jackson, Mississippi; the hideous martyrdom of Clyde Kennard; the terrible revelations of James Baldwin and Martin Luther King, Jr., have shocked Americans. We are now a deeply concerned people, but we are not well informed.

White Americans and Negro Americans, communicating at only the most superficial level, tend to see the same event in entirely different lights. Whites view the growing Negro militancy with fear. Negroes view it as the only solution, because they can see little hope that whites will voluntarily grant them their rights—and they can no longer live without these rights. Negroes grow more determined as they grow more disillusioned by the cheating, the continued harassments, the obstructionism that is openly

FROM *SIGN*, AUGUST, 1963. REPRINTED WITH PERMISSION OF THE AUTHOR, JOHN HOWARD GRIFFIN.

practiced all over America against any move to exercise their civil rights.

Negroes are well-informed, through their own news media, of the constant racist depredations. Since newspapers seldom carry controversial material, the non-Negro public is only vaguely informed. I have seen in Mississippi the same brutality that I have seen in New York City. I have seen the same lack of communication between Negro and white citizens in Cleveland, Detroit, Los Angeles, Rochester, and Buffalo that I have seen in Alabama.

Uninformed, the national conscience cannot manifest itself. We remain two groups of citizens with two different sets of information who do not trust one another and who cannot discuss our problems at a sufficiently profound depth.

I Lived as a Negro in the South

My information about and attitude toward the crisis today are deeply influenced by an experience three years ago when I had a dermatologist darken my skin, and I lived as as a Negro in the Deep South. Behind this sociological experiment there lay the profound conviction that America's most corrosive problem was not a racial problem but a problem of racism and that unless this problem of racism were understood, it could destroy us.

In my teens, as a medical student in France, I had seen the extremes to which racism could lead when I helped smuggle German and Austrian Jews from the Nazi "final solution." I had seen men and women of great quality destroyed because they were born of Jewish parents. Later, in America, I had made studies of crisis community patterns in areas where racial prejudice subverted justice. These studies showed appalling parallels to the growth of racism I had witnessed in Germany. Mental attitudes were similar. In Germany, a man was condemned, not by his qualities as a human being, but because he was Jewish. In America, skin pigmentation was enough to condemn a man to second-class citizenship.

The folly of racism which discriminated against a man because of the color of his skin was dramatically illustrated to me during ten years when I was blinded by a brain injury. The blind learn to judge an individual by his qualities as a human. To the sightless we are all human individuals, more or less good, more or less cultivated, more or less intelligent. Our physical attractiveness, lightness or darkness do not enter the picture.

When I was blind, it seemed to me a grotesque abuse of the gift of sight to prevent any man from fulfilling his human potential merely because his skin was dark. Yet we were doing this in America and bringing up our children to follow in our footsteps, despite the fact that scientists were every day denouncing concepts of racial inferiority or superiority. Listening one evening to the Beethoven *Opus 132 Quartet*, one of the sublimest utterances in all music, I realized that if Beethoven lived in the South today, he would be considered a Negro, a second-class human. I, as a white man in the South, could not sit down at a restaurant table with Martin of Porres or Benedict the Moor, though I could eat there with the most derelict white.

I decided that the only way to demonstrate what racism does to a human being was to become a Negro and experience it from the side that no white man can really know. I had a deep concern for the Negro as a victim of racism, but I had an equally deep concern for the white who, whether he realized it or not, was also a victim of racism. Obviously, the situation that warps and handicaps the Negro child must — perhaps even more terribly — warp and handicap the white child.

On a chilly November night in New Orleans, after ten days of treatments by a dermatologist, I was ready to enter the world as a Negro. I was evenly dark from head to foot, and I had shaved my head. Otherwise, I was the same. I retained my name, my credentials, my speech pattern. I decided that if I were questioned, I would answer truthfully. In the next seven weeks, no white man asked my name; no one questioned my identity as a Negro.

But if I remained essentially the same man, everything about my life was drastically altered. Doors of dignity and self-respect that had been opened to me as a white man were closed to me as a Negro.

The full impact of it hit me that first night when I was directed to the best hotel accommodations for Negroes. It was a wretched little place in the ghetto area. I asked for the best room and paid in advance. The proprietor led me up the rickety stairs to the second floor. My "best room" was a cubicle scarcely larger than a double bed. It had no windows. I locked the door and began to undress. Noises of talk, laughter, and juke-box jazz from a nearby tavern drifted through the thin clapboard walls. I turned out the light and crawled into bed. A dog yowled somewhere in the distance. I lay awake in the oppressive closeness and felt desolation spread through me. For the first time, a statement came from my lips that I have heard Negroes utter countless times since: "It doesn't make any sense."

What sense did it make? Here I was, the same John Griffin who had often been an honored guest in New Orleans. I had been there on concert tours with the French pianist Robert Casadesus. I had been received in the finest homes, the finest hotels, the finest restaurants. I was that same man, with the same characteristics, even the same wallet and the same money. But because my skin was black, all of these doors were closed to me. No amount of money could buy me better accommodations. I lay in a wretched hole, because I was a Negro. I realized that if my pigmentation were permanently dark, my wife and children would have this sort of accommodations. I would have to see them deprived, because they were of my flesh and blood.

In the next few days, I looked for jobs. I answered some want ads by telephone. My credentials often elicited interest, and I was virtually assured of the job, until I appeared for an interview. Then, when they saw I was a Negro, I was courteously turned away. There is no question but what I could have earned a decent living as a white man. As a Negro, the best jobs I had were shining shoes and unloading trucks. Only in the professions or after a long period of working oneself up could a Negro make a decent living. So I worked hard for my three or four dollars a day.

In this economic bracket, my diet was largely reduced to the sempiternal rice and beans of the area. This was delicious and cheap, but after a week of eating little else, my mind tended to pray, "Give us this day our daily beans...."

Many whites are poor, of course, and subsist on inadequate diets. The important difference is that they are not kept poor because of the color of their skin.

And yet, New Orleans was a disarmingly courteous city. Individual whites treated me with great courtesy. But all of the courtesies in the world do not long mask the one massive discourtesy of segregation that inexorably banishes the Negro to humanity's junkheap.

This involves being the victim of what Negroes call the "System." This System is a complex of customs and traditions so deeply ingrained in the southern white that they have the force of law, plus the actual Jim Crow ordinances. Though it may vary in its details from locality to locality, the System says in effect that American Negroes are indeed citizens, and, as such, should pay taxes and defend their country from its enemies but that they should not vote or have equal protection under the law or equality of educational or job opportunities and that they should not have the use of public parks and beaches (even though their tax dollars help maintain these) or of public eating places, hotels, libraries, concert halls, and hospitals. The System contrives, in a thousand subtle ways, to defraud Negroes of constitutional rights, to kill their incentive to struggle for something better, and to deprive them of opportunities of developing their full human potential, thereby depriving this country of their full contribution as citizens.

The System plunges a whole group of citizens into intimate misery. As a Negro, I soon felt this misery. It consisted in facing daily the mountain of rebuffs that struck me from the very core of the System.

These rebuffs are unknown to the white man. As a white, I had always been free to walk into a nearby door whenever hunger, thirst, or restroom needs made themselves felt. As a Negro, I quickly learned what it meant not to be free to walk into such doors. It can be a humiliating frustration to need restroom facilities and to discover that you must go halfway across town to find a place that will accommodate men of your color. Getting a drink of water was no longer simple. It meant searching, asking questions, locating places.

I began to see WHITE ONLY signs in a new way — as a cruel rebuff to nature and humanity. This is not a mere physical inconvenience. It goes far deeper. Life turns somber when a man is never for a moment free from this grinding concern over the purely animal aspects of his existence. The white hand kept my mind crammed down into my viscera, and I grew to hate the senseless degradation of it. All Negroes do. Life seldom rises above a mood of smouldering resentment over such indignities. The fact that Negroes often hide this resentment in order to survive does not mean that they become inured to it. The "Problem" is the obsession at all levels of society in the Negro community.

Like all other Negroes, I soon found myself imprisoned in the stereotype. And yet I never encountered a Negro who fitted this stereotype which white men have contrived in order to justify racist injustice and salve their consciences.

My soul shriveled to sit with a group of Negroes, sensitive human beings, and listen to what the radio told us of our plight. A white woman with a marvelously patronizing voice spoke of our "earning" our rights to full citizenship — this in a country where every American is born with those rights and where Negroes have fought in wars to defend them for all. One night, we sat in the ghetto squalor and heard a politician warn the public that any move toward racial justice that might give us the hope of human dignity was "playing into the Communists' hands." And he concluded that the System was "for the Negro's own good."

We stared at our dark hands and wondered if he had any idea what a massive crime he was committing. The deepest irony for us was to see white racists act always under the guise of patriotism and Christianity.

Many whites came to our shoe-shine on a skid row street in New Orleans. Many wanted us to help them find immoral pleasures—girls, gambling, obscene photographs. We learned to spot them, for they treated us with a conniving friendliness and "equality." I mentioned this to my partner, an elderly veteran who had lost a leg in World War I.

"Oh, yes," he remarked astutely. "The whites are much more democratic in their sinning than in their worship."

I did not immediately realize the profound scandal involved in his words, and certainly I did not connect it with the Catholic Church. What struck me was that the racist, who spoke so often of the lower morals of Negroes, appeared to live on a much lower moral level than I found among Negroes. His concern for "racial purity" did not extend to the colored race, as any Negro soon learns.

That afternoon, as we prepared to quit work, I asked my shine partner where I could find the nearest Catholic church.

"I guess the closest colored Catholic church would be way over on Dryades Street," he said.

"There's no such thing as a colored Catholic church," I replied quickly.

He looked at me in astonishment. "You don't really believe that, do you?"

I assured him I did. "I know some churches practice segregation," I said. "But Archbishop right here in New Orleans has declared segregation a grave mortal sin."

"You're black now, John," my companion said in a gentle voice. "And this is the South. You're going to find that a lot of white Catholics look on you as a nigger first and a Catholic second, no matter what the Archbishop says. And a nigger Catholic's got to stay in his place, just like any other nigger."

Segregation in the Church
On Dryades Street, in the Negro section, I mounted the

230

steps of St. John the Baptist Catholic Church and opened one of the heavy doors. Street noises were muffled with its closing. Soft light filtered through magnificent stained-glass windows in the oldest of New Orleans' churches — once a church for Catholics, now a church for Negro Catholics.

I sat in a pew, dwarfed in the vast structure, and leaned forward with my head against the bench in front. Glancing down at my hands, I saw each black wrinkle, each dark pore. This blackness condemned me out in the world, but the blessed illusion of sanctuary within the church was so intense that I could not believe it condemned me here. I was home. I belonged here as much as any man. I felt superbly safe from that incessant threat of humiliation which daily accompanies the American Negro. I knew the Church's teaching allowed for no racial distinction between members of the human family. It regarded man as a *res sacra*, a sacred dignity. God created all men with equal rights and equal dignity. The color of skin did not matter. What mattered was the quality of soul. I recalled a statement made by Father J. Stanley Murphy, C.S.B. "Whenever any man permits himself to regard any other man, in any condition, as anything less than a *res sacra*, then the potentiality for evil becomes almost limitless." Remembering this in the skin of a Negro, I saw that it summed up the racist fallacy and its effects on us.

Later, as I made my way slowly through the more deprived areas of the South, I learned some of those burningly shameful contradictions that Negro Catholics have to face. If it is painful to see that your country does not practice what it preaches, it is infinitely more painful to see that your Church does not. Though we deny that segregation exists in the Catholic Church, it does in effect exist.

I learned the humiliating protocol. In areas where there was a Negro Catholic church, it was made clear to me that I had better attend that one and no other. In areas where no such provision existed, I attended a "white" church. But I was instructed by other Negro Catholics: I was to sit to one side. If I wanted to receive Christ, I waited until the last white person had received Him and had returned to his seat before I approached the altar rail. Otherwise, I was warned, I would risk being passed at the altar rail. Negroes are constantly affronted by this. It either drives them deeper into the faith or it drives them away.

How can the Catholic Church be God-centered and yet practice this sort of segregation which it denounces as a "grave sin"? The point was clear. The Church did not practice this sort of segregation—this was the practice of bad Catholics, pure and simple. They persisted in a sin which their religion abominated. Knowing this, however, was strangely poor consolation. In such areas, the blessed illusion of sanctuary within the Church was shattered. We were hurt there in our deepest selves. We were, in effect, second-class Catholics, as we were second-class everything else. It was the same for all other Christian religions, of course, but that did not help either. And when we Negroes heard priests and bishops quietly explain their hesitancy to repudiate such attitudes "for fear of alienating souls," we knew they were referring to the souls of prejudiced white Catholics. And we wondered why they appeared to have so little "fear" of alienating the souls of Negroes.

How did otherwise decent white Christians justify such things? They said: "Why Negroes are more comfortable in their place. They like it that way. It's a kindness, really." I never heard a Negro say such a thing or in any way act as though he "liked it that way." One of our greatest problems was the white's willingness to solve our problems according to his comforts. This is true in the North, South, East, and West.

In the many rural areas and small towns, the "wonderfully harmonious relations" whites claimed to enjoy with Negroes resembled those one might enjoy with an animal beaten into utter submission. Here we knew that if we did not grin and say "Yes, yes, yes" to everything the white man wanted, we would be taught a lesson. We "accommodated," but when we went home in the evenings, we wept and said how could the white man twist his mind enough to think this death of our manhood, our hopes, and our dignity—this slavery—was for our own good.

232

As a stranger in their midst, I was taken in by Negroes and treated with the sort of protective tenderness that comes only from those who have suffered to the point of despair.

One night, I watched a mother feed mashed yellow beans in Carnation milk to bright-eyed youngsters who did not yet know that doors into wonderlands of education and justice and employment opportunity were barred to them. They reminded me of my own white children who could enter all of those doors. And I wondered how any human parent could tolerate a System that arbitrarily marked my children for deprivation. I said to myself: "We are not that evil. It's because we don't know, don't understand what a killing thing it would be to look into your children's eyes and know they didn't have a chance." I told myself that we would shout our outrage if anyone advocated that we physically maim these children. Yet we daily implicated ourselves in the vaster crime that saw them spiritually maimed.

At that moment, I saw the lamplit wretchedness in sharp focus, saw my hosts' faces flattened of all expression, dulled of hope or enthusiasm. I saw my black hands clenched in my lap and was torn to remember that I was once white. And I realized with sickening horror, that we whites have permitted ourselves to allow fellow human beings to be burned into the burnt-out shells who sat with me in that shanty. And I asked myself what great thing have we gained that was worth making them pay this kind of price.

These were people of quality. With education, the incentives of fair employment, a chance at human dignity, all of this would have been different. But we had condoned the System that deprived them of any chance to fulfill themselves. And then, unbearable irony, we had attributed their nonfulfillment to radical defect.

I could not understand how Negroes resisted the temptation to hate. They have a remarkable record for resisting subversion, for manifesting a deep love of country. But this is a love of what the country is supposed to be,

233

the American dream—not what it is where racism is practised. No, even in despair, Negroes could resist the temptation to hate White, and this for two reasons.

First, Negroes understood clearly what whites are only beginning to understand—that whites are as helplessly entrapped by the "System" as Negroes are and are as handicapped by it.

Second, Negroes believed that their misery comes from the "white trash" and that the trash, though powerful and unscrupulous, were a minority as oppressive and painful to the "good whites" as to the Negroes. We Negroes seldom met these good whites, but we were sure they were there and could be counted on to behave correctly and to call for justice when the time came. A handful of them had stood up and been counted. Lillian Smith, that great and brave Georgia woman of prophetic vision, has warned that those who embraced the strangely shallow dream of white supremacy were killers of the American Dream of a society based on freedom, equality, and justice and had been slashed to bits by racist reprisals. P. D. East, in Mississippi, had spoken and suffered, Sara Patton Boyle, in Virginia, had spoken and been devastated.

But since I returned to the white society, all of this has changed, is now changing. The changes are so drastic that those who knew something about the South ten years ago, or even two years ago, are misinformed if they rely on that information today.

Can the wounds be cured? Is death to be the only effective educator? We go on speaking of gradualism, but in the skin of a Negro and through his eyes, it has become obvious that gradualism can stretch on to eternity. We go on speaking of Negro crime, when Negroes know that these are not the crimes of Negroes but the crimes of men, the crimes of the ghetto where we have so long forced Negroes to remain. We go on in the euphoric illusion of progress, while the Negro cries, "It looks like all Africa is going to be free before we can get a lousy cup of coffee in America." Can we draw love out of this cauldron of growing hatred, before it dehumanizes all of us? These are the questions that lead to the core of the problem. It is a moral problem, and unless we attack it at this level, we have no chance of evading the nation-wide explosion that must occur.

If Negroes have been embittered by the "white man's Christianity," they have been made deeply cynical by the "white man's politics." Demagogues have ridden to political power through appeals to popular prejudice and racist villification. National political leaders have talked timidly about justice and acted even more timidly to implement it. White men have consistently decided what Negroes want, what is good for them, and how their problems should be solved—but always according to the white man's lights. Even in intergroup councils, Negroes seldom choose their own representatives. The whites choose those Negroes whom they want on the councils. As one Negro minister put it: "They always talk for us and to us but never *with* us."

In the early days of the Kennedy administration, despite some implementation that appeared catastrophically radical to segregationists, Negroes viewed the Administration's refusal to "go all the way" as merely more tokenism. There lingered the suspicion that the President's civil-rights stance was a matter of political manoeuver rather than statesmanship. After so many disappointments with past presidents, few dared hope that President Kennedy's affirmations of right would stand the acid tests that would prove them true principles. When the showdown came, would he relax into the safety of non-action or would he act as a man of principle?

The showdown clearly came during the recent Alabama crisis. For the first time in history, a President of the United States spoke on the matter of civil rights without equivocation, without those fatal "if's, and's and but's," and he followed through with a civil-rights bill that had the ring of authentic statesmanship.

"We face," he said, "a moral crisis as a country and as a people. It cannot be met by repressive police action.

It cannot be left to increased demonstrations in the streets. It cannot be quieted by token moves or talks. It is time to act in the Congress, in your state and local legislative body, and, above all, in our daily lives."

The President did not speak of Negroes as Negroes but as men, as citizens. He made no mention of the "Negro Problem" but spoke clearly of America's problem and of the problems of every individual American. "A great change is at hand," he said, "and our task, our obligation, is to make that revolution, the change, peaceful and constructive for all."

The President is giving leadership, and he is asking for leadership at the regional, the sectional, the local, and the individual level. The issues are clear, and they have been clearly stated: we must choose to embrace the sanity of justice, or we will perish as a nation in the insanity of violence. Negroes and most whites, surely, realize that we hang in the balance now. Yet the President's words have been obstreperously repudiated by the Southern bloc, with a veritable orgy of question-begging epithets that any unprejudiced twelve-year-old of normal intelligence could recognize as such. If the bill falls into the hands of Senator Eastland and is killed, it will show that one man can have tossed into the wastebasket the strongest move toward right that this nation has made in modern times.

Religion, in the eyes of many, has been a failure. When asked what he thought of the contributions of Christian ministers to the solution of our racist problems in the South, P. B. East replied, "Very damn little. I always thought ministers of God were supposed to be leaders, not followers."

Many religious leaders have remained silent out of fear of precipitating violence. Others, ministers of the Protestant faiths, have often remained silent because they know they would be put out by their conregations, which would demand ministers with the "right kind of religion." The growing, new sentiment, however, suggests that the time is so critical that ministers must speak up in an attempt to clear the consciences of their congregations and let the chips fall where they may. In Mississippi, twent-eight Methodist ministers spoke up. So far, six have been fired. Their Bishop was tentative in his support. Presbyterians, Episcopalians, Quakers, and many others have spoken up and have suffered the consequences. Among Catholics, the archbishops of New Orleans and Atlanta have been notable exceptions to a dreary picture. The National Catholic Conference for Interracial Justice reports that twenty Catholic dioceses of the twenty-five stretching from West Virginia to Texas have announced a school-integration policy.

In other areas, the scandal of silence prevails in most churches, Catholic and Non-Catholic. Where tensions are extreme, the encyclicals *Mater et Magistra* and *Pacem in Terris* appear to be ignored.

There are many reasons for this silence. The bishops are in a difficult position where almost any overt movement would create chaos. However, we must face the painful fact that to the Negro Catholic and to many white Catholics, these reasons are obscure and they suffer the bitter disillusion of seeing that Holy Mother Church does not speak up for her children and that she appears prudent to the point of paralysis and overly patient with injustice. This is an agony for many priests. Individual Catholics, and also groups like the Grail and Caritas, are throwing their lives into this shallow reservoir of charity in a desperate attempt to stem the tide of conflict. Often they ask in anguish, "Why doesn't the Church here speak *now*?"

This year, I have had close contact with some of the best-informed people in the world: Jacques Maritain, Thomas Merton, Louis Lomax, Killian Smith, P. D. East, Sarah Patton Boyle, Professor Dwight L. Dumand. All have said the same thing. Time is running out in America. We have been subverted by expediency and compromise faster than we are being converted to ethical principles and wisdom. All agree that we are faced with two basic alternatives.

We can look beyond the accident of skin color and view

one another simply as humans and as citizens and join together in repudiating every injustice suffered by every citizen. Or we can deny the humanity that lies beneath our skins and set about the insane business of killing one another.

Letter From Birmingham City Jail

Martin Luther King, Jr.
BIRMINGHAM CITY JAIL
APRIL 16, 1963

BISHOP C. C. J. CARPENTER
BISHOP JOSEPH A. DURICK
RABBI MILTON L. GRAFMAN
BISHOP PAUL HARDIN
BISHOP NOLAN B. HARMON
THE REV. GEORGE M. MURRAY
THE REV. EDWARD B. RAMAGE
THE REV. EARL STALLINGS

My dear Fellow Clergymen,
While confined here in the Birmingham City Jail, I came across your recent statement calling our present activities "unwise and untimely." Seldom, if ever, do I pause to answer criticism of my work and ideas. If I sought to answer all of the criticisms that cross my desk, my secretaries would be engaged in little else in the course of the day and I would have no time for constructive work. But since I feel that you are men of genuine goodwill and your criticisms are sincerely set forth, I would like to answer your statement in what I hope will be patient and reasonable terms.

I think I should give the reason for my being in Birmingham, since you have been influenced by the argument of "outsiders coming in." I have the honor of serving as president of the Southern Christian Leadership Conference, an organization operating in every Southern state with headquarters in Atlanta, Georgia. We have some eighty-five affiliate organizations all across the South— one being the Alabama Christian Movement for Human Rights. Whenever necessary and possible we share staff, educational, and financial resources with our affiliates. Several months ago our local affiliate here in Birmingham invited us to be on call to engage in a nonviolent direct action program if such were deemed necessary. We readily consented and when the hour came we lived up to our promises. So I am here, along with several members of my staff, because we were invited here. I am here because I have basic organizational ties here. Beyond this I am in Birmingham because injustice is here. Just as the eighth century prophets left their little villages and carried their "thus saith the Lord" far beyond the boundaries of their home town, and just as the Apostle Paul left his little village of Tarsus and carried the gospel of Jesus Christ to practically every hamlet and city of the Graeco-Roman world, I too am compelled to carry the gospel of freedom beyond my particular home town. Like Paul, I must constantly respond to the Macedonian call for aid.

Moreover, I am cognizant of the interrelatedness of all communities and states. I cannot sit idly by in Atlanta and not be concerned about what happens in Birmingham. Injustice anywhere is a threat to justice everywhere. We are caught in an inescapable network of mutuality tied in a single garment of destiny. Whatever affects one directly affects all indirectly. Never again can we afford to live with the narrow, provincial "outside agitator" idea. Anyone who lives inside the United States can never be considered an outsider anywhere in this country.

You deplore the demonstrations that are presently taking place in Birmingham. But I am sorry that your statement did not express a similar concern for the conditions that brought the demonstrations into being. I am sure that each of you would want to go beyond the superficial social analyst who looks merely at effects, and does not grapple with underlying causes. I would not hesitate to say that it is unfortunate that so-called demonstrations are taking place in Birmingham at this time, but I would say in more emphatic terms that it is even more unfortunate that the white power structure of this city left the Negro community no other alternative.

In any nonviolent campaign there are four basic steps: (1) collection of the facts to determine whether injustices are alive; (2) negotiation; (3) self-purification; and (4) direct action. We have gone through all of these steps in Birmingham. There can be no gainsaying of the fact that racial injustice engulfs this community. Birmingham is probably the most thoroughly segregated city in the United States. Its ugly record of police brutality is known in every section of this country. Its unjust treatment of Negroes in the courts is a notorious reality. There have been more unsolved bombings of Negro homes and churches in Birmingham than any city in this nation. These are the hard, brutal, and unbelievable facts. On the basis of these conditions Negro leaders sought to negotiate with the city fathers. But the political leaders consistently refused to engage in good faith negotiation.

Then came the opportunity last September to talk with some of the leaders of the economic community. In these negotiating sessions certain promises were made by the merchants—such as the promise to remove the humiliating racial signs from the stores. On the basis of these promises Rev. Shuttlesworth and the leaders of the Alabama Christian Movement for Human Rights agreed to call a moratorium on any type of demonstrations. As the weeks and months unfolded we realized that we were the victims of a broken promise. The signs remained. As in so many experiences in the past we were confronted with blasted hopes, and the dark shadow of a deep disappointment settled upon us. So we had no alternative except that of preparing for direct action, whereby we would present our very bodies as a means of laying our case before the conscience of the local and national community. We were not unmindful of the difficulties involved. So we decided to go through a process of self-purification. We started having workshops on nonviolence and repeatedly asked ourselves the questions, "Are you able to accept blows without retaliating?" "Are you able to endure the ordeals of jail?"

We decided to set our direct action program around the Easter season, realizing that with the exception of Christmas, this was the largest shopping period of the year. Knowing that a strong economic withdrawal program would be the by-product of direct action, we felt that this was the best time to bring pressure on the merchants for the needed changes. Then it occurred to us that the March election was ahead, and so we speedily decided to postpone action until after election day. When we discovered that Mr. Conner was in the run-off, we decided again to postpone action so that the demonstrations could not be used to cloud the issues. At this time we agreed to begin our nonviolent witness the day after the run-off.

This reveals that we did not move irresponsibly into direct action. We too wanted to see Mr. Connor defeated; so we went through postponement after postponement to aid in this community need. After this we felt that direct action could be delayed no longer.

You may well ask, "Why direct action? Why sit-ins, marches, etc.? Isn't negotiation a better path?" You are exactly right in your call for negotiation. Indeed, this is the purpose of direct action. Nonviolent direct action seeks to create such a crisis and establish such creative tension that a community that has constantly refused to negotiate is forced to confront the issue. It seeks so to dramatize the issue that it can no longer be ignored. I just referred to the creation of tension as a part of the work of the nonviolent resister. This may sound rather shocking. But I must confess that I am not afraid of the word tension. I have earnestly worked and preached against violent tension, but there is a type of constructive nonviolent tension that is necessary for growth. Just as Socrates felt that it was necessary to create a tension in the mind so that individuals could rise from the bondage of myths and half-truths to the unfettered realm of creative analysis and objective appraisal, we must see the need of having nonviolent gadflies to create the kind of tension in society that will help men rise from the dark depths of prejudice and racism to the majestic heights of understanding and brotherhood. So the purpose of the direct action is to create a situation so crisis-packed that it will inevitably open the door to negotiation. We, therefore, concur with you in your call for negotiation. Too long has our beloved Southland been bogged down in the tragic attempt to live in monologue rather than dialogue.

One of the basic points in your statement is that our acts are untimely. Some have asked, "Why didn't you give the new administration time to act?" The only answer that I can give to this inquiry is that the new administration must be prodded about as much as the outgoing one before it acts. We will be sadly mistaken if we feel that the election of Mr. Boutwell will bring the millennium to Birmingham. While Mr. Boutwell is much more articulate and gentle than Mr. Conner, they are both segregationists dedicated to the task of maintaining the status quo. The hope I see in Mr. Boutwell is that he will be reasonable enough to see the futility of massive resistance to desegregation. But he will not see this without pressure from the devotees of civil rights. My friends, I must say to you that we have not made a single gain in civil rights without determined legal and nonviolent pressure. History is the long and tragic story of the fact that privileged groups seldom give up their privileges voluntarily. Individuals may see the moral light and voluntarily give up their unjust posture; but as Reinhold Niebuhr has reminded us, groups are more immoral than individuals.

We know through painful experience that freedom is never voluntarily given by the oppressor; it must be demanded by the oppressed. Frankly I have never yet engaged in a direct action movement that was "well timed," according to the timetable of those who have not suffered unduly from the disease of segregation. For years now I have heard the word "Wait!" It rings in the ear of every Negro with a piercing familiarity. This "wait" has almost always meant "never." It has been a tranquilizing thalidomide, relieving the emotional stress for a moment, only to give birth to an ill-formed infant of frustration. We must come to see with the distinguished jurist of yesterday that "justice too long delayed is justice denied." We have waited for more than three hundred and forty years for our constitutional and God-given rights. The nations of Asia and Africa are moving with jet-like speed toward the goal of political independence, and we still creep at a horse and buggy pace toward the gaining of a cup of coffee at a lunch counter.

I guess it is easy for those who have never felt the stinging darts of segregation to say "wait." But when you have seen vicious mobs lynch your mothers and fathers at will and drown your sisters and brothers at whim; when you have seen hate filled policemen curse, kick, brutalize, and even kill your black brothers and sisters with impunity; when you see the vast majority of your twenty million Negro brothers smothering in an air-tight cage of poverty in the midst of an affluent society; when you suddenly find your tongue twisted and your speech stammering as you seek to explain to your six-year-old daughter why she can't go to the public amusement park that has just been advertised on television, and see tears welling up in her little eyes when she is told that Funtown is closed to colored children, and see the depressing clouds of inferiority begin to form in her little mental sky, and see her begin to distort her little personality by unconsciously developing a bitterness toward white people; when you have to concoct an answer for a five-year-old son asking in agonizing pathos: "Daddy, why do white people treat colored people so mean?"; when you take a cross country drive and find it necessary to sleep night after night in the uncomfortable corners of your automobile because no motel will accept you; when you are humiliated day in and day out by nagging signs reading "white" men and "colored"; when your first name becomes "nigger" and your middle name becomes "boy" (however old you are) and your last name becomes "John," and when your wife and mother are never given the respected title "Mrs."; when you are harried by day and haunted by night by the fact that you are a Negro, living constantly at tip-toe stance never quite knowing what to expect next, and plagued with inner fears and outer resentments; when you are forever fighting a degenerating sense of "nobodiness";— then you will understand why we find it difficult to wait. There comes a time when the cup of endurance runs over, and men are no longer willing to be plunged into an abyss of injustice where they experience the bleakness of corroding despair. I hope, sirs, you can understand our legitimate and unavoidable impatience.

You express a great deal of anxiety over our willingness to break laws. This is certainly a legitimate concern. Since we so diligently urge people to obey the Supreme Court's decision of 1954 outlawing segregation in the public schools, it is rather strange and paradoxical to find us consciously breaking laws. One may well ask, "How can you advocate breaking some laws and obeying others?" The answer is found in the fact that there are two types of laws: There are *just* laws and there are *unjust* laws. I would be the first to advocate obeying just laws. One has not only a legal but moral responsibility to obey just laws. Conversely, one has a moral responsibility to disobey unjust laws. I would agree with Saint Augustine that "An unjust law is no law at all."

Now what is the difference between the two? How does one determine when a law is just or unjust? A just law is a man-made code that squares with the moral law or the law of God. An unjust law is a code that is out of harmony with the moral law. To put it in the terms of Saint Thomas Aquinas, an unjust law is a human law that is not rooted in eternal and natural law. Any law that uplifts human personality is just. Any law that degrades human personality is unjust. All segregation statutes are unjust because segregation distorts the soul and damages the personality. It gives the segregator a false sense of superiority. To use the words of Martin Buber, the great Jewish philosopher, segregation substitutes an "I-it" relationship for the "I-thou" relationship, and ends up relegating persons to the status of things. So segregation is not only politically, economically, and sociologically unsound, but it is morally wrong and sinful. Paul Tillich has said that sin is separation. Isn't segregation an existential expression of man's tragic separation, an expression of his awful estrangement, his terrible sinfulness? So I can urge men to obey the 1954 decision of the Supreme Court because it is morally right, and I can urge them to disobey segregation ordinances because they are morally wrong.

Let us turn to a more concrete example of just and unjust laws. An unjust law is a code that a majority inflicts on a minority that is not binding on itself. This is *difference* made legal. On the other hand a just law is a code that a majority compels a minority to follow that it is willing to follow itself. This is *sameness* made legal.

Let me give another explanation. An unjust law is a code inflicted upon a minority which that minority had no part in enacting or creating because they did not have the unhampered right to vote. Who can say the legislature of

Alabama which set up the segregation laws was democratically elected? Throughout the state of Alabama all types of conniving methods are used to prevent Negroes from becoming registered voters and there are some counties without a single Negro registered to vote despite the fact that the Negro constitutes a majority of the population. Can any law set up in such a state be considered democratically structured?

These are just a few examples of unjust and just laws. There are some instances when a law is just on its face but unjust in its application. For instance, I was arrested Friday on a charge of parading without a permit. Now there is nothing wrong with an ordinance which requires a permit for a parade, but when the ordinance is used to preserve segregation and to deny citizens the First Amendment privilege of peaceful assembly and peaceful protest, then it becomes unjust.

I hope you can see the distinction I am trying to point out. In no sense do I advocate evading or defying the law as the rabid segregationist would do. This would lead to anarchy. One who breaks an unjust law must do it *openly, lovingly* (not hatefully as the white mothers did in New Orleans when they were seen on television screaming "nigger, nigger, nigger") and with a willingness to accept the penalty. I submit that an individual who breaks a law that conscience tells him is unjust, and willingly accepts the penalty by staying in jail to arouse the conscience of the community over its injustice, is in reality expressing the very highest respect for law.

Of course there is nothing new about this kind of civil disobedience. It was seen sublimely in the refusal of Shadrach, Meshach, and Abednego to obey the laws of Nebuchadnezzar because a higher moral law was involved. It was practiced superbly by the early Christians who were willing to face hungry lions and the excruciating pain of chopping blocks, before submitting to certain unjust laws of the Roman Empire. To a degree academic freedom is a reality today because Socrates practiced civil disobedience.

We can never forget that everything Hitler did in Germany was "legal" and everything the Hungarian freedom fighters did in Hungary was "illegal." It was "illegal" to aid and comfort a Jew in Hitler's Germany. But I am sure that, if I had lived in Germany during that time, I would have aided and comforted my Jewish brothers even though it was illegal. If I lived in a communist country today where certain principles dear to the Christian faith are suppressed, I believe I would openly advocate disobeying these anti-religious laws.

I must make two honest confessions to you, my Christian and Jewish brothers. First I must confess that over the last few years I have been gravely disappointed with the white moderate. I have almost reached the regrettable conclusion that the Negroes' great stumbling block in the stride toward freedom is not the White Citizens' "Counselor" or the Ku Klux Klanner, but the white moderate who is more devoted to "order" than to justice; who prefers a negative peace which is the absence of tension to a positive peace which is the presence of justice; who constantly says "I agree with you in the goal you seek, but I can't agree with your methods of direct action"; who paternalistically feels that he can set the time-table for another man's freedom; who lives by the myth of time and who constantly advises the Negro to wait until a "more convenient season." Shallow understanding from people of good will is more frustrating than absolute misunderstanding from people of ill will. Lukewarm acceptance is much more bewildering than outright rejection.

I had hoped that the white moderate would understand that law and order exist for the purpose of establishing justice, and that when they fail to do this they become the dangerously structured dams that block the flow of social progress. I had hoped that the white moderate would understand that the present tension in the South is merely a necessary phase of the transition from an obnoxious negative peace, where the Negro passively accepted his unjust plight, to a substance-filled positive peace, where all men will respect the dignity and worth of human personality. Actually, we who engage in nonviolent direct action are not the creators of tension. We merely bring to the surface the hidden tension that is already alive. We bring it out in the open where it can be seen and dealt with. Like a boil that can never be cured as long as it is covered up but must be opened with all its pus-flowing ugliness to the natural medicines of air and light, injustice must likewise be exposed, with all of the tension its exposing creates, to the light of human conscience and the air of national opinion before it can be cured.

In your statement you asserted that our actions, even though peaceful, must be condemned because they precipitate violence. But can this assertion be logically made? Isn't this like condemning the robbed man because his possession of money precipitated the evil act of robbery? Isn't this like condemning Socrates because his unswerving commitment to truth and his philosophical delvings precipitated the misguided popular mind to make him drink the hemlock? Isn't this like condemning Jesus because His unique God-consciousness and never-ceasing devotion to His will precipitated the evil act of crucifixion? We must come to see, as federal courts have consistently affirmed, that it is immoral to urge an individual to withdraw his efforts to gain his basic constitutional rights because the quest precipitates violence. Society must protect the robbed and punish the robber.

I had also hoped that the white moderate would reject the myth of time. I received a letter this morning from a white brother in Texas which said: "All Christians know that the colored people will receive equal rights eventually, but is it possible that you are in too great of a religious hurry? It has taken Christianity almost 2000 years to accomplish what it has. The teachings of Christ take time to come to earth." All that is said here grows out of a tragic misconception of time. It is the strangely irrational notion that there is something in the very flow of time that will inevitably cure all ills. Actually time is neutral. It can be used either destructively or constructively. I am coming to feel that the people of ill will have used time much more effectively than the people of good will. We will have to repent in this generation not merely for the vitriolic words and actions of the bad people, but for the appalling silence of the good people. We must come to see that human progress never rolls in on wheels of inevitability. It comes through the tireless efforts and persistent work of men willing to be coworkers with God, and without this hard work time itself becomes an ally of the forces of social stagnation.

We must use time creatively, and forever realize that the time is always ripe to do right. Now is the time to make real the promise of democracy, and transform our pending national elegy into a creative psalm of brotherhood. Now is the time to lift our national policy from the quicksand of racial injustice to the solid rock of human dignity.

You spoke of our activity in Birmingham as extreme. At first I was rather disappointed that fellow clergymen would see my nonviolent efforts as those of the extremist. I started thinking about the fact that I stand in the middle of two opposing forces in the Negro community. One is a force of complacency made up of Negroes who, as a result of long years of oppression, have been so completely drained of self-respect and a sense of "somebodiness" that they have adjusted to segregation, and of a few Negroes in the middle class who, because of a degree of academic and economic security, and because at points they profit by segregation, have unconsciously become insensitive to the problems of the masses. The other force is one of bitterness and hatred and comes perilously close to advocating violence. It is expressed in the various black nationalist groups that are springing up over the nation, the largest and best known being Elijah Muhammad's Muslim movement. This movement is nourished by the contemporary frustration over the continued existence of racial discrimination. It is made up of people who have lost faith in America, who have absolutely repudiated Christianity, and who have concluded that the white man is an incurable "devil." I have tried to stand between these two forces saying that we need not follow the "do-nothingism" of the complacent or the hatred and despair of the black nationalist. There is the more excellent way of love and nonviolent protest. I'm grateful to God that, through the Negro church, the dimension of nonviolence entered our struggle. If this philosophy had not emerged I am convinced that by now many streets of the South would be flowing with floods of blood. And

I am further convinced that if our white brothers dismiss us as "rabble rousers" and "outside agitators"—those of us who are working through the channels of nonviolent direct action—and refuse to support our nonviolent efforts, millions of Negroes, out of frustration and despair, will seek solace and security in black nationalist ideologies, a development that will lead inevitably to a frightening racial nightmare.

Oppressed people cannot remain oppressed forever. The urge for freedom will eventually come. This is what has happened to the American Negro. Something within has reminded him that he can gain it. Consciously and unconsciously, he has been swept in by what the Germans call the *Zeitgeist*, and with his black brothers of Africa, and his brown and yellow brothers of Asia, South America, and the Caribbean, he is moving with a sense of cosmic urgency toward the promised land of racial justice. Recognizing this vital urge that has engulfed the Negro community, one should readily understand public demonstrations. The Negro has many pent-up resentments and latent frustrations. He has to get them out. So let him march sometime; let him have his prayer pilgrimages to the city hall; understand why he must have sit-ins and freedom rides. If his repressed emotions do not come out in these nonviolent ways, they will come out in ominous expressions of violence. This is not a threat; it is a fact of history. So I have not said to my people, "Get rid of your discontent." But I have tried to say that this normal and healthy discontent can be channeled through the creative outlet of nonviolent direct action. Now this approach is being dismissed as extremist. I must admit that I was initially disappointed in being so categorized.

But as I continued to think about the matter I gradually gained a bit of satisfaction from being considered an extremist. Was not Jesus an extremist in love? "Love your enemies, bless them that curse you, pray for them that despitefully use you." Was not Amos an extremist for justice—"Let justice roll down like waters and righteousness like a mighty stream." Was not Paul an extremist for the gospel of Jesus Christ—"I bear in my body the marks of the Lord Jesus." Was not Martin Luther an extremist—

"Here I stand; I can do none other so help me God." Was not John Bunyan an extremist—"I will stay in jail to the end of my days before I make a butchery of my conscience." Was not Abraham Lincoln an extremist—"This nation cannot survive half slave and half free." Was not Thomas Jefferson an extremist—"We hold these truths to be self evident that all men are created equal." So the question is not whether we will be extremist but what kind of extremist will we be. Will we be extremists for hate or will we be extremists for love? Will we be extremists for the preservation of injustice—or will we be extremists for the cause of justice? In that dramatic scene on Calvary's hill three men were crucified. We must never forget that all three were crucified for the same crime—the crime of extremism. Two were extremists for immorality, and thus fell below their environment. The other, Jesus Christ, was an extremist for love, truth, and goodness, and thereby rose above His environment. So, after all, maybe the South, the nation, and the world are in dire need of creative extremists.

I had hoped that the white moderate would see this. Maybe I was too optimistic. Maybe I expected too much. I guess I should have realized that few members of a race that has oppressed another race can understand or appreciate the deep groans and passionate yearnings of those that have been oppressed, and still fewer have the vision to see that injustice must be rooted out by strong, persistent, and determined action. I am thankful, however, that some of our white brothers have grasped the meaning of this social revolution and committed themselves to it. They are still all too small in quantity, but they are big in quality. Some like Ralph McGill, Lillian Smith, Harry Golden, and James Dabbs have written about our struggle in eloquent, prophetic, and understanding terms. Others have marched with us down nameless streets of the South. They have languished in filthy, roach-infested jails, suffering the abuse and brutality of angry policemen who see them as "dirty nigger lovers." They, unlike so many of their moderate brothers and sisters, have recognized the urgency of the moment and sensed the need for powerful "action" antidotes to combat the disease of segregation.

Let me rush on to mention my other disappointment. I have

been so greatly disappointed with the white Church and its leadership. Of course there are some notable exceptions. I am not unmindful of the fact that each of you has taken some significant stands on this issue. I commend you, Rev. Stallings, for your Christian stand on this past Sunday, in welcoming Negroes to your worship service on a non-segregated basis. I commend the Catholic leaders of this state for integrating Springhill College several years ago.

But despite these notable exceptions I must honestly reiterate that I have been disappointed with the Church. I do not say that as one of those negative critics who can always find something wrong with the Church. I say it as a minister of the gospel, who loves the Church; who has nurtured in its bosom; who has been sustained by its spiritual blessings and who will remain true to it as long as the cord of life shall lengthen.

I had the strange feeling when I was suddenly catapulted into the leadership of the bus protest in Montgomery several years ago that we would have the support of the white Church. I felt that the white ministers, priests, and rabbis of the South would be some of our strongest allies. Instead, some have been outright opponents, refusing to understand the freedom movement and misrepresenting its leaders; all too many others have been more cautious than courageous and have remained silent behind the anesthetizing security of stained glass windows.

In spite of my shattered dreams of the past, I came to Birmingham with the hope that the white religious leadership of this community would see the justice of our cause and, with deep moral concern, serve as the channel through which our just grievances could get to the power structure. I had hoped that each of you would understand. But again I have been disappointed.

I have heard numerous religious leaders of the South call upon their worshipers to comply with a desegregation decision because it is the law, but I have longed to hear white ministers say follow this decree because integration is morally right and the Negro is your brother. In the midst of blatant injustices inflicted upon the Negro, I have watched white churches stand on the sideline and merely mouth pious irrelevancies and sanctimonious trivialities. In the midst of a mighty struggle to rid our nation of racial and economic injustice, I have heard so many ministers say, "Those are social issues with which the Gospel has no real concern," and I have watched so many churches commit themselves to a completely other-worldly religion which made a strange distinction between body and soul, the sacred and the secular.

So here we are moving toward the exit of the twentieth century with a religious community largely adjusted to the status quo, standing as a tail light behind other community agencies rather than a headlight leading men to higher levels of justice.

I have traveled the length and breadth of Alabama, Mississippi, and all the other Southern states. On sweltering summer days and crisp autumn mornings I have looked at her beautiful churches with their spires pointing heavenward. I have beheld the impressive outlay of her massive religious education buildings. Over and over again I have found myself asking: "Who worships here? Who is their God? Where were their voices when the lips of Governor Barnett dripped with words of interposition and nullification? Where were they when Governor Wallace gave the clarion call for defiance and hatred? Where were their voices of support when tired, bruised, and weary Negro men and women decided to rise from the dark dungeons of complacency to the bright hills of creative protest?"

Yes, these questions are still in my mind. In deep disappointment, I have wept over the laxity of the Church. But be assured that my tears have been tears of love. There can be no deep disappointment where there is not deep love. Yes, I love the Church; I love her sacred walls. How could I do otherwise? I am in the rather unique position of being the son, the grandson, and the great-grandson of preachers. Yes, I see the Church as the body of Christ. But, oh! How we have blemished and scarred that body through social neglect and fear of being nonconformist.

There was a time when the Church was very powerful. It

was during that period when the early Christians rejoiced when they were deemed worthy to suffer for what they believed. In those days the Church was not merely a thermometer that recorded the ideas and principles of popular opinion; it was a thermostat that transformed the mores of society. Wherever the early Christians entered a town the power structure got disturbed and immediately sought to convict them for being "disturbers of the peace" and "outside agitators." But they went on with the conviction that they were a "colony of heaven" and had to obey God rather than man. They were small in number but big in commitment. They were too God-intoxicated to be "astronomically intimidated." They brought an end to such ancient evils as infanticide and gladiatorial contest.

Things are different now. The contemporary Church is so often a weak, ineffectual voice with an uncertain sound. It is so often the arch-supporter of the status quo. Far from being disturbed by the presence of the Church, the power structure of the average community is consoled by the Church's silent and often vocal sanction of things as they are.

But the judgment of God is upon the Church as never before. If the Church of today does not recapture the sacrificial spirit of the early Church, it will lose its authentic ring, forfeit the loyalty of millions, and be dismissed as an irrelevant social club with no meaning for the twentieth century. I am meeting young people every day whose disappointment with the Church has risen to outright disgust.

Maybe again I have been too optimistic. Is organized religion too inextricably bound to the status quo to save our nation and the world? Maybe I must turn my faith to the inner spiritual Church, the church within the Church, as the true *ecclesia* and the hope of the world. But again I am thankful to God that some noble souls from the ranks of organized religion have broken loose from the paralyzing chains of conformity and joined us as active partners in the struggle for freedom. They have left their secure congregations and walked the streets of Albany, Georgia, with us. They have gone through the highways of the South on torturous rides for freedom. Yes, they have gone to jail with us. Some have been kicked out of their churches and lost the support of their bishops and fellow ministers. But they have gone with the faith that right defeated is stronger than evil triumphant. These men have been the leaven in the lump of the race. Their witness has been the spiritual salt that has preserved the true meaning of the Gospel in these troubled times. They have carved a tunnel of hope through the dark mountain of disappointment.

I hope the Church as a whole will meet the challenge of this decisive hour. But even if the Church does not come to the aid of justice, I have no despair about the future. I have no fear about the outcome of our struggle in Birmingham, even if our motives are presently misunderstood. We will reach the goal of freedom in Birmingham and all over the nation, because the goal of America is freedom. Abused and scorned though we may be, our destiny is tied up with the destiny of America. Before the pilgrims landed at Plymouth, we were here. Before the pen of Jefferson etched across the pages of history the majestic words of the Declaration of Independence, we were here. For more than two centuries our foreparents labored in this country without wages; they made cotton "king," and they built the homes of their masters in the midst of brutal injustice and shameful humiliation—and yet out of a bottomless vitality they continued to thrive and develop. If the inexpressible cruelties of slavery could not stop us, the opposition we now face will surely fail. We will win our freedom because the sacred heritage of our nation and the eternal will of God are embodied in our echoing demands.

I must close now. But before closing I am impelled to mention one other point in your statement that troubled me profoundly. You warmly commended the Birmingham police force for keeping "order" and "preventing violence." I don't believe you would have so warmly commended the police force if you had seen its angry violent dogs literally biting six unarmed, nonviolent Negroes. I don't believe you would so quickly commend the policemen if you would observe their ugly and inhuman treatment of Negroes here in the city jail; if you would watch them push and curse old Negro women and young Negro girls; if you would see them slap and kick old Negro men and young Negro boys; if you will observe them, as they did on two occasions, refuse to give us food because we wanted to sing our grace together. I'm sorry that I can't join you in your praise for the police department.

It is true that they have been rather disciplined in their public handling of the demonstrators. In this sense they have been rather publicly "nonviolent." But for what purpose? To preserve the evil system of segregation. Over the last few years I have consistently preached that nonviolence demands that the means we use must be as pure as the ends we seek. So I have tried to make it clear that it is wrong to use immoral means to attain moral ends. But now I must affirm that it is just as wrong, or even more so, to use moral means to preserve immoral ends. Maybe Mr. Connor and his policemen have been rather publicly nonviolent, as Chief Pritchett was in Albany, Georgia, but they have used the moral means of nonviolence to maintain the immoral end of flagrant racial injustice. T. S. Eliot has said that there is no greater treason than to do the right deed for the wrong reason.

I wish you had commended the Negro sit-inners and demonstrators of Birmingham for their sublime courage, their willingness to suffer, and their amazing discipline in the midst of the most inhuman provocation. One day the South will recognize its real heroes. They will be the James Merediths, courageously and with a majestic sense of purpose, facing jeering and hostile mobs and the agonizing loneliness that characterizes the life of the pioneer. They will be old, oppressed, battered Negro women, symbolized in a seventy-two-year-old woman of Montgomery, Alabama, who rose up with a sense of dignity and with her people decided not to ride the segregated buses, and responded to one who inquired about her tiredness with ungrammatical profundity: "My feets is tired, but my soul is rested." They will be young high school and college students, young ministers of the gospel and a host of the elders, courageously and nonviolently sitting in at lunch counters and willingly going to jail for conscience sake. One day the South will know that when these disinherited children of God sat down at lunch counters they were in reality standing up for the best in the American dream and the most sacred values in our Judeo-Christian heritage, and thus carrying our whole nation back to great wells of democracy which were dug deep by the founding fathers in the formulation of the Constitution and the Declaration of Independence.

Never before have I written a letter this long (or should I say a book?). I'm afraid that it is much too long to take your precious time. I can assure you that it would have been much shorter if I had been writing from a comfortable desk, but what else is there to do when you are alone for days in the dull monotony of a narrow jail cell other than write long letters, think strange thoughts, and pray long prayers?

If I have said anything in this letter that is an overstatement of the truth and is indicative of an unreasonable impatience, I beg you to forgive me. If I have said anything in this letter that is an understatement of the truth and is indicative of my having a patience that makes me patient with anything less than brotherhood, I beg God to forgive me.

I hope this letter finds you strong in the faith. I also hope that circumstances will soon make it possible for me to meet each of you, not as an integrationist or a civil rights leader, but as a fellow clergyman and a Christian brother. Let us all hope that the dark clouds of racial prejudice will soon pass and the deep fog of misunderstanding will be lifted from our fear-drenched communities and in some not too distant tomorrow the radiant stars of love and brotherhood will shine over our great nation with all their scintillating beauty.

Yours for the cause of
Peace and Brotherhood
MARTIN LUTHER KING, JR.

Following is a verbatim copy of the public statement by eight Alabama clergymen which occasioned Dr. King's reply.

We the undersigned clergymen are among those who, in January, issued "An Appeal for Law and Order and Common Sense," in dealing with racial problems in Alabama. We expressed understanding that honest convictions in racial matters could properly be pursued in the courts, but urged that decisions of those courts should in the meantime be peacefully obeyed.

Since that time there had been some evidence of increased forebearance and a willingness to face facts. Responsible citizens have undertaken to work on various problems which cause racial friction and unrest. In Birmingham, recent public events have given indication that we all have opportunity for a new constructive and realistic approach to racial problems.

However, we are now confronted by a series of demonstrations by some of our Negro citizens, directed and led in part by outsiders. We recognize the natural impatience of people who feel that their hopes are slow in being realized. But we are convinced that these demonstrations are unwise and untimely.

We agree rather with certain local Negro leadership which has called for honest and open negotiation of racial issues in our area. And we believe this kind of facing of issues can best be accomplished by citizens of our own metropolitan area, white and Negro, meeting with their knowledge and experience of the local situation. All of us need to face that responsibility and find proper channels for its accomplishment.

Just as we formerly pointed out that "hatred and violence have no sanction in our religious and political traditions," we also point out that such actions as incite to hatred and violence, however technically peaceful those actions may be, have not contributed to the resolution of our local problems. We do not believe that these days of new hope are days when extreme measures are justified in Birmingham.

We commend the community as a whole, and the local

news media and law enforcement officials in particular, on the calm manner in which these demonstrations have been handled. We urge the public to continue to show restraint should the demonstrations continue, and the law enforcement officials to remain calm and continue to protect our city from violence.

We further strongly urge our own Negro community to withdraw support from these demonstrations, and to unite locally in working peacefully for a better Birmingham. When rights are consistently denied, a cause should be pressed in the courts and in negotiations among local leaders, and not in the streets. We appeal to both our white and Negro citizenry to observe the principles of law and order and common sense.

Signed by:

C. C. J. CARPENTER, D.D., LL.D., Bishop of Alabama
JOSEPH A. DURICK, D.D., Auxiliary Bishop, Diocese of Mobile-Birmingham
RABBI MILTON L. GRAFMAN, Temple Emanu-El, Birmingham, Alabama
BISHOP PAUL HARDIN, Bishop of the Alabama-West Florida Conference of the Methodist Church
BISHOP NOLAN B. HARMON, Bishop of the North Alabama Conference of the Methodist Church
GEORGE M. MURRAY, D.D., LL.D., Bishop Coadjutor, Episcopal Diocese of Alabama
EDWARD V. RAMAGE, Moderator, Synod of the Alabama Presbyterian Church in the United States
EARL STALLINGS, Pastor, First Baptist Church, Birmingham, Alabama

Why Don't Negroes . . .

BAYARD RUSTIN

HAVE MORE RESPECT for law and order? . . . straighten up their family life and stop asking for handouts? . . . do something to help themselves, the way other minorities have? These questions, lurking in the minds of many white men, are answered honestly and frankly by one of the most prominent leaders of the civil rights movement.

Television viewers were shocked some weeks ago to see Negroes attending a conference of the Citizens Crusade Against Poverty demonstrate against Sargent Shriver. To most Americans, I'm sure, this was another demonstration of Negro irrationality, ingratitude and lack of self-discipline.

I opposed and tried to curb the demonstration because it allowed a handful of people to obscure the fundamental criticisms most conference participants had of the anti-poverty program. In Indianola, Miss., for example, the chief of police is head of the antipoverty board; in Selma, Ala., Jim Clark controls much of the funds, and for the most part the concept of maximum feasible participation has not been implemented.

I recall the incident because it brought to the fore once again the questions white people often raise about Negroes. For instance: "Why don't Negroes respect law and order?" "Why don't they straighten up their families and stop asking for handouts?" "Why don't they pull themselves up by their bootstraps as we did?"

I don't want to belittle these questions, for even religious people are deeply confused about some of them. Men of good will cannot sit by, however, and allow programs that were well-intentioned to flounder, nor should they accept unsubstantiated or unthought-out statements about law and order, the breakdown of the Negro family and self-help.

FROM *AMERICA*, JUNE 4, 1966. REPRINTED WITH PERMISSION FROM *AMERICA*, THE NATIONAL CATHOLIC WEEKLY REVIEW, 106 W. 56th STREET, NEW YORK, N.Y. 10019.

I am going to address myself to those questions in the following pages, but before I do so, I want to say that there are two things I believe we can all accept. The first is that the Negro family can be reconstructed only when the Negro male is permitted to be the economic and psychological head of the family. The second, that racism is a blasphemy against the fundamental oneness and unity that the world and all its people derive from their Creator; that racists are, in a very precise sense of the term, blasphemers who set themselves up as gods over their fellow men and worship not a human nature created in the divine image, but the accidents of skin color, of nation, of ethnic background. These people would annul that great and enormous truth which is so central to the Judeo-Christian tradition: that God is not the talisman of a tribe, a sort of good-luck charm for one's warriors as against the warriors of some other god, but that God is indeed one.

The racists, for all their Scriptural quoting, would belittle God, for they turn human beings into non-souls and thus seek to diminish the divine work.

Who is to blame for ghetto violence?

Anatole France once wrote that it is illegal for rich men and poor men alike to sleep under bridges or to steal a piece of bread. At the heart of this wise witticism, there is an understanding of the way in which all the noble words — equality, justice, freedom — have definitions that vary according to one's misery or prosperity. And this sad truth holds most profoundly in the racial ghettos of America, where millions of black citizens live out poverty-stricken lives. In these man-made jungles, there are many who cannot comprehend the very meaning of a phrase like "law and order," for it does not correspond to anything that has ever happened in their lives. Such people are not stupid; far from it. They are being ruthlessly logical in generalizing from their own experiences, for they have seldom seen the least shred of empirical evidence that there is such a thing as "law and order."

But then, there are those who say that when I talk in this way I somehow "excuse" the violence and nihilism that sometimes erupt in the Negro slum. And that, of course, is not the case at all. It would take a fool or a sadist to celebrate the involuntary, spastic violence of the ghetto or to say that it was a means toward any good. The real issue is: Who is to blame? Is it the Negro man or woman who was born into a miserable, vermin-infested apartment, sent to an overcrowded, inadequate school, not really taught to read, write or count, and actually educated, for all practical purposes, in the street? Is this the autonomous, morally choosing individual whom we shall not excuse for his free choice of violence?

My question should answer itself. But more than that, this line of inquiry should indicate the profound limits on the moralistic advocacy of respect for law and order. The disorder, the alienation, the violence of the ghetto are, to a considerable degree, social consequences that are imposed upon people. It is thus a waste of time to give beautiful sermons filled with words that may make some sense in suburbia, but that the daily reality of slum life had rendered meaningless. Moreover, the root of the violence is in the economic order of the ghetto. The policeman who arrests a young man for selling marijuana, numbers or women is not only preventing crime; he is in fact stopping that young man from earning a living.

The great lesson one could teach would be to create a decent, integrated environment in which man's potential for brotherhood, reason and cooperation was a deduction from firsthand experience, rather than an incomprehensible pronouncement broadcast into chaos by philosophers who live in ordered comfort. For, as Western philosophy has understood as far back as Aristotle, the hungry man, the freezing man, the sick man, does not have time or inclination to speculate upon the higher things. He is consumed by his immediate misery, which is the only reality he knows. And so for millions of people living in ghettos, a discussion of law and order is misleading. For where there is justice and just law, order can exist; where there is injustice and an unjust administration of law, disorder is inevitable. What are a Negro's job prospects?

Two decades ago, in the Irene Morgan case, Jim Crow was

illegalized in interstate transportation. The Supreme Court decision outlawing segregation was handed down almost twelve years ago. The Montgomery bus protest was won eleven years ago. The sit-in movement swept through the lunchrooms and bus stations of the South five years ago. The dogs were unleashed in Birmingham three years ago. It is a year since Selma. And during all this time, while thousands and tens of thousands suffered and faced death — and while some died — the economic and social position of the Negro relative to that of the white has declined. When general unemployment was high, the Negro rate was double the white; when progress in reducing joblessness was made, as in the last two years, the Negro gains were half those of the white. At the same time, New York (where liberal pieties on the race issue are required of all serious candidates for office) maintains ghetto schools that actually work a deterioration on the intellectual ability of a growing number of black students each year.

This situation becomes all the more pathological when one looks at the job prospects of the young, systematically uneducated Negro from the black ghetto. In the next five years, according to the President's Manpower Report of last year, Negroes, who are approximately 10 percent of the population, will be almost 20 percent of the entrants to the labor force. In part, of course, this figure simply reflects the ability of the whites to prolong education (and in their case, more effective education: Scarsdale spends twice as much per capita on education for its children as Harlem). But beyond that, what is going to happen to these hundreds of thousands of young Negroes?

One grim possibility is discernible in the recent government reports of progress in reducing unemployment. The over-all jobless level has fallen to around 4.2 percent; the Negro rate, at well over 8 percent, is as usual double. But — and this is an explosive fact — the Negro teen-age percentages have hardly declined at all, and remain in the neighborhood of 25 percent. In other words, at the very moment when the New Economics was successfuly rescuing whites and some Negroes from unemployment (the Negroes returning to work were laid-off workers, usually with skills), Negro youth was continuing to inhabit a world where work was as hard to find as in the Depression of the 1930's.

It should be emphasized, however, that even the positive figures are overly optimistic. A number of economists have convincingly argued that Washington's unemployment statistics do not take into account those driven out of the labor market (there have been estimates as high as a million and a half) and do not compute the cumulative effect of part-time unemployment and various other forms of under-employment. As a result, Leon Keyserling has concluded that the "true" unemployment rate, even with the much vaunted progress we have recently made, is around 8 percent and all the numbers for Negroes would show a substantial increase. Beyond this, as the testimony that Clarence Mitchell of the NAACP presented on behalf of the civil rights leadership last year shows, working Negroes are, to an unusually high degree, concentrated in "poverty jobs": domestic work, the janitorial occupations in the service trades, laundry work, etc. These are people who often labor a full two thousand hours a year and who are, nevertheless, bitterly poor. They are in jobs not covered by Federal legislation at all, or in those that pay the official, legal and impoverishing minimum of $2,600 a year, or $500 under the poverty line for a man with a wife and two children.

But, then, perhaps Watts can be taken as a summary—and utterly persuasive statement—of my themes. The Los Angeles ghetto was, and is, a way station on the terrible above-ground railway that this economy runs for Negroes. Literally tens of thousands of black men are forced to migrate from the South. They come North to "freedom," where they are packed together in slums and sent out to compete on the labor market with the black generation that arrived a decade or two ago (Jeremy Larner has estimated that over half the adult population of Harlem is made up of migrants who were not born there). And they also must contend, of course, with white competition. In Watts, then, one found jobless rates—according to the official figures—of nearly 40 percent. And since the flaming outbursts of last summer, many agencies, public and private, have gone into Watts to talk to Negroes there about work. The one thing they have not provided is jobs.

In one form or another, the reality I have described is now common knowledge in the civil rights movement and in the Federal government. What, then, are we going to do about it—besides writing sociological descriptions of it?

The debate over the "Moynihan Report" focuses on one approach. As is generally known by now, one of the principal authors of the report was Daniel Patrick Moynihan, then Assistant Secretary of Labor.

Let me make it clear at the outset that I feel it is unfair to charge Moynihan with being a racist, open or covert, and that, as a matter of fact, he was trying in his report to insist on the social and economic dimension of the race issue—for example, in his showing that prolonged unemployment tended to disintegrate the white family structure and to place particularly difficult psychological burdens on the male. The Negro family, Moynihan shows, has lived in a depression-like atmosphere ever since the 1930's, and the result has been a predictable breakdown. Now, this point has been made previously by Negro scholars—the late Franklin Frazier comes to mind in particular—and it has also emerged from studies of the heritage of American slavery.

But the Moynihan data were presented in a form guaranteed to promote confusion. An intra-office memo on one aspect of a problem, it was taken by many, both friends and foes, as a comprehensive statement. Thus, even though the report made it clear that Negro family stability had always increased when Negro economic opportunity was on the rise, there were those who claimed that Moynihan had demonstrated that the real problem was a Negro deficiency in facing reality. Don't talk about "handouts," these sermonizers and moralists said whenever anyone spoke of the job of generating programs that could provide a basis for Negro family stability. And they concluded: just have Negroes put their own house in order! Thus chaotic aspects of Negro life that are the direct consequence of the economic and social discrimination practiced by white America were turned into bogus evidence of some kind of Negro inferiority.

And the truncated form of the Moynihan Report also meant

that it concentrated almost solely upon what is negative in Negro life. There was no examination of the degree to which the "abnormality" of some of the ghetto mores, when seen from the point of view of a secure white middle class, represents a desperate, but intelligent, attempt on the part of a jobless Negro to adapt to a social pathology. There was no assessment of the extraordinary accomplishment of the civil rights movement in summoning so many to sacrifice and to idealism despite these indignities.

Breakdown of the Negro Family
In 1962, Abram Kardiner, M.D., and Lionel Ovesey published their study of the personality of the American Negro, *The Mark of Oppression.* The section in their book that deals with the breakdown of the Negro family is a scientific and compassionate description; it explains a great deal about the interrelationship between personality and economics.

When a Negro male abandons his wife and children, the authors point out, he is blamed for having no sense of responsibility—something generally considered a character trait of Negroes. Research has shown, however, that such a man himself is more often than not the product of a broken home. He had no father to set him a pattern of stability and protection, and his overburdened mother was irritable and demanded strict obedience. He was thrown into competition with his mother's other children. Hearing men disparaged by his female relatives, and without affectionate attention from anyone, his self-esteem was lowered. The submissive attitude he thus developed toward women limited his ability to enter into a satisfactory marital relationship. When he married, he knew that his wife had much better chances economically than he did. Moreover, neither he nor his wife had much tolerance for each other's faults. Even if he found work, it was hardly ever permanent. Often he tried hard to fulfill his obligations, but he failed continuously. Thereupon his wife began berating and browbeating him. Finally, either she invited him to leave, or he himself abandoned his family.

When a husband moves out, the authors continue, he is generally a defeated man. He drifts from job to job. Often

266

he seeks escape in drink, or satisfaction through expensive clothes or through pleasure with women. Even if he stays married, the husband remains subordinate to his wife. Though he is submissive toward her, he may become domineering over the children. An abandoned wife, on the other hand, usually marries—and often successfully—a second time. If that marriage fails, her lot from then on is one of ceaseless toil. Usually she cannot give her child either attention or love. Often a sister or brother has to take care of the child, who is thus exposed to bitter rivalries with other children. The male child of a broken marriage takes to the streets. Here he elevates his self-esteem through exploits with other boys, obtaining rewards he cannot get at home. Without his knowing it, many of his satisfactions are bought through anti-social acts.

If we study this description of the breakdown of the American Negro family, we find that there is a common reality-factor in that cycle: the economic position of the Negro male. We could attempt to psychoanalyze poor Negroes, to improve their self-image and self-esteem, but in the face of the economic realities, all our effort would be futile.

That is why A. Philip Randolph has proposed a "Freedom Budget," a multibillion-dollar social investment to destroy the racial ghettos of America, house the black and white poor decently and create full and fair employment in the process. His approach is fundamental if we are serious about reconstructing the Negro family and allowing the Negro male to be the head of the household.

"Help Yourself, Like We Did"
Misconceptions about Negro family life are often compounded by admonitions to Negroes to help themselves "like we did" (the "we" are the Poles, Jews, Irish, Italians, etc.)

Michael Harrington pointed out, in a recent issue of *Dissent,* that the old immigrant groups came to America when an expanding blue-collar economy had work for grade school dropouts and men who could not even speak English, while the Negro has come to the city as an internal alien in a time of automation, a time when the number of available jobs is decreasing. (Oscar Handlin points out in his book *Race, Nationality and American Life* that without the immigrant labor supply, the development of the cotton goods industry to its present status in New York and other North Atlantic States could not have taken place.)

Saying this does not mean that Negro self-organization is irrelevant. Far from it. It is only when the black ghetto of the North, which has yet to be organized massively by *any* civil rights group, comes to conscious political life that the full impact of the Negro revolution will be felt. But first of all, the economic and social setting in which such organization becomes possible and even probable has to be created. Just as the semi-skilled factory workers did not create the CIO at the bottom of the Depression in 1932, but only when times were getting better a few years later, so the black masses require some tangible signs of hope and success before they are going to move.

For that matter, the white immigrant groups from Europe, which are so often held up as images of the "self-help" process, benefited from massive government intervention. The great advance made by the first and second generation workers took place, of course, in the 1930's, and the most important new institutions they created were precisely the industrial unions. But this did not happen in a vacuum. There was the Wagner Act, which, if it did not immediately guarantee collective bargaining rights, put the moral and psychological authority of the government on the side of the labor movement ("Mr. Roosevelt wants you to join," John L. Lewis said in those days). And there were the various programs—the climate of economic hope. Some Negroes participated in this progress; most were excluded because racism had kept them out of the factories, where the decisive events occurred.

In short, the CIO had to organize itself, but it did so under circumstances of Federal intervention that made the momentous task easier to perform. Negroes have to organize themselves. And the Freedom Budget, which is their New Deal 30 years late, will not simply provide full and fair employment and lay the basis for the destruction of the physical environment of poverty. Like the Wagner Act and the social investments of the New Deal, it should also evoke a new psychology, a new militancy and sense of dignity, among millions of Negroes, who will see something more concrete and specific than a promise of eventual freedom.

But secondly, when I talk of the self-organization that the Freedom Budget should make possible, I am not talking about "self-help" in the neighborhood improvement sense. In *Dark Ghetto*, Kenneth Clark tells of how one New York block got together to clean up the street. In the doing, Clark rightly remarks, these Negroes gave tacit assent to the charge that it was their *fault* that the street was dirty, thus accepting one more of the white man's stereotypes about the Negro (i.e., he is guilty of non-cleanliness). What is more, the energy was misdirected. It should have been directed to City Hall as a demand that the city clean up the streets of Harlem the same way it cleans up the streets of the white middle class.

From the time of the American Revolution until the rise of the NAACP in the first decade of this century, Negroes have followed the advice of the self-helpers. When Negroes were thrown out of the Methodist Church in the 18th century, they established the African Methodist Episcopal Church. When they were not allowed to attend white universities, they set up Wilberforce University in Ohio. When insurance companies would not insure Negroes, fraternal organizations and social clubs took on the task. The history of the Negro people in the United States is a history of attempting to build separate self-help organizations. At the end of World War II, the Urban League and the National Council of Negro Women formed "Hold Your Job Committees." The committees conducted educational campaigns in the factories and the Negro community to urge Negroes not to give employers any excuse for discharging them after the war.

More recently, Black Nationalists and Muslims have believed that if Negroes would only follow the Protestant ethic and "Buy Black" (while a number of confused whites have said: "Be frugal"), they could end their economic independence. But the fact is that if millions of Negroes are to change the conditions of their life, it will be not by becoming shopkeepers or by cleaning up their block, but by winning full and fair employment for black men as well as white.

Negroes, I am saying, should be individually virtuous — and so should whites. But the Negro movement's future does not lie along the line of making over millions of black personalities, one by one. The European immigrants and their children ceased being rude peasants not because they got religion or psychology, but because they got economic opportunity and hope. The Negro movement must now struggle against economic injustices that are more deeply rooted in the management and structure of our technology than anything the immigrants ever faced. And it can win this perilous fight only by way of militant political organization and through national programs.

[BAYARD RUSTIN is the executive director of the A. Philip Randolph Institute. His article is based on a study paper that he prepared for a recent conference of the John La-Farge Institute.]

Unchanging Duty
in a Changing World

1961 STATEMENT OF THE BISHOPS OF THE UNITED STATES

FEW NATIONS of the world can look back on their historic origins with such justifiable pride as the United States. That pride, in large measure, finds its justification in the high moral principles which guided our Founding Fathers in laying the foundations of our government and in launching this Nation on its history. Our first legal documents, the Declaration of Independance and the Constitution with its first ten Amendments, marked us from the beginning as a nation committed to the principles of the moral law.

Those principles and the religious beliefs that underlie them continued to guide our people in their national development. At a time when our country was emerging from infancy into vigorous youth, De Tocqueville, in his still widely read *Democracy in America*, said: "Religion in America takes no direct part in the government of society, but it must be regarded as the first of their political institutions. I do not know whether all Americans have a sincere faith in their religion—but I am certain that they hold it to be indispensable to the maintenance of republican institutions." (1)

Later at the end of the 19th century when our country was entering upon its maturity, another European observer, James Bryce, still could write: "Religion and conscience have been a constantly active force in the American Commonwealth . . . not indeed strong enough to avert many moral and political evils, yet at the worst times inspiring a minority with a courage and ardor by which moral and political evils have been held at bay and, in the long run, overcome." (2) In the present century it was not without a sense of moral duty that the United States became an arsenal of defense against totalitarian aggression, a storehouse to feed the hungry and starving world, a Samaritan helping defeated enemy nations to rehabilitate themselves

SIGNED BY MEMBERS OF THE ADMINISTRATIVE BOARD, NATIONAL CATHOLIC WELFARE CONFERENCE, IN THE NAME OF THE BISHOPS OF THE UNITED STATES, 1961.

(1) De Tocqueville: *Democracy in America*, Vintage Books, Vol. I, p. 310
(2) James Bryce: *The American Commonwealth*, Macmillan Company, Third Ed. Vol. II, p. 599

in peace. The history of our country has been generally infused with an ideal based on moral principles.

The time has come to confess, however, that our national ideal no longer rests upon a foundation of broad and solid popular morality. Ignorance of moral principles and the rejection of the very notion of morality are on the rise today and threaten to undermine our nation and its most sacred traditions. The evidences of our moral decline are everywhere to be seen: in the alarming increase in crime, particularly among the young; in the sensational treatment of violence and sexuality in literature, on the stage, screen and television; in the disclosures of greed and cynicism government, labor and business; in the stubborn continuance of race prejudice and injustice; in the multiplication of divorce and in the rapid disintegration of the family; in a harsh and pagan disregard of the sacredness of human life concealed under the mantle of science.

This present moral deterioration cannot be interpreted as a mere temporary relaxation of standards which will be followed by the sort of moral reform past experience would lead us to expect. The conditions we face are unique; for them, the past gives neither precedent nor guide. Many men are questioning and often denying the objective distinction between good and evil and the ability of human reason to know with certainty what is right and wrong. They are cutting themselves off completely from moral traditions. For the first time in history they find themselves without a moral law to break.

The reasons for this moral revolution can be ascertained at least in part. Just as the high morality of our early history found its strength in religion, so now the rejection of morality finds its most basic cause in the denial of God. Here, too, is something quite new. In the past there have always been men who for various reasons have denied the existence of God. But the present atheism is different. Now not only do many act and live as if there were no God to Whom they are responsible, but a steadily increasing number— some individuals of great influence—proclaim the nonexistence of God to be a scientifically established fact. The consequences of such an attitude are inescapable. If there is no God, then the old morality based on God is not valid. The whole of human life has to be reorganized on a new basis. Many modern men find themselves without God and religion, on a lonely eminence of their own making, left to create their own moral values, forced to determine for themselves what is good and evil, right and wrong.

In their newly proclaimed independence, modern men have tended to place their main reliance on physical science. While the enemies of religion and morality have attempted to make science the principal weapon of their attack, actually science itself has no part in this warfare. "Science, " says one of its most eminent scholars, Dr. Vannevar Bush, "does not exclude faith . . . science does not teach a harsh materialism. It does not teach anything beyond its boundaries and those boundaries have been severely limited by science itself." (3) But many who have taken science as their creed and their cult do not share the humility of the scientist. With invincible self-assurance and with an air of unchallenged authority, they teach a scientism that denies God and makes sport of the moral law. From positions many of them occupy in schools and universities, in literature and journalism, with all the modern media of communication at their command, they succeed in impressing their doctrine on great numbers of misled minds.

Toward the present moral decline, the modern media have done more than supply instruments for the spread of unbelief and moral revolt. Although the communications industry through many sincere and admirable leaders has made valuable contributions to human welfare, yet it has also inflicted on the modern world a pernicious cult of the "image." Submerged beneath waves of publicity from "image-makers" and "hidden persuaders" modern man tends to become a victim of the image. Whether a thing is true is less important than the impression it creates. Man's moral focus is distorted. For nations as well as individuals the all-important thing is the image that is projected on the minds of others. The rosy deception is rated good if it succeeds—in selling

(3) Vannevar Bush: *Modern Arms and Free Men*, p. 78

more products, in winning more votes, in convincing more taxpayers.

Popular education also bears a measure of responsibility for the decline and rejection of moral principles. At first, there was no intention of excluding either religion or morality from the common tax-supported school. But the diversity of our religious pattern and the rising pressure of secularism have produced the school without religion, and it was idle to suppose that this school could long inculcate in American youth moral convictions which would be firmly held. The result is that our society is now faced with great numbers of young people almost completely devoid of religious belief and moral guidance— young people who are causing increasing concern at every level of the community and in all parts of our country.

Beneath these present trends and pervading all modern society has been the influence of secularism—the banishment of God from public and private life and the enthronement of human nature in His place. Born in the "Enlightenment" of the 18th century, deriving its great impetus from the French Revolution, adopted and fostered by 19th century Liberalism, it became and still remains the principal characteristic of modern society. Under its influence, men may not perhaps deny God; on formal occasions, they may even mention His name. In practice, however, they simply ignore His existence. They do not openly reject moral principles; they may even pay them lip-service. But they disregard them or reduce them to hazy generalities. In general, the only sanctions they recognize are those supplied by individual taste, public opinion and the power of the state.

The result of these trends has been, even among those who have not rejected moral principles, a widespread moral apathy which touches practically every group: citizens who are not concerned enough to exercise the right to vote; elected officials who are interested only in their "public image," their personal power; union members, labor leaders, and industrialists who place their selfish interests above national security and the common good. Harmful as these weaknesses are, our acknowledgment of them can give no real comfort to our enemies.

It is the American tradition to look at ourselves, to examine our conscience, to reappraise our moral position. In a dictatorship this is impossible. In a democracy it is a constant necessity.

Both apathy and amorality certainly run counter to the American tradition. Because we have been a moral people, it has been characteristic of Americans ultimately to be guided by moral considerations and, even in periods of laxity, to respond vigorously to moral appeals. Our best traditions have been based on moral principles and ideals. We must remain true to them. We of the household of the faith have a special obligation to promote them. What, then, are our particular duties in the face of present conditions?

In today's world, our most obvious duty is to speak out, to make open profession of religious beliefs and moral convictions, to reaffirm morality as the foundation of our nation's past greatness and of its future aspirations. We must indeed be prepared to demonstrate the falseness of the claims of scientism, the hollowness and futility of the cult of the image, the corrosive effect of secularism on both the individual and society. Especially we must recognize and affirm the essential place of religion and morality in the formation of the human personality if we are to survive as a moral people. But over and above all this, the temper of the times demands that, by our words and acts, we bear personal witness to the existence of moral principles grounded on religious belief. In a world in which individual obligation is being denied, we must show the reality of personal responsibility—transcendent responsibility to God for all acts and attitudes, personal accountability for self, for family, for community, for nation. In particular, our teaching, our influence, and our conduct must show that the soundness of society depends on the principles of family life: the unity and sanctity of marriage, parental duty and authority, filial reverence and obedience.

As God-fearing people we must not only bear witness to those principles governing personal and family life; we must also give testimony to the reality and importance of those moral principles which govern man's wider social relationships. Pope John has recently reminded all Catholics of this obligation. "The social teaching proclaimed by the Church," he tells us, "cannot be separated from her traditional teaching regarding man's life." The norms of justice contained in the great social encyclicals of the Popes during the past 70 years are vital moral principles, just as are the principles of individual morality. We have the duty to know these principles through study and reading, through reflection and prayer. Nor can these principles be allowed to lie idle. "Social norms of whatever kind," says Our Holy Father, "are not only to be explained but also applied. This is especially true of the Church's teaching on social matters, which has truth as its guide, justice as its end, and love as its driving force." (4) The moral influence of these social principles must be made to permeate all of society and its institutions. The laborer must bring them to his union meetings; the industrialist, to the business world; the teacher, to his class; the parent, to his home—each to the sphere of life in which he moves. Only in this way will each religious person become involved with his fellow-citizens in constructing a "public philosophy" based on a frank acceptance of God and the moral law.

In rebuilding a sound religious and moral foundation for America, a special difficulty arises from the varied character of our society. Since we are a people of many religious beliefs, of diverse racial and national origins, there will undoubtedly always be tensions and some misunderstandings. But these differences will not constitute insurmountable barriers to national peace and cooperation if we are faithful to the moral principles which are the foundation of our traditions—particularly if we complement justice with charity. This is true of the racial issue which continues to rise and plague our country; it is true of other issues which divide us.

Our moral responsibility, however, transcends the limited circle of our individual lives and the confining borders of our country. Our interests and our obligations are world-wide—indeed our horizons are no longer confined

(4) *Mater et Magistra*, NCWC Edition. No. 222 and 226

to this earth, they have been projected into the uncharted seas of space. In its earlier years, our nation—young in its freedom and confident in the nobility of its democratic ideals—stood as an inspiration to all those who suffered in bondage and hoped for freedom. Country after country, encouraged by the success of our endeavors, threw off their shackles and asserted their independence. Millions flocked to our shores as to the haven of freedom and hope. Now, in our more mature years, the newer nations as well as some of the older impoverished ones have looked to us for material help and for the most part they have received from us a ready response. But they—particularly the emerging peoples—have needs that go deeper than the requirements for mere material help. They want more positive evidence of our understanding. They seek a recognition of their dignity, both individual and national. They crave the knowledge and technical skill which will enable them to help themselves. They need the vision which comes from faith, and the encouragement that comes from hope. They must have spiritual ideals and spiritual leadership. Our own freedom sprang in large measure from religious and moral sources. We must inspire these nations wherever possible to build on a religious and moral foundation if we are to contribute significantly to the achievement of their national aspirations. Meanwhile, we must be willing to open our hearts and our homes to those who come to our shores; to make room for them in our schools and universities; even to send our own sons to their lands to assist them. All these things we must do, not as mere counter-moves against communism, but for their essential rightness, as expressions of our highest principles: love of God and love of neighbor.

Because we have so often faltered in our course, and because the communist nations have profited by our mistakes to inspire false ideals and to awaken glittering but barren hopes, we must not be discouraged, imagining that our hour of opportunity has passed. It has not passed. The hour of greatest opportunity is striking now, as the forces of freedom and of tyranny gird for a decision. America's strength, bestowed by Divine Providence, has been given for this hour—that freedom may not fail. The exercise of our national strength, in order to achieve its true purpose, must be guided by those principles on which our strength was built. We must apply those principles in both national and international affairs. We shall be worthy of world leadership only if we are willing to pledge "our lives, our fortunes, and our sacred honor" in behalf of the right.

At present, when America is beset by so many frustrations, when there are so many temptations to despair, all who believe in God have the special duty of keeping alive within their own hearts and within the hearts of all free men a true and undying hope. Our hope will not be for a Utopia of material well-being, although we do look forward to a world in which science and technology will be used to the full in eliminating needless poverty, hunger and disease. Nor do we expect a world in which all will be morally and socially perfect. Our hope is for a world in which men, imperfect though they be, will accept the reign of God—a world in which the principles of the natural law and of the Christian dispensation will be recognized as the norm of moral judgment and the basis of the social order. Should such an order take hold on the world of today, there is not a single problem, no matter what its magnitude, which would not admit of a reasonable and, on the whole, a satisfactory solution.

Above all, the Christian today must have a profound sense of mission, which will cause him to bear witness to his religious faith and his moral convictions as the early Christian did—by deed and affirmation, even by death. Such was St. Paul's program of action; such, too, was St. Augustine's. Like Paul, we face a world largely paganized. Like Augustine, we see the encroachment of barbarism. Like both, we must be dauntless in proclaiming Christ.

In this way, we shall be true to our Christian duty in preserving God's moral order as man's standard of action. Only in this way shall we preserve the religious and moral traditions in which our country was born, and without which our country cannot survive.

SUPPLEMENTARY READINGS

Since this issue is so current, the daily newspapers, weekly and monthly magazines, and television news programs and documentaries supply much excellent material for classroom presentation.

Luka, Ronald L. "WE MARCHED THE MASS: AUGUST 28TH MARCH," AVE MARIA *(November 2, 1964), 10–11. This article emphasizes the connection between liturgy and life.*

"NOT WORDS BUT ACTS: *Religious Participation in Civil Rights Demonstrations,"* COMMONWEAL *(July 26, 1963), 444.*

Stringfellow, William. "THE ANATOMY OF POVERTY," JUBILEE, *12 (July 1964). A young white lawyer gives a description of life in Harlem with emphasis on the personal element in the poverty experience.*

"WHY WE CAN'T WAIT," LIFE *(May 15, 1964), 98–100.*

POINTS FOR DISCUSSION

The following "Interracial Examination of Conscience"* provides much pertinent material for thoughtful reflection and discussion.

Interracial Examination of Conscience
I. FAITH
1. *Do I profess to believe all the teaching of the Catholic Church, yet in practice deny:*
   a) *The unity of the human race? "For you are all one in Christ Jesus."*
   b) *The equality of all men in the eyes of Almighty God and before the Catholic Church?*
   c) *The dignity of every human soul ransomed by the blood of Jesus Christ and destined for an unsegregated seat before the throne of God?*

2. *Do I profess to believe all the teachings of the Catholic Church, yet in practice assert that:*
   a) *The Catholic Church is primarily a "white" church in which*

---

* Composed by the Catholic Interracial Conference, Washington, D.C. Reprinted with permission.

all races should not have equal treatment? *"Those who enter the Church, whatever be their origin or their speech, must know that they have equal rights as children in the House of the Lord, where the law of Christ and the peace of Christ prevail." Summi Pontificatus: Pope Pius XII.*

b) *I am free to adopt one set of moral principles governing my actions toward members of my own race and another governing my actions toward members of a different race?*

II. HOPE

1. *Do I presume that I am without fault if I attempt to do nothing to right the wrongs inflicted on my fellow men because there is no solution to the race problem?*

2. *Do I feel that it is useless to try to lead a Christian life because of the burden of injustice placed upon me as a result of racial discrimination?*

III. CHARITY

1. *Knowing that love of my fellow men is a gift from God, do I make frequent use of the Sacraments, particularly the Blessed Eucharist, as means He has placed at my disposal to obtain and increase Divine Charity?*

2. *Do I pray daily for the spread of Christian Charity throughout the world and for the destruction of the kingdom of satan which incites race prejudice?*

3. *Do I consider that the Divine command to love all men does not bind me as regards those who have sinned against me?*

4. *Am I patronizing or condescending in my dealings with those differing from me in color or race, who work with or under me?*

5. *Do I help perpetuate race prejudice by encouraging and re-telling jokes in which the Negro is always inferior, or the white man a fiendish monster?*

6. *Do I leave unchallenged such statements as:*
   a) *All white people are hypocrites?*
   b) *All Negroes are immoral?*
   c) *All whites are cruel and unjust?*
   d) *All Negroes are dirty, lazy and unreliable?*

7. *Do I practice Christ-like charity toward the Negro at all times on the street, on public conveyances, in the office and in church?*

IV. PRUDENCE

1. *Have I seriously studied the teachings of the Catholic Church regarding race?*

2. *Do I realize the grave danger to my soul in sinning against racial justice and racial charity?*

3. *Has my conduct been regulated by a worldly type of prudence or expediency so that I have been completely indifferent and inactive in overcoming racial injustices?*

4. *Has my unreasonable aggressiveness in my contacts with those of another race seriously endangered the eventual harmony of all races?*

5. *Do I realize that, as a member of a democratic community, I share in responsibility before God for the poor living conditions, job discrimination and inadequate health facilities of the Negro people in this city?*

6. *What am I doing to correct these injustices and to help the Negro to win his natural and constitutional rights?*

7. *Am I making any attempt to combat racial prejudice in my home, among those with whom I work, and among my fellow parishioners?*

V. JUSTICE

1. *Do I pay equal wages to white and Negro for equal work?*

2. *Do I provide equal accommodations for Negro and white employees doing the same work?*

3. *Do I serve my employer to the best of my ability, fulfilling all my obligations, and justifying the responsibility placed in me?*

4. *Am I as careful in my conversation not to injure the reputation of those of another race as those of my own race?*

VI. FORTITUDE

1. *Have I the courage of my convictions in my daily life? Do I practice justice and charity toward the Negro, even though I may be jeered at, scorned, or even discriminated against for so doing?*

2. *Have I the courage to challenge race prejudice wherever it is found—at work, among my friends, in my church and school?*

3. *Do I unite the many sufferings with which I am afflicted because of my race with the sufferings of Our Lord Jesus Christ, thus increasing my reward in Heaven?*

4. *Am I discouraged and disheartened by racial injustice and uncharitableness?*

VII. TEMPERANCE

1. *Do I pride myself on what I erroneously deem virtuous moderation as regards race, and as a result, do nothing and say nothing which might help solve the problem?*

2. *Is my personal conduct such, particularly in public, that it will not antagonize persons of another race against me and against my people?*

3. *Am I boisterous, careless about my personal appearance, uncouth in my language when in public places, thus strengthening the prejudices of others against people of my own race?*

chapter 9
ECUMENISM

The 20th century can be aptly described as the century of vast and rapid change. Within a single person's lifetime revolutions have taken place in air and space travel, in the field of communications, in industry, and in the many areas of scholarly study and research. Change, and even revolutions, have taken place within religious bodies during this century as well. The World Council of Churches and Vatican Council II have been living examples of the work of the Spirit in adapting and reforming the Church of God. One of the biggest changes in attitudes and practices within both Church groups has been in their attitudes toward each other. Another description of the 20th century which is often heard in ecclesiastical circles is to call it "The Age of Ecumenism." Since this movement within the Church today is so important and does have such far-reaching consequences, as well as some built-in difficulties and dangers, it is most fitting to spend more than a few classes in an attempt to understand the many facets of the movement and to form proper attitudes and practices toward it. Two extreme positions are to be avoided: first, a lack of proper respect for the religious beliefs and practices of other faiths springing from ignorance, arrogance, prejudice, or intolerance; second, a religious indifferentism which looks upon all religions in the same way and holds the opinion that "one religion is as good as another." While respectful of all religions and tolerant of man's right to go to God according to the light of his conscience, the fundamental question each man must ask, and whose answer he must discover for himself, is how has God willed that man should worship and serve Him in this life. Each man has the responsibility to search for the answer to this basic question of life and to live it fully.

The following two articles are by theologians active in ecumenical affairs. Father Baum outlines the changing attitudes toward ecumenism among Catholics; Father Conley describes five suggested steps to be taken toward unity with other Christians. Both articles provide much food for reflective thought and discussion.

Christian Unity

There was a time when we thought of Christian unity in terms of conversions to the Catholic Church. The efforts of those concerned with the reunion of Christians in the one fold of Christ were directed to one single aim: to make as many converts as possible among Protestant Christians. This attitude was even reflected in our prayers. Praying for Christian unity such as we did, and still do, during the Unity Octave simply meant asking God to give grace and light to Protestant Christians that they may discover their error and return to the Catholic Church. If we read the "intentions" which were attached to the different days of the Octave, we find in them a perfect expression of this attitude to Christian unity.

While as Catholics we still believe, and always believe, that the Roman Catholic Church is the unique community of Jesus Christ, our approach to Christian unity has undergone a great change. What exactly has happened? This is the question I wish to answer in this article.

First of all we have begun to look at our separated brethren more dispassionately. We have examined their teachings and their ways of life more carefully and made the startling discovery that much that is Christian and supernatural is alive among them. This is true especially of the older and more traditional Protestant Churches. Taking for granted their faith, we must conclude that many elements which have come into this world through the Gospel of Jesus Christ have retained their vitality among Protestants. We are often impressed by their spirit of faith, the firmness of their hope, and the amplitude of their charity. Among them we often find prayer, sacrifice, a deep appreciation of sacramental baptism, and a love for the breaking of the bread described in the Gospel. It is true, we also find other elements among Protestants, scepticism and unbelief, a disregard of the faith of the New Testament Church, doubts about the divinity of Our Lord Jesus Christ . . . This is especially true of a kind of Protestantism we find so widely

FROM *THE CATHOLIC MESSENGER*. REPRINTED WITH PERMISSION.

spread in our own country. Yet we know that salvation and holiness will come to Protestant Christians, if they follow what is authentically Christian in their denominational traditions. More than that, we believe that Protestant Christians who, with supernatural charity, are faithful to Jesus Christ and His call move along a road which brings them closer to the fullness of truth in the Catholic Church. For this reason we must be very careful not to offend Protestant Christians by our way of speaking about them; for by offending them we could impede their progress on the road to the fullness of truth. Being unappreciative of their Christian spirituality and continually stressing their need of conversion must offend Protestant Christians and thus render a disservice to Christian unity.

It may be mentioned in this connection that the great amount of Catholic "convert-making" is made not among believing Protestants, but in the enormous crowd of people who have neither faith nor hope in this world.

There is a second factor which has contributed to the change in our approach to Christian unity; we have begun to take seriously Protestant criticism of ourselves. I do not mean that we should pay attention to the voices of bigotry and prejudice which still abound in the Protestant world, or rather, to use a phrase of Professor Bennett, in the Protestant underworld. But we should take very seriously the intelligent and thoughtful criticism offered by Protestant leaders, especially by their great theologians. We certainly are in need of criticism. We can never relax with the feeling that we have got it all. While we believe that the Catholic Church has received the fullness of Christ, we also believe that we are sinners, that we have not lived up to this fullness, that we have presented a one-sided picture of it, have over-emphasized certain aspects of divine truth and neglected others. For this reason, then, we can learn from the criticism of Protestants.

Let me give two simple examples. If we read in the best of Protestant writers that the Catholic Church has given a place in religion to Mary which is out of proportion to her place in the Gospel, we acknowledge that this accusation brings to light a deep divergence between the Protestant and our understanding of divine Revelation. At the same time we must recognize with humility and shame that there are certain popular devotions and prayers to Mary which obscure the full Catholic teaching on Mary's dependence on her divine Son. Can we not learn from Protestant criticism to speak about Mary with more moderation and precision, as it is done by our popes, by never separating her from the mystery of human redemption in Jesus Christ? Or, when we read that Protestants are afraid of Christian unity of the Catholic type because they dread centralization and the lack of freedom granted to the local churches, can we not admit that the present centralization of the Catholic Church is not a dogmatic necessity but an accident of history? The present centralization is not essential to the Church's divine structure, nor does the supreme jurisdiction and the infallible teaching of the pope imply that all relevent changes and significant movements in the Church must come from Rome. There are many voices today, even among Catholic hierarchy, advocating a decentralization of ecclesiastical government. The supreme power of the pope would in no way be slighted if the bishops of the various countries received the freedom to adapt their churches to the needs of the people in which they exist.

These considerations lead us to a third factor which has produced a change in our approach to Christian unity. Being aware on the one hand of the Christian values, however limited, alive among Protestants and on the other of the possibility of learning from their critical remarks, we come to the conclusion, painful though it may be, that we too must change. This sentence must be understood correctly. The Catholic Church cannot change in its divine structure, we cannot change our teaching nor our sacraments, but there is a large area of life where changes are possible, normal, and necessary. In the above paragraph I have suggested some of these "changes": a more Christological way of venerating our Lady and a greater freedom for the initiative of the local churches. There are many others that could be named. At present Catholic literature is full of critical examinations and constructive suggestions.

The urgent demand of Pope John XXIII that the life of the

Church be adapted to the needs of the modern world—the word adaption is continually on the lips of the Holy Father—indicates his wish to work for Christian unity precisely by introducing changes and improvements in various areas of Catholic practice. Our present Pope is fully aware that many barriers which prevent others from understanding the true nature of the Church are barriers which we have put up ourselves. Whether the forthcoming Ecumenical Council really will adapt the Church to the demands of our century and the interests of Christian unity no man can foresee. The outcome of a Council is not up to the pope; it is the work of the bishops meeting in council.

Apart from the great changes that can only be initiated by the Catholic hierarchy, there are other smaller yet still significant changes in the Catholic life that are up to our priests and the laity. For the sake of Christian unity, we all can make our spiritual life more liturgical. We can try always to put the emphasis on what is central in our Catholic faith, on our redemption in Jesus Christ, and understand the other elements of our faith for their relationships to this central mystery. Our moral life must spring from our incorporation in Christ, not simply from a submission to a set of laws. Our devotions must be fed from our access to the One mediator, not simply from a seeking of personal blessings. The words of our creeds must be sources of life for us, not the passive acceptance of a formula. This is the way of the New Testament and this is the way of the Catholic liturgy. This, incidentally, is also the approach of the great encyclical of Pius XII.

Summing up, then, there are three factors which have altered our attitude toward Christianity in recent years: the appreciation of the authentically Christian among Protestants, a serious consideration of their criticisms, and the willingness on our part to struggle for a more balanced possession of Catholic spirit. Much more then can be done in favor of Christian unity than persuading a few Protestants to become Catholics. While we have no right to disparage individual conversions to the Church, we feel that our first duty in regard to Christian unity is to exchange ourselves. We must discover to what extent the image of the Church which we create really manifests her true nature and to what extent it deforms it; and then have the humility to change, to improve, to grow spiritually.

With this "new" attitude in the heart even the prayer for unity which we offer during the Unity Octave takes on a different quality. Praying for the unity of Christians we do not simply ask God that Protestants may discover their error and be converted; we ask with an even greater intensity that we may discover our own shortcomings and receive the grace to improve. That Christians are disunited is a terrible sin before God, but why should we in our prayers point an accusing finger at others? Should we not rather admit that we too are responsible for Christian divisions, not only in the past, but even in the present whenever our pride creates an obstacle to the unity that Christ desires for his people? Only if we are humble will God hear our prayer THAT ALL MAY BE ONE.

Common Prayer and Worship in an Ecumenical Age

KIERAN CONLEY, o.s.b.

Among the many areas of co-operation open to Christians in an ecumenical age, none is more important or more pressing in urgency than that of common prayer and worship.

At the outset I should like to stress what Pope Paul VI has said in the third section of *Ecclesiam Suam* when he refers to the deep responsibility that is ours in the whole ecumenical movement. We cannot stand idly by and let others take the initiative. We cannot close our hearts and minds to the problem. And the source of our responsibility is in that final prayer of Christ, "That all may be one!" (JOHN 17:21).

The tragedy today is not so much that Christians are divided. This of course is disastrous enough. But the real tragedy is that we, as Christians, do not really suffer from the incredible scandal of our disunity. If we were genuinely concerned, the topic of this paper would present fewer difficulties.

The question before us is really part of a much broader question: What are the areas of co-operation we can enter into with non-Catholic Christians? I say non-Catholic Christians because for the moment this particular discussion should be kept in a Christian context. The problem of common worship and prayer with non-Christians is much more complex and might be unnecessarily confusing for us.

Much has already been done ecumenically in the social order, where co-operation is obviously possible, to alleviate hunger, disease, poverty. At least we recognize here the possibility of co-operating. Christians could and should also co-operate far more adequately to erase the stigma

FROM *PROCEEDINGS OF THE LITURGICAL CONFERENCE, 1964*.
REPRINTED WITH PERMISSION.

of anti-Semitism among Christians and to promote civil rights. All this is evident. At another level, there is the familiar area we call dialogue, of which Pope Paul speaks throughout his encyclical. Here we encounter individual Christians who see their commitment to Christ through a lens which may differ from ours, and yet with them we share the same commitment and we meet them with understanding, with compassion, sincerity, and respect, and above all, with love.

But the question before us now is, "Can we move beyond mere dialogue?" Are we not obliged to move toward common worship and prayer together with other Christians?

If we read the New Testament and ask ourselves what prayer and worship should be, we find Christ first in the Sermon on the Mount telling His disciples, "When you pray, do not be like the hypocrites who love to pray standing in the synagogue or on the street corners, in order that they might be seen by men. But when you pray, go into a room by yourself and shut the door, and pray to your Father in secret. And your Father who sees in secret shall reward you" (Matt. 6:5-6). This is the New Testament mandate for personal, private prayer. There is another side, however, to the coin of prayer in the New Testament. We find it later in St. Matthew's Gospel, in Chapter 18, where Christ says, "If two of you agree about any request you have to make, that request will be granted by my Father in heaven. For where two or three are gathered together in my name, there am I in the midst of them" (Matt. 18:19-20). In other words, we have here an obvious allusion to social prayer. The prayer is to be intelligible because the individual must agree. They cannot agree unless they can communicate. And this will demand intelligible signs.

Such a concept of prayer will of course be completed by what we learn regarding the institution of the Eucharist. In Chapter 2 of 1 Corinthians, we find Paul recounting the institution, and we hear Christ's words saying, "Do this in commemoration of me. For as often as you eat this bread and drink the cup, you proclaim the death of the

Lord until he comes" (1 Cor. 11:25-26). Christ's command to perpetuate, to renew, to enter into the celebration of the Last Supper, adds a fulfillment, a completion to what we heard in Matthew, "where two or three are gathered in my name . . ." And we find the early Christian community carrying out this mandate for social or communal prayer as they listen to the teaching of the apostles, breaking bread and praying (Acts 2:42). It is in this context and against this background that we must understand what we are doing when we worship, and why it is that we should either close our worship to others, or open it to others. The most important thing is to see the necessity of intelligibility which the Constitution on the Sacred Liturgy refers to as the ideal of an honest sign. This theme can be found throughout the entire treatment of the liturgy. Its purpose, to make it possible for people to understand what they are doing.

We must ask the question, then, whether or not in our liturgy, as we close it or open it to others, or as we join or do not join with others, we are being really true to the necessity of worshiping with intelligible signs. But first we must ask, what is it that God has done for us? What is it that keeps us really interested in making it possible for Christians to become truly one?

If we look back at what God has done in history, we find Him exercising His selective purpose, leading to our becoming one in Christ. We see Him create. We see Him create man as special within the whole of creation. "Let us make man to our image and likeness" (Gen. 1:26). We see Him choose Israel, becoming present in a special way to Israel. "I will dwell in the midst of the Israelites, and will be their God" (Ex. 29:45). Within Israel He chooses prophets, priests and kings to keep alive the covenant He has made with His people, to guide that people, to teach that people, to lead that people in worship. And finally out of Israel He selects Judah; and within Judah the faithful remnant continues until Christ. In Christ God speaks His final Word and performs His final saving action. He had spoken and acted earlier in history, but this is His definitive word and action. He will never say anything more; He will never do anything more. He has made himself perfectly at one with His people, perfectly in communion with them. And from that time onward it is simply that people must come into contact with this saving word and action of God in Christ. All this is the great at-one-ment.

If we think of history, then, as a progressive immersion of God into the world, a progressive making Himself present and at one with His people, we are at the heart of the ecumenical problem. Because this is precisely what we ask: how can we become at one — not merely in our diverse ways, at one with Christ personally on different channels, but how can we become more obviously one together in our commitment to Christ? The thrust of God's love in giving Himself to us urges us to seek a more evident unity. "The love of Christ impels us" (2 Cor. 5:14).

Present canonical legislation, of course, is severe in its restrictions regarding *communicatio in sacris* — the sharing in sacred things. But perhaps the legitimate reasons which prompted those restrictions no longer carry their original force.

The present legislation is found primarily in Canons 731 and 1258 of the Code. In the first, we are forbidden as Catholic ministers to administer sacraments to those who are not Catholics, even when they ask for them, even when they are well disposed. They must first be reconciled to the Church completely before we can administer the sacraments to them.

In Canon 1258, we are forbidden as Catholics to take active part in any non-Catholic service. But we can attend, for a grave reason, if we remain passive, if we sit back, rather inhumanly perhaps, and watch. This may be for weddings, funerals, dedications, civil celebrations, and the like. Such is the present legislation of the Church. It has had some exceptions, however, e.g., in the case of dying persons.

Father Gregory has an excellent article in *The Ecumenist* *where he comments on communicatio in sacris* in the light of the schema on ecumenism to be discussed at the third session of Vatican II. He discusses the background of liturgical legislation and the reasons for this legislation. He does point out, of course, that certain decisions of the Roman congregations have permitted us to administer sacraments to non-Catholic baptized Christians; e.g., penance, anointing, even Viaticum. Therefore, we are not facing a question of intrinsic impossibility, of complete dogmatic closure, as we look to the possibilities of worship together, even ultimately to communion together.

For the moment, the reasons behind the Church's legislation are in effect threefold. First, when we take part in a church's worship service we are proclaiming our acceptance of the faith proclaimed in that liturgy or worship. And the claim is made that since the integrity of a church's faith is being proclaimed in its liturgy, unless we can admit everything that is involved in that faith, we should not take part.

A second reason: since the unity of Christians is not obvious, if we were to come together in any sense for public worship, we would be lying, because we would be setting forth or presenting a deceptive sign. The worship as a sign of unity suggests that we are one. But we are not obviously one, so how can we worship together?

The third reason for the present legislation, observes Father Baum, is indifference. This is the pragmatic reason in the background of most of the Church's decisions on this question in the past. We are afraid that if we open up the possibility of worship with other Christians in their public worship services, there is a real danger that we may become indifferent to the unity of the Church and to what that unity must consist in.

Such are the reasons that stand behind the Church's legislation: integrity of faith, worship as a sign of unity, and the danger of indifference. But we must see if we are not being a bit too closed in attitude when we say there is no unity of faith, that there is no avenue by which we can express honestly the unity we already enjoy, and that there is serious danger of indifference.

The reasons supporting the legislation are really no longer

susceptible of univocal interpretation. When we speak of integrity of faith, we must not forget that faith is first of all a personal commitment to a personal Christ. Our assent to truths is always consequent upon that commitment. This means that there is but one Christian faith, subjectively the same in all Christians, even though each Christian may view his surrender to Christ through a different lens. St. Paul writes of "One Lord, one faith, one baptism" (Eph. 4:5), and all Christians enjoy this threefold unity.

St. Thomas points out what is primary in faith is our acceptance of the person through whom and because of whom we make our intellectual assent. Theologians distinguish carefully between *fides qua,* the subjective commitment, and *fides quae,* the objective extension of truths to which one assents. The first is the same for all Christians; the second may be different for different people, either as communities or as individuals within communities. The true Christian faith of an Orthodox, an Anglican, a Lutheran, or another Protestant, is the same Christian faith of the Catholic, subjectively, the *fides qua.* The *fides quae* is different because we, as Catholics, assent to certain things which others do not accept, and they may assent to certain things which we do not accept.

However, there is but one Lord to whom we commit ourselves, one faith by which we commit ourselves, one baptism through which we are incorporated into that one Lord, unto the one God and Father of all, who is above all and through all and in all. Evidently, then, what we have in common is far greater than that which distinquishes us. And how can we possibly move sincerely toward full Christian unity without prayer together? In any case, the lack of more complete unity in faith should not prevent that common worship.

But what of hypocrisy in the sign? Would a sign of unity be presented when we are really not one? We must realize that we are already, in some sense, one. "One Lord, one faith, one baptism." We are also one in the sense that we are zealous for that for which Christ prayed: "That all may be one." Because of this deep, though partial, unity, common worship would not be hypocritical. It might be limited and qualified to protect the truth of the sign, but such common worship seems not only permissible theologically but absolutely mandatory, There is but one body, one Spirit, one hope of our calling, and how can Christians hope to attain the unity prayed for by Christ without common prayer to His Spirit?

This is the background against which we should examine the possibilities of common prayer and worship among Christians. We should remember, however—and this should appear obvious in the conciliar decree on ecumenism—that liturgy or worship is not merely sign; it is also cause. It is not only a sign of the family of God, God's people, being at one; it is a cause bringing that people of God into deeper unity. And if we already share with other Christians a real unity in faith and in baptism, then what better way is there to become more perfectly one than by entering into common prayer and worship to the degree that this is theologically tenable and ecumenically practical?

Finally, the danger of indifference has been all but eliminated by the contemporary ecumenical atmosphere. At long last we recognize the greatest tragedy of all, namely, that Christians do not really suffer from the awful scandal of their disunity. But as we meet each other at every level of the Christian experience, we learn little by little to feel deeply the sadness of separation. Rather than indifference resulting from common worship with other Christians, its effect will rather be genuine concern, concern for all the things which might hasten the day of full Christian unity.

In the light of all this, where do we stand? Between the Our Father prayed in common at ecumenical meetings— as allowed by the 1949 Instruction of the Holy Office—and full communion (Eucharistic participation), there is a wide range of possibilities with regard to common worship. But between these extremes, where should our stance be taken? Should we say that we will never do anything more than say an Our Father in the garage with a friend, quietly, in the dark? Or should we say, "Let us all get together. Bring in all the non-Catholic Christians to our Masses and give them Communion, and every now and then, or as a regular thing, we shall take part in their eucharistic celebrations." These are the two extremes; and neither one, of course, is adequate. The first is insufficient because of our commitment to Christ and our awareness of the imperative in Christ's final prayer for unity; the second would be completely unintelligible theologically, because to make the sign so completely one, that is, communion as a normal, regular thing, would be a complete lie. The latter may not be dogmatically impossible, because when someone is baptized and has faith in Christ, who is to keep that someone from celebrating Christ's Eucharist? But such procedure would certainly be remarkably imprudent. What, therefore, should be said?

As we look at the problem we face today, our guide is the new liturgical Constitution and we are pushed forward by *Ecclesiam Suam*. We realize that the responsibility for ecumenical endeavor must be ours. And we are deeply aware that nothing in Christianity is effected without prayer. In the light of this, I would make the following proposals—they look to immediate implementation . . .

First, there should be a common Bible acceptable to all Christians. This has already been realized in Scotland where Catholic bishops have agreed to the use of the Revised Standard Version, a text compiled by American Protestant biblical scholars. The same arrangement could be made in this country as we await the completion of The Anchor Bible from Doubleday.

Secondly, there should be a common hymnal. St. Augustine's remark, *amantis est cantare*—song is for the one who loves—is not only pertinent; it is imperative. Ecumenism, as Christianity, is dead without love, and if singing together will help us love more deeply, then by all means let us sing together. Some attempts have been made in the direction of securing a common hymnal but they have not yet taken hold.

Thirdly, there must be possible a true familiarization of Catholics with non-Catholic worship practices, and non-Catholics with Catholic practices. Encouragement should be given to interested, intelligent Catholics to acquaint themselves with non-Catholic liturgies by qualified participation in them. As was indicated earlier, in our contemporary ecumenical atmosphere, the danger of indifference should no longer be significant. With a better educated clergy and laity, we could feel free to allow our people to take a limited part in non-Catholic services. The unity of baptism and faith in the one Lord which we already enjoy is surely adequate support for this proposal. And ignorance of each other's worship is hardly an ideal.

Fourthly, with a common Bible and a common hymnal there could be common non-eucharistic services. If these were held in every major city in the Christian countries of the world three or four times a year, the effect of such participation upon the desire for unity would be unbelievable. And there is nothing dogmatically against this, nothing theologically against it. For the time being there are laws against it, yes, but these are diverse questions. We are asking all kinds of questions of the present Council, and out of these questions, or the answers to these questions, certain canons will have to be changed. Here we are suggesting a rather abrupt and extensive change of the canons which concern common worship.

A fifth stage, after common Bible, common hymnal, familiarization, and a non-eucharistic service which we could participate in publicly, would be a Eucharistic service — Catholic or non-Catholic — where there might be arranged what was done in Germany by the Una Sancta group, involving an inner circle and an outer circle of worshipers. The inner circle communicates completely. The outer circle takes part but does not communicate. For example, at a Catholic Mass, the Catholics were around the altar on the inside, the Lutherans, theologians, and laymen were around the altar on the outer ring. And they all took part in the Mass, in the singing and the hearing of the Word; but the Lutherans did not communicate. This would bring Christians together around the eucharistic table and they would suffer more poignantly the fact that they are not one. But the Lord of the Eucharist would be there, not only by their prayer — where two or three are gathered together in His name — but by His Eucharistic presence as well.

The final stage I am going to leave in question. I am firmly convinced that the stages already suggested are possible; they are commendable; they are necessary. Our love in Christ demands them. But whether or not we can take the next step is another question. Can we ever really enter into communion, that is, enter into a full celebration of the Eucharist, with each other? Remember, it is obviously not intrinsically wrong. We give Communion to dying Orthodox; we give Communion to dying baptized Christians, if we interpret the legislation more liberally. But it is not a question of whether or not inter-communion is intrinsically wrong, but whether it is really theologically pragmatic.

All I can say is that there seems to be reasons for intercommunion; there seems to be reasons against it. One reason for it, of course, would be the Eucharist itself, which is not only sign but cause as well. And perhaps we should not let the sign value completely outweigh the effectiveness. The Eucharist is the greatest source of unity. But would we be telling too great a lie by entering into communion with each other at the Eucharistic services? This is the question. We have the unity of baptism and faith in the one Lord, and this partial unity must be expressed. Perhaps this partial unity could be expressed by making intercommunion only occasional—at weddings, funerals, ecumenical gatherings, church dedications. I am not so sure. There are those who would suggest it. Just not having it as a normal thing would be enough to protect the sign as indicating only partial unity.

On the other hand, we have to ask the question: Might this not be too hypocritical? Might it not be too great a lie? As I say, I do not know. Also, perhaps the ultimate question: Would it really be good for ecumenism? Because, if we are really trying to intensify the pain of suffering as we confront the sundial of our disunity, perhaps by never allowing intercommunion we can keep that pain alive. As I say, I do not know. There seems to be arguments on both sides. And I am certainly open to appreciating very deeply the effectiveness of the Eucharist. I will leave it to your discussion.

But as we consider these various proposals, I think we

should realize that common worship and common prayer, although suspect in recent tradition, are a matter of real obligation. Because if we have fallen in love with the truth which is Christ, and if we are indeed living that truth in love, then we must pray together. If the one Holy Spirit is guiding the Christian churches to unity, and we all are convinced that He is, how can we refuse to come together more fully, more completely as a community, in order to beg Him to bring us to perfect unity?

Ecumenism is a concern of persons, diverse persons all committed to one Person. We Catholics must realize our responsibility here. As we are committed to this Person who is Christ, we must live our lives open to others, above all to those others who are equally committed to Christ. The openness for which I plead is to prayer and worship in common among those who have encountered a Person and who live in His love.

SUPPLEMENTARY READINGS

Bea, Augustine Cardinal. THE POSITION OF CATHOLICS RE-
GARDING UNITY. Glen Rock, N.J.: Paulist Press, 1961. Cardinal
Bea stresses the role that love must play in our efforts to achieve
Christian Unity.

DECREE ON ECUMENISM (November 21, 1964). This was issued
by Pope Paul VI, together with the Fathers of the Second Vatican
Council. There are at least three good editions in circulation:
(a) DOCUMENTS OF VATICAN II from America Press, 106 West
56th Street, New York, New York 10019; (b) THE NATIONAL
CATHOLIC WELFARE CONFERENCE EDITION from NCWC,
1312 Massachusetts Avenue, N.W., Washington, D.C. 20005;
(c) STUDY CLUB EDITION from The Paulist Press, Glen Rock,
New Jersey.

GRASS-ROOTS ECUMENISM. Ecumenical Projects of Formation
and Action for Lay People, Parish, Diocese, Organization, School.
Published by The National Council of Catholic Men and The
National Council of Catholic Women, 1312 Massachusetts Avenue, N.W., Washington, D.C. 20005. This kit includes key Church
documents on ecumenism, several explanatory articles by ecumenical experts and, finally, practical suggestions for various
approaches to ecumenical activity.

Shehan, Lawrence Cardinal. AMERICAN CATHOLICS AND
CHRISTIAN REUNION. Peekskill, N.Y.: Graymoor Press, 1961.
Cardinal Shehan stresses the role of the laity in Christian reunion.

POINTS FOR DISCUSSION

1. Is this whole question of ecumenism and the existing separa-
ration within the Christian family of any real concern to Catholic
teenagers today? Why? Why not? Should it be?

2. Do you feel that the Ecumenical Movement includes a danger
of religious indifferentism arising in the Catholic community?
Why? What can be done to forestall such possible danger?

3. What would you say to some Catholics who, in this Ecumenical
Age, say that it would almost be better to be a Protestant—no
confession, possibilities of divorce and remarriage, legitimacy of
birth control, etc. Is this a real problem in the practical order?

4. What is your attitude towards Catholics and non-Catholics coming together for some form of common worship? How do you explain the fact that the Church today is permitting and even encouraging such practices when in former years it forbade them, sometimes under pain of sin?

5. Do you feel that the fact that we as Catholics, have our own parochial and private system of education poses a problem for the Ecumenical Spirit and Movement and is more divisive than unifying? Explain your reasons for either point of view. What can be done to offset such difficulites if they exist, granted the continued reality of the Catholic School System?

6. What do you feel is the best way to promote a truly Ecumenical Spirit among Catholic and non-Catholic teenagers? Whose responsibility is it to inaugurate meetings and the like to foster such a spirit?

7. What obstacles do you feel are present generally, and in yourself particularly, which hinder the promotion of this Ecumenical Spirit?

8. Discuss Father Kieran Conley's five steps toward union among Christians. Do you think these steps are possible and practical in your local Church area?

9. The Decree on Ecumenism issued by Vatican Council II stresses the fact that the liturgy of the Eucharist is not only a sign of union but a cause of it. In the light of Father Conley's article discuss how it can be both a sign of disunity and unity at the present time of our ecumenical dialogue. What is his point regarding the need to suffer disunity in order to desire unity? Is there such real suffering on the part of Catholics generally? On your part? Should there be? Why?

10. List and discuss the similarities of belief within various Christian denominations, i.e., Lutheran, Baptist, Episcopalian, Methodist, Presbyterian.

11. In the light of the ecumenical age and spirit comment on these two statements frequently heard in Catholic circles during the past: "Error has no rights," and "No salvation outside the Roman Catholic Church."

12. *The two main dangers to be squarely faced during this ecumenical age are religious intolerance on the one hand and religious indifference on the other. Discuss some concrete instances where both extreme positions are experienced today and indicate ways in which such extremism can and should be guarded against.*

chapter 10
THE CHURCH AND THE WORLD COMMUNITY

The Church, as the People of God, is a "called community" — a community called from the broader expanse of the human family which makes up the world community. It is called to be of service to this world community. This service goes far beyond merely telling its members what is right and what is wrong, what they should and should not do in their private lives in order to gain heaven. The church is an integral part which presently is undergoing vast and rapidly sweeping changes. It is the mission of the Church, which is universal and which cuts across all national boundaries of particular self-interest, to be a voice and a force for wisdom, truth, prosperity, peace, justice, and charity on a human and on a divine level.

It is in this spirit and with this intent that recent popes, and most notably Pope John XXIII, have addressed some of their encyclicals and other writings and speeches to the world community, "to all men of good will." The decrees of Vatican Council II also bear the stamp of this concern for the world community; this is seen very clearly in the decree on the Church in the Modern World as the Fathers of the Council gave expression to the Church's concern and teaching on the pressing problems of today's world which affect all men as members of the human family. The spirit of this decree aims at making a contribution to the alleviation, and hopefully to the ultimate solution, of such international problems as peace, nuclear disarmament, poverty of underprivileged peoples, world population, etc.

In this section of the religious program it will be fitting and helpful to make a general study of the leading ideas expressed in Pope John's classic encyclical *Pacem in Terris*. These ideas touch upon each of the world problems mentioned above. The articles which follow focus on the two central world issues of war and poverty.

303

Pacem in Terris Convocation

POPE JOHN'S ENCYCLICAL ON PEACE IS
DISCUSSED BY EXPERTS FROM THIRTEEN COUNTRIES

A group of American scientists who met quietly in 1961 to discuss the possibility of rational life in other solar systems found themselves asking, only half-jokingly, "Is there intelligent life on Earth?" Man's cruelty, hatred and intransigence are unending and despite his professed desire to preserve peace he seems equally intent on blowing up the world and everyone in it. It was in hopes of rousing men to halt their apparent drift toward destruction and to join together in working for peace that Pope John XXIII, shortly before his death two years ago, issued his great encyclical, Pacem in Terris. It was greeted by the world with more interest and enthusiasm than any other papal statement has commanded in hundreds of years. Paradoxically, however, Catholics, perhaps especially in the United States, have been reluctant to acclaim it, possibly because Pope John asked for discussions even between men of diametrically opposed ideologies and for the subordination of national sovereignty to an international authority when necessary for the good of humanity. A few weeks ago at least part of Pope John's urgent plea was heeded. Politicians, scientists, government leaders, educators, lawyers and a noted Protestant theologian met in New York City to discuss the requirements for achieving world peace; they used Pacem in Terris as the basis for their talks. Attending the convocation were about two thousand guests, among them a large number of priests, religious and Catholic laymen. (Earlier some Catholics had opposed the very idea of the meeting, perhaps because some of the speakers represent political systems or profess political opinions which many Catholics find unacceptable.) The discussions ranged from predictable apologies for cold war positions (Vice President Humphrey and the Russians on Viet Nam, for instance, or the Polish and German speakers on their traditional enmities) to profound and moving analyses of the present human predicament, such as those given by theologian Paul Tillich and Israel's Deputy Prime Minister, Abba Eban. The general impression was

FROM *JUBILEE*, APRIL, 1965. REPRINTED WITH PERMISSION.

one of striving for a common understanding in the light of Pope John's encyclical; that there must be communication before communion.

On the following pages, JUBILEE presents some of the diverse and interesting statements delivered at the Pacem in Terris Convocation.

—ED.

Major Points of the Convocation

For thirty centuries, humanity has been searching for an ideal Jerusalem that lives forever in the hearts and minds of men, symbol in every land and every tongue of the quest for individual and human perfection.

Peace is the destination of that quest. It is now the central idea, but also the central interest of mankind. It was not always so. War has too often been regarded as a part of man's essential nature, the source of nobility, heroism and redeeming sacrifice. Literature is full of such images of war. Today, the ideal of peace converges with its necessity. Whether men are moved by hope or fear, by active ideals or a passive acceptance of survival, the result is the same.

Everything in history that once made for war now makes for peace. In this I include our new and all-pervading vulnerability. Peace is not something to be inherited by aspiration alone. It will be attained, if at all, by action in its service. This implies a duty to look at structures, institutions and laws. This is the first era of global history—the first in which an event happening anywhere has effects and echoes everywhere. There is an ecumenical spirit in modern life and thought and letters—a new pluralism, diversity and tolerance. No ideological camp believes any longer that its doctrine must either perish or conquer all mankind. And yet the structures, institutions and laws of peace are in disarray.

— ABBA EBAN

Although we have abjured war as an instrument of policy, all nations have not yet abjured the state of mind that has so often led to war—the nationalistic urge to dominate and extend, by various means, their spheres of influence, and the conviction of the unquestionable superiority of their own particular traditions, forms of government and ways of life. Nor has it been possible effectively to eliminate the use of force, whether openly or covertly, as a means of furthering political or other ends. Such attitudes inevitably breed in other nations the fears, resentments and suspicions which historically have also created the atmosphere of tension in which wars break out. Again, although we speak loudly for equal rights and against discrimination, there are still many nations and groups throughout the world, which are not prepared to accept the practical consequences of these ideals, while an even greater number still suffer from discrimination or lack of equal opportunity. It is this failure of everyday, practical behavior to keep pace with professed ideals and aims, which makes the promise of our infinitely promising world a mockery for so many of its inhabitants.

We have to work toward a world order in which aggressive nationalism or expansionism are banished as a means of promoting or protecting national interests, where fanaticism is no longer necessary to support a different point of view and where diversity can be preserved without resort to prejudice and hatred. All of our high aims, our vaunted technology, our skill and our real desire to co-operate and to help one another will be of no avail if this adaptation to new circumstances, this general accommodation, this real change of heart, does not come about.

—U THANT

The American Position

It is the intention of the United States government to pursue every reasonable avenue toward agreement with the Soviet Union in limiting the nuclear arms race.

Today we must recognize that the next major step in controlling the nuclear arms race may require us to look beyond the narrow U.S.-Soviet competition of the past. For the explosion of a nuclear device by Communist China has impressed us once again that the world of today is no longer the bi-polar world of an earlier decade. Nuclear competition is no longer limited to two super-powers.

If the need for preventing the proliferation of nuclear weapons is more immediate in Asia today, it is no less important in Latin America, Africa and the Near East. All of these areas are ripe for regional arms pacts which would prevent these countries from developing nuclear weapons. Nuclear weapons would serve no useful purpose in preserving their security. The introduction of these weapons would imperil the peace of Latin America and Africa and intensify the present rivalries in the Near East. It would endanger the precarious economies of countries which already possess military forces too large for their security needs and too expensive to be maintained without outside assistance.

In Latin America, in Asia and Africa, another threat to peace lies in the shocking inequality between privileged and impoverished, between glittering capitals and festering slums, between boom-ing industrial regions and primitive rural areas. A real threat to peace in these areas is the revolutionary challenge of an unjust social order in which true peace—peace based on justice—is impossible.

Those who have been "more blessed with this world's goods" must heed the Pope's plea to assist "those political communities whose citizens suffer from poverty, misery and hunger and who lack even the elementary rights of the human person."

We must do this out of compassion—for we are our brother's keeper. And we also do it out of self-interest as well—for our lot is their lot, our future their future, our peace their peace. This planet is simply too small for the insulation of the rich against turbulence bred of injustice in any part of the world.

—HUBERT HUMPHREY

The Russian Position

It is necessary to have a clear idea of the aims and views of each other, to understand them unequivocally. Permit me to explain our aims with all frankness. We have never tried to conceal that we believe the Socialist system to be a higher form of social and economic structure of society than capitalism, that we strive to achieve the victory of communism. This attitude of ours is, however, a testimony of our deepest concern for peace, not of a desire for a new world war.

On the international scene there has appeared and developed a large group of Socialist states, which do not have the notorious "military-industrial complex," have no classes and social groups that are directly interested in war or secure their well-being from the armaments race.

Ideological opponents of Communists make use of assertions that "war and Socialist revolutions are synonymous notions," that "Communists advocate armed violence everywhere at all times" and that Communists allegedly believe that "every means is justified for the sake of the triumph of revolution."

There is nothing more alien to the spirit of Marxism than the doctrine of the export of revolution and "revolutionary wars." Socialist and national liberation revolutions result from the most acute class antagonisms of the capitalist society, as an expression of the impact of internal forces and the struggle of popular masses in each of the countries.

Marxists resolutely oppose the export of revolution. But they nonetheless oppose the export of counter-revolution, of forceful interference in the domestic affairs of any nation in order to support a regime that a nation abhors.

The struggle for freedom and independence is a legitimate struggle; it is always met with understanding and support by all Soviet people.

One can either "accept" or not the national-liberation struggle, but it is a real factor of a present life; and there can be no real policy while denying the historic necessity of such a struggle.

The Soviet Union did not and is not concealing its intention to win the economic competition with the capitalist world. But it does not mean at all any abandoning of economic cooperation. The principle of peaceful coexistence provides for the developmént of normal economic and political relations between states of different social systems, the development of various forms of international cooperation.

The Soviet Union is always prepared to consider with understanding constructive proposals of the Western powers and to achieve mutually acceptable solutions. The Soviet foreign policy never renounces reasonable compromise if it takes into account the opinions and legitimate interests of the contracting parties and promotes peaceful settlement of major issues.

—N. N. INOZEMSTEV

Pope Paul's Message

"Glorious things are said of you, O city of God! (PS. LXXXVI, 3). Mankind will be united into that city when it accepts God as the foundation of all justice and of all brotherhood; under Him and with His grace, men will associate into a universal and peaceful society. The recognition of this divine plan must then be followed by its execution through good will among men, the brotherhood and fraternal love of the sons of one heavenly Father.

Particularly during the present grave international crisis is it necessary to invoke higher principles of the moral order and to recall the collective responsibility of all nations for the preservation of friendly relationships and the avoidance of armed conflict, which in our day would have incalculable and frightful results for all mankind. Increasingly more important, then, is the irreplaceable mission of the United Nations in promoting mediation of disputes and restoration of peace, and we pray in the words of our venerated predecessor, Pope John XXIII, in his encyclical Pacem in Terris, that soon "every human being may find in this organization an effective safeguard of his personal rights," and we add, every nation a forum in which right and reason may replace force and might as principles of justice and peace.

—POPE PAUL VI

(Statement read to the Convocation)

Discussion of the Issues

I believe that it is a violation of natural law for half of the people of the world to live in misery, in abject poverty, without hope for the future, while the affluent nations spend on militarism a sum of money equal to the entire income of this miserable half of the world's people.

—LINUS PAULING

Few aspects of modern life are more repellent than the spectacle of governments proclaiming peace while they are armed to the teeth, while they are busily trying to get into the nuclear arms race or forge ahead in it, and while they are assuring their peoples that others cannot be trusted.

In 1962 a United Nations study reported that the world was spending $120 billion annually on military account. It also said, "A substantial part of the world's labor force now earns its living, directly or indirectly, in meeting military demands. To re-deploy this force for non-military purposes is an operation large enough to give rise to important problems of economic and social adjustment."

John XXIII says, as Thomas Aquinas did before him, that peace is the work of charity and [the fruit of] justice. Peace is not merely the absence of war; it is the nurture of human life everywhere. It is no accident that Pacem in Terris begins with a list of human rights. The Pope says, "The fundamental principle upon which our present peace depends must be replaced by another." The principle upon which our present peace depends is fear, for that is what the theory of deterrence amounts to. The principle that must replace it is justice.

The Pope consigns nuclear arms, nationalism, colonialism, racism, and non-constitutional regimes to the wastebasket of history. He rejects the devil theory of politics. He asserts the unfashionable doctrine that "the same moral law which governs relations between individual human beings serves also to regulate the relations of political communities with each other."

He is equally unfashionable in refusing to see power as the object

310

of politics. The object is the common good, that good which accrues to every person because he is a member of the community and which he would not have if the community did not exist. And finally the Pope maintains that no nation is any longer capable of serving the common good. We are all members of one community, we share one common destiny, the common good we seek is the good of the human community. We must now supply the political fabric of an existing world community, and the place to begin, the Pope says, is the United Nations.

—ROBERT M. HUTCHINS

A Theologian's View

The appearance of the encyclical, Pacem in Terris, is an important event in the history of religious and political thought and may have practical consequences for man's historical existence. Most valuable seems to me the way in which is emphasized throughout the document the ultimate principle of justice, the acknowledgment of the dignity of every man as a person, from which follow his rights and his obligations in the manifold encounter of man with man.

However, the determining principle of the encyclical reaches only as far as the Western, Christian-humanist culture, but not essentially beyond it. Therefore, if we envisage "peace on earth," we must remain aware of the fact that there are large cultural groups, some of them shaped by thousands of years of different religious tradition, in which the principle of the dignity of the individual man is not ultimate. Only a prolonged mutual interpenetration, in which the West must take as well as give can change the situation. This should restrain those who adhere to the spirit of the encyclical from attempts to force some of its consequences, e.g., particular ideas of freedom and equal rights, upon people with other principles. Such attempts are hopeless even if they lead to external victory.

The second problem concerning the encyclical is the question of resistance against those who violate the dignity of the individual. Such resistance unquestionably belongs to the rights of the person as well as of the group which has accepted and is willing to

311

defend the dignity of the person and the principles following from it. But such resistance can become rebellion, and rebellion can become revolution, and revolution can become war; and history leaves no doubt that the wars over contrasting ideas of justice are the most cruel, most insistent and the most devastating ones. So it was with the truth about man. So it is now in the ideological wars when the rights of man are identical with the social organization which guarantees these rights. And there is hardly a situation in which the dignity of the person is more deeply violated than in the struggles for the establishment of conditions under which this dignity shall be guaranteed. This is true of person-to-person relationships as well as of the relation of individuals to groups and of groups to groups. There are situations in which resistance without armed violence is possible; but even then, destructive consequences are hardly avoidable, be it through psychological, through economic or through sociological forms of compulsion. And there are situations in which nothing short of war can defend or establish the dignity of the person. Nothing is more indicative of the tragic aspect of life than the unavoidable injustice in the struggle for justice.

A third problem is the role of power in relation to force and the principles of justice. Power can neither be identified with force nor with authority. In several statements of the encyclical, this has been done, and a direct discussion of the ambiguities of power is lacking. But without it, a realistic approach to the peace problem is impossible.

There is no effective authority without a structure of power behind it; and under the conditions of existence, no power can become effective without coercion applied against those who try to undercut it. For power is something positive; it is a basic quality of being. It is the power to resist what tries to distort or annihilate the structures of being. In every individual and in every group is some power of being and the affirmation of this power and the drive to defend and to increase it. In the encounters of power with power, union as well as conflict arises and the conflicts lead to the use of force for the sake of coercion. Then the great question arises: When is coercion a just expression of power, when an unjust one? We acknowledge ust coercion in the enforcement of the law. Is there a just enforcement in the relation of power groups? This question has been answered for many centuries by the concept of the just war. But this concept has lost its validity through the fact that in a serious atomic conflagration, there is no victor and no vanquished, in other words, neither a coercer nor a coerced will be left.

Only in minor conflicts has the old concept meaning and may lead to a kind of world police. But a conflict between those who give power and authority to such a police force could not be solved in this way. The problem is neither power nor coercion, but the use of coercion with or without justice in the necessary exercise of power.

In this connection, a fourth problem arises: the question to what degree a political group, for instance a social group with a center of power, able to act politically, can be judged in the way in which one judges human individuals. Such analogy, if taken seriously, has dangerous consequences. It considers a contingent government as the deciding and responsible center of the group. This makes it possible that the government is asked to follow moral laws like the Ten Commandments, or the Sermon on the Mount or the natural moral law for individuals — as is often demanded by a legalistic pacifism. But no government can make a total sacrifice of its nation, such as an individual can and sometimes ought to make of himself. However, this does not and should not prevent a government to induce its nation to bring the sacrifice of self-restriction for the common good of a group of nations, including itself, even if some loss of the questionable and pernicious possession, called prestige, is involved. There is another consequence which the personification of a group can have. If the government is considered as the deciding center of the social body, no individual has the right to resist it. And this is the surest and most frequently used road to despotism. The group lies in another dimension of being than the individual; and the moral laws, valid for the latter, can be applied to the former only indirectly and with essential qualifications. A direct application of the rights and duties of the individual to the rights and duties of a group is impossible. This fact, together in unity with the three other problems we have mentioned, show the limits of any realistic hope for peace on earth.

This statement forces me to lead you into a more universal and more basic consideration of the question of peace on earth. We must ask: which are the predispositions for the fulfillment of this aim in human history? Most differences about the problems of peace are rooted ultimately in different interpretations of human nature and consequently of the meaning of history. At this point I must speak both as a Protestant theologian and as an existentialist philosopher. I see human nature determined by the conflict between the goodness of man's essential being and the ambiguity of his actual being, his life under the conditions of existence. The goodness of his essential nature gives him his greatness, his dignity, the demand, embodied in him, to be acknowledged as a person. On the other hand, the predicament in which he finds himself, the estrangement from his true being, drives him in the opposite direction, preventing him from fulfilling in actual life what he essentially is. It makes all his doings and all that which is done by him, ambiguous, bad as well as good. For his will is ambiguous, good as well as bad. And one would not appeal to "all men of good will" as the encyclical does. One should appeal to all men knowing that in the best will, there is an element of bad will and that in the worst will there is an element of good will. This view of the ambiguity of man's moral nature has direct consequences for the way a peace conference should look at the chance for a future state of peace.

—PAUL TILLICH

The less developed countries could well take advantage of a situation in which they are being subjected to the most intense pressures by the nuclear powers. Instead, their policy is undergoing a process of demoralization, and they have become the victims of an utterly shameless opportunism on both the international and domestic levels. Their contribution to peace is zero. Instead they perform adequately as the chorus in a tragedy that could unfold at any moment. In this sense, they are greatly abetting the possible outbreak of war. In addition, they are willingly offering themselves as a stage on which the nuclear powers can test their strength and make their decisions. They are a laboratory, just as Spain, before World War Two, served as a testing ground for the effectiveness of new military devices and the degree of reaction of a frightened Europe.

It is the duty of the developing nations to raise their voices loudly and clearly in quest of the strict observance of the rights of individuals and peoples without discrimination. Too often we tend to apply a very high standard of performance to those powers that have done most throughout history to comply with their national and international obligations even as we acquiesce in the fact that a huge part of the world is governed, as a matter of principle, without any respect for the rights of human beings or nations. This hypocritical tendency of some of the non-nuclear countries has done a great deal of damage to the cause of peace. For peace, as John XXIII conceived of it, is the product of a social order based on truth. The truth is that in more than half of the world respect for human rights is unknown and governments derive their stability and their strength from this very phenomenon. The truth is that the rest of the world lives in an atmosphere of instability and of an unceasing struggle for a better, freer and more just life. In such an åtmosphere, governments surely don't become any stronger. Countries in the middle, but especially in the less developed regions, which speak of non-alignment in this fight between the two great powers, give up the quest for the triumph of human rights and jeopardize the right of nations to be free.

— ALBERTO LLERAS CAMARGO

Some Tentative Solutions

I do not believe that mere coexistence is going to be possible for much longer in the new kind of world into which we have now moved.

The accelerating pace of technological advance is making it increasingly difficult to solve our problems on any scale short of a world-wide one. We have to make war impossible, we have to save the human race from being poisoned by the waste product of "atoms for peace," and we are soon going to have to feed three or four times as many people as are now alive. I believe these jobs can be dealt with only by world-authorities with effective power to override the national governments.

The mutual interest of all nations is that the human race shall survive. If the nations destroy the human race, they will be destroying themselves with it. Therefore it is the mutual interest of the nations to subordinate their national sovereignty to world-authorities. This is the only condition on which the nations can survive in the atomic age.

There is always conflict in human affairs; it is important that it be dealt with by free discussion carried on under agreed forms of constitutional procedure.

The status quo cannot be frozen, and we ought not to try to freeze it. This is anyway doomed to failure, because constant change is of the essence of life. What we have to do is not to try to stop change, but to try to carry out the inevitable changes without violence and bloodshed. In our time, the revolutionary development of technology is producing rapid change in all departments of life. But we are now in the atomic age, so we cannot survive if we continue to carry out our changes by the old senseless and barbarous method of resorting to force.

The prophet of the atomic age is surely the Mahatma Gandhi. He has demonstrated that radical political changes can be carried out without resort to violence.

— ARNOLD TOYNBEE

The era of the atom demands that all nations be completely disarmed and that a world authority taking care of the security of each nation effectively be established.

We can hardly expect that such a vision of the future world can be realized in a revolutionary fashion. However, it is a sign of the times that the statesmen both of the United States and the Soviet Union, however different in their ideologies, have agreed that this should be our ultimate goal. How to attain that goal is the thorniest question which we have to solve.

One line of approach has been suggested to me by the Japanese experience during the post-war period: Article 9 of the new Constitution of Japan contains a highly idealistic provision, abolishing war as a sovereign right of the nation, and banning the maintenance of armed forces in all forms. This apparently fantastic provision originated from a proposal made by the Japanese Prime Minister Shidehara and was sponsored with much enthusiasm by General MacArthur. Shidehara and MacArthur were thinking in terms of the shape of things to come in the atomic era. They thought that Article 9 should serve as a model for the future constitutions of all nations and that otherwise mankind might perish. This Article has, moreover, served to reduce military budgets to the minimum, and has played no small part in Japan's economic recovery and cultural development.

Now, the method I humbly suggest for attaining the final goal: a multilateral treaty for constitutional amendment to be recommended by the United Nations to its member states. Its contents should not be too idealistic.

They must be such as to appeal to the common sense of ordinary citizens. Such an amendment may well contain such provisions as the banning of nuclear weapons, reduction of armed forces to the extent necessary for territorial defense against foreign aggression, prohibition of the employment of armed forces outside territorial limits, except in cases where such is requested by the United Nations, and so on. The contents must, of course, be carefully worked out by experts. It seems wise to leave a wide margin of discretion about the coming into effect of the amendment, so that each nation can fully inquire whether or not its security is assured under such amendment.

This plan will keep alive the issue of general and complete disarmament, as a condition for human survival by lively debates which would take place in every country prior to the ratification of such a treaty. This would check a dangerous tendency to view the disarmament question solely in the light of the balance of armed forces, which brings about "a fatal drift toward tolerance of the ultimate intolerance."

Pope John said, "Is there anyone who does not ardently yearn to see war banished, to see peace preserved and daily to be more firmly established?" With such a background, if disarmament is presented as a question affecting the private life of citizens, may not strong public opinion be formed in each country in favor of the reduction of armament, escalating ultimately to general and complete disarmament? Would not, moreover, such public opinion in each country facilitate its leaders to cooperate with those of other nations to attain the goal of total disarmament?

The unorganized peace-loving sentiment of ordinary people in every land might thus be mobilized effectively for meeting one of the basic and minimum conditions for human survival and that by the consensus of all mankind.

—DR. KENZO TAKAYANAGI

National sovereignty, international organization, peace-keeping and the rule of law are interrelated ideas.

Fortunately, the ideal of world peace has inspired the slow and painful elaboration of an incipient institutional structure: the United Nations. If up to now the UN has not succeeded in destroying the fears and possibilities of war, it simply means that the statesmen of our international society must reconsider the nature and functions of the UN, so as to enable it fo fulfill its vital historical mission: that of maintaining a permanent international peace.

For the sake of argument and as things presently stand, the United Nations could be considered a rather queer and timid beginning of what eventually could become a positive world government.

Those who, in absolute good faith, seem alarmed at the very mention of "world government," must understand that "government" simply means "organization"; and that without social organization, which requires some sort of a political structure, no civilized society, whether national or international, can hope to develop.

Life is, indeed, dynamic. It is always on the march. And when social conditions happen to change, reason cannot ignore these changes. Those who insist upon ignoring history and its evolutionary or revolutionary process will simply stay behind. Each of us, therefore, must contribute to help history find a solution to that which is unquestionably the most important problem of our age; concretely, a modernized and efficient world structure, capable of avoiding wars and ensuring permanent peace among nations of good will.

—LUIS QUINTANILLA

The problem of peace will not be advanced unless it exercises the minds of nations at their highest level of responsibility. This is not the position today. Diplomacy is still conservative in its traditions, methods, and above all, its range. It is concerned with the crisis of today and the explosions of tomorrow—Vietnam, Cuba, Congo, Cyprus, the Near East. Diplomacy is local, not universal in its habit of mind and in its techniques of solution. Diplomacy is still obsessed by the old myths.

The new reality lies in the existence of problems which cannot be solved except on a global scale.

Just as the leaders of communities within our nations assemble to survey the national problems, so should the leaders of nations come together for the first time in history to review the total human destiny. By this I mean a review of problems and action facing the City of Man during the next quarter of a century.

I propose for discussion that the heads of all sovereign governments, within and outside the U.N., devote a week of their time to consider the problems not of any nation but of the human nation. An agenda for such an encounter must include:

1) The prospect opened up by the new technologies—both the danger and the hope.

2) The world will very nearly double its population within the next three decades. Is this a problem for our presidents and premiers in comparison with what exercises them now?

3) Over 1.5 billion people suffer from malnutrition. There was a "campaign against hunger" conference a few years ago, but its participants were not heads of government with a capacity for action and commitment.

4) In this golden age of knowledge there are 700 million adults entirely illiterate—one-third of the world's adult population—and a similar number at a low level of literacy. There is as yet an inadequate flow of scientific and educational skills from the advanced to the developing worlds.

5) Among the 115 sovereign states, ostensibly equal in their rights and status, there is a vast disparity of income and resources. There are groups of states where income is 2000 per cent higher than that of others. Within a national community such disparities would lead to violent upheavals. Are we sure that the same is not true of the international community? There should be a blueprint of a Great Society in international terms.

6) The fabric of our planet—its soil, water, minerals and air—face depletion or pollution or both. Our generation has no special right to hand the planet onto our children in a worse natural condition than that in which we found it.

7) The future of international organization—and especially in the problem of peace-keeping—needs long-term planning by those who have knowledge both of the central political realities and of technical developments. Disarmament is a vain discussion unless we devise instruments of security, beyond the national deterrents of sovereign states.

In proposing that the heads of 115 governments give a week to the survey of these vistas, I do not delude myself by the view that a solution will be found. The world was created, according to Biblical imagery, in six days. It will take longer to repair the damage that we have been doing ever since.

But there have been, in each of our national histories, occasions of assembly to which we look back as points of departure towards uncharted seas. Let there be the first assembly of governmental leaders to survey, not the state of any nation, but the state of mankind.

—ABBA EBAN

There are, of course, many avenues of approach to peace. Each man is entitled to believe his own is the most effective, and it might be. I happen to believe that the basis for an ordered world is law. The laws of the universe keep the celestial cosmos in order. The laws of nature make life possible on this earth. Civilized man has always recognized the necessity for law in an ordered society. Every nation has a body of law. Menes, the first ruler of Egypt over three thousand years before the Christian era, ruled his country through law. Hammurabi of Babylon, almost two millenia before Christ established his code that "the weak might be protected against the strong."

Since those days, domestic law has made great progress, and most nations have a viable system of law and order. However, this cannot be said of international law, although the ancients recognized the necessity for law and order between nations to be equally as important as domestic law.

If we really want peace on earth, if we believe that order is achieved through law, then we should make world peace through law our preoccupation. First we must agree upon the principles that are essential to peace in our twentieth-century civilization.

Then we must advocate and promulgate laws that will make those principles the guiding force in the lives of nations and people everywhere. Lastly we must have forums for their interpretation and enforcement.

This is not merely the job of governments. It is the job of the religions of the world and of every moral force that can be brought to bear in order that the will for peace may abide in the hearts of men everywhere on this globe.

—EARL WARREN

In Conclusion

There is a profound analogy between the history of the religious hope in Israel and the history of the secular hope in the Western world from the great Utopias of the Renaissance up to our day. In the movements which were striving for a state of peace and justice in modern times, hope was partly based on the belief in a universal law of progress, partly on the belief of man's growing reasonableness. Both hopes were disappointed, perhaps most profoundly in our century. We cannot close our eyes any longer to the fact that every gain produced, e.g., by scientific and technical progress, implies a loss; and that every good, achieved in history, is accompanied by a shadow, an evil which uses the good and distorts it. And we know just through our better understanding of man's personal and social life that human reason is not only determined by the natural laws of reason but also by the dark elements in his total being which struggle against reason. In view of the two main examples for this predicament of man, the ambiguity of blessing and curse in the scientific penetration into the atomic structure of the universe, and the well reasoned outbreak of destructive anti-rationality in Hitlerism and fascism, it is understandable that hopelessness has grasped large masses in the Western nations, especially in the younger generations.

But there are not only utopian expectations, there is also genuine hope in our time and in what we are trying to do—here and now—just as in the men of the Old Testament. A realistic view of man and history need not lead to cynicism. But it may often ask for hope against hope, and certainly demands the courage to risk, even if failure is more probable than success.

321

Where then lies the difference between utopian expectations and genuine hope? The basis for genuine hope is that there is something present of that which is hoped for, as in the seed something of the coming plant is present, while utopian expectations have no ground in the present. So we must ask: What are the seeds out of which a future state of peace can develop?

The first basis for genuine hope is something negative which, however, can have and partly has had positive effects: The atomic threat and the fear of mutual destruction. The limited peace, forced upon us by the threat, is in itself merely negative. But it does something which is somehow positive: It makes the conflicting groups of mankind feel that there is mankind with a common destiny. This experience of a "community of fear" is still weak and easily overwhelmed by a stronger feeling of national and ideological conflict. But it does exist as a small seed.

A second basis of genuine hope for peace is the technical union of mankind by the conquest of space. Of course, nearness can intensify hostility; and the fact that the first manifestation of the technical oneness of our world were two world wars proves this possibility. But nearness can also have the opposite effect. It can change the image of the other as strange and dangerous; it can reduce self-affirmation and effect openness for other possibilities of human existence and—particularly as in the encounter of the religions—of other possibilities of genuine faith.

A third basis for genuine hope for peace are the increasing number of cross-national and cross-ideological fields of cooperation, some of them desirable, as e.g. exchange in the humanities and religion, some of them essential, as e.g. collaboration in the sciences, some of them necessary for the future of mankind, as e.g. the problems of food, medicine, overpopulation, conservation of nature.

A fourth basis of genuine hope is the existence and effectiveness, however limited, of a legal roof for all these types of limited groups. But man can extend the realm of peace which nature cannot. He can establish a legal structure which guarantees peace among those who are subject to it, not absolutely but to a certain degree. Not absolutely, for everyone subjected to the legal structure can break through it for his own interest or his conviction.

Therefore, something more than the legal structure for peace is needed. One has called it "consensus." But it is not something as intellectual as this word indicates. It is communal eros, that kind of love which is not directed to an individual but to a group. It is said that one cannot love another nation. One can have eros towards them in their uniqueness, their virtues, their contributions, in spite of their shortcomings and vices. It seems that no world community is possible without this eros which trespasses interest as well as law. Every expression of such eros is a basis of hope for peace, every rejection of such eros reduces the chances of peace.

And now a last word about what we as a peace conference can hope for. First of all: we can only hope. We cannot calculate, we cannot know. The uncertainty remains. All the seeds of hope mentioned can be destroyed before they come to fulfillment. And further: there is no hope for a final stage of history in which peace and justice rule. History is not fulfilled as its empirical end; but history is fulfilled in the great moments in which something new is created, or, as one could express it religiously, in which the Kingdom of God breaks into history, conquering destructive structures of existence, one of the greatest of which is war. This means that we cannot hope for a final stage of justice and peace within history; but we can hope for partial victories over the forces of evil in a particular moment of time.

—PAUL TILLICH

The papal message Peace on Earth was governed by deep compassion for man in his vulnerability. There is also a sense, in this wondrous age, of what man can achieve in his redeeming moments of grandeur. As we look out on the human condition, our consciences cannot be clean. If they are clean, then it is because we do not use them enough. It is not inevitable that we march in hostile and separated hosts into the common abyss. There is another possibility—of an ordered world, illuminated by reason and governed by law. If we cannot yet touch it with our hands, let us, at least, grasp it in our vision.

—ABBA EBAN

Human beings are not insects caught on the flywheel of history. They make history. Pacem in Terris has already given an historic turn to international affairs. The Pope did not wait for a consensus. He decided to take the lead in forming one. His example deserves emulation.

Cornford, the great Greek scholar, said the way of avoiding action in the Cambridge of his day was to refer to the Principle of Unripe Time. He concluded that the time was never ripe until it was time to do something else. One thing is clear: the Principle of Unripe Time has no application today. The world is in disarray. Its principal hope, the United Nations, seems to face a new threat every day. The thermonuclear menace is mounting; we may expect, if we survive, to see the number of nations with hydrogen bombs double within five years. This is International Co-operation Year, a year so far marked by the steady deterioration of international co-operation. Time presses. It is time to open a new conversation about the requirements of peace on a level somewhere between apathy and panic, and this side of the irrelevance of propaganda. We may justify the words of Pope John who, in commenting on Pacem in Terris just before his death, said of it, "We are convinced that in years to come the doctrine it offers to the world will prevail by its very clarity. Presented to our contemporaries without partisan bias, it cannot but foster the growth in the world of those who worthily and with glory will be called builders and makers of peace."

—ROBERT M. HUTCHINS

Commencement Address
Georgetown University, June 1964

SARGENT SHRIVER

IT IS EMBARRASSING for me today to confess that I remember only one quotation from St. Ignatius. Fortunately it is only one word: "magis!" — "more."

The watchword of the Jesuit order has always been: *Ad majorem Dei gloriam.* But Ignatius was a man of action. His personal watchword was *magis:* More. More work, more sacrifice, more men to serve the greater glory of God.

And that is my message now. We need more.

We need more men and women schooled in the tradition of Ignatius and Xavier. We need more like the 238 Peace Corps Volunteers now serving overseas who came from Jesuit schools. And we need more like the thirty-eight Peace Corps Volunteers who studied at Georgetown, who are serving in towns and villages of twenty-three countries in Africa, Asia and Latin America. I have seen them work. I can testify to their spirit and dedication.

As a matter of fact these robes I am wearing here today are evidence of their dedication. These were given to me at Chulalongkorn University by the Foreign Minister of Thailand. He was awarding me an honorary degree to honor the Peace Corps and the 265 Volunteers serving in Thailand. Three of those Volunteers studied here at Georgetown. In his speech commending them, the Foreign Minister called the Peace Corps "the most powerful idea in recent times."

Let me tell you about eight other Volunteers — eight of the first 300 Volunteers for Ethiopia who took their Peace Corps training here at Georgetown. I last saw them in the little provincial town of Debra Marcos, near the blue Nile,

THE ADDRESS DELIVERED BY MR. SHRIVER AT THE ONE HUNDRED SIXTY-FIFTH ANNUAL COMMENCEMENT OF GEORGETOWN UNIVERSITY, JUNE 8, 1964. REPRINTED WITH PERMISSION.

in October 1962. We sent men only to that post because it was considered the most difficult, most isolated one in Ethiopia. I will never forget the rocky ride from the strip of grass on which we landed to their school—the cobblestones on the main street were put in with the smooth side down and the pointed, spike side up. I wondered how these eight men, thrown together like that, without any American women around, would get along.

Here is what one of them, Dick Lipez, wrote recently. "Through some unimaginable fluke we got along. We were not only friends, but we stimulated one another intellectually in a way that perhaps no eight people in the same house ever have. Last year, I did more reading and more talking about what I had read than during any three years of college. We talked politics endlessly, we talked about history, travel, sports, women, literature." The liberals, he said, became more conservative and the conservatives more liberal. "If anyone in Lock Haven, Pennsylvania," Dick wrote, "discovered four or five men sitting around a Coleman lantern in the middle of the night reading and talking about poetry, the scandal would shake the town from the first island bridge to Crow's Diner!"

Those eight men who went from this campus in 1962 to Debra Marcos, Ethiopia, are now coming home. One of them, a white boy from Alabama, has volunteered to teach in an all-Negro slum high school in Washington, D.C. Another will work for the Peace Corps. All of them are interested in the War on Poverty. Why is this?

Dick Lipez in his letter tried to explain why they were coming home with a new sense of responsibility. "Peace Corps life tempers one by its sheer and irresistible intensity," he says. They look forward to coming home, but "missing," he says, will be "the adventure, the thrill that none of us will ever be able to live again with such intensity, such freedom. We had great responsibilities—to our students, to one another, to ourselves—and in meeting these responsibilities we found a kind of freedom greater than any we could have imagined."

Soon Dick Lipez will be home, and so will 3000 of our first

Volunteers. You will see how much they have learned. They have learned about the world—not in an abstract way, not in books, but in service—in service of the poor: the poor in education, the poor in health, the poor in spirit. They have learned how to serve. They have learned responsibility. They are coming home feeling responsible for their own country. They now feel responsible for poverty in America.

My question today is: Why should they? Why should you? Why should I? President Johnson has made me responsible for doing something about poverty. But who is really responsible for poverty—who is responsible for the poor?

Is Georgetown University responsible for the poor? Is it responsible even for the poor of the nation's capital— the community in which the University was born and has grown to international eminence? Its primary responsibility is surely to its students and to the educational process. Our academic gowns remind us of the high educational purposes of the university. Is it fair to ask to distract itself from these noble purposes?

Is this faculty responsible for the poor? Surely, the task of educating young men and women should consume practically all its time and energy. Are the students of this University responsible? What time do they have to spare when they should devote themselves fully to their studies— to the academic excellence this nation needs and this school must require?

Are the alumni responsible? You are about to become alumni. I am told that forty percent of you will go straight to graduate school, twenty-eight percent of you will enter the armed forces, and thirty-two percent of you will take on jobs in business, in teaching, or in government. How responsible for the poor can you be while embarking on such commendable pursuits and professions? A lawyer's first responsibility is to his client, a doctor's is to his patient. These are high professional duties. Then what about the businessman? His duty is to make profits for his stockholders, his partners, his family. Even his duty to his Alma Mater, to a school like this, may strain his resources!

Who then is responsible for the poor? That leaves only the poor themselves. But they cannot all be responsible for their poverty. One-third of today's poor are children. Can anyone claim they came to be poor because they are lazy, shiftless, drunken, or profligate? They were born poor. And most of their parents were born into poverty. You will find millions of American children who represent the third or fourth generation of poverty in their families. We cannot hold these children responsible.

Many of the poor are Negroes. They are born with a legacy worse than mere poverty. They are born with the mark of slavery and discrimination — with skin that for five generations has shut doors to them. The old signs "Irish Not Wanted" are gone now, but the doors of many schools and many jobs and many neighborhoods are not yet open to someone whose skin is black. A Negro cannot be held responsible for the color that God gave him. Who, then, is responsible? Is anyone responsible? You can point to me and say President Johnson made you responsible. But to have you do that makes me feel like Lady Astor on the sinking ship *Titanic.* As the iceberg crashed through the ship's wall, she said, "I asked for ice, but this is ridiculous."

Poverty is like an iceberg. Although submerged, cold, and impersonal, it can crash into our lives. When a woman is attacked on a city street, when a gang holds up a subway car, when a bystander is killed in a riot, when little girls are bombed in a church, we suddenly feel one cutting edge of poverty.

Poverty is like an iceberg because if it chills us, it freezes our hearts, it makes us cold and impersonal! It is so frightening that we turn our eyes away from the human constituents of poverty, the people who are drowning in the sea of poverty — the men without jobs, the mothers without a man, or money, the children on the streets. These are the ones who feel the sharpest edge of poverty.

The worst news story of the year was about the murder of a woman in New York who could have been saved by onlookers. But not one of the thirty-eight witnesses came to her aid, not one raised a hand, not one even uttered a cry or called the police until it was all over. No one was ready to go out into the night! No one felt responsible!

When we reach this pit, this bottom, there can be no way but up. This kind of irresponsibility is the great pitfall of our complex modern civilization. The way up and out is not easy. But if any graduating class should know the answer, if any university should teach it, it should be here! For out of the books you read, among the words you ponder, are these ancient ones, "For what does it profit a man, if he gain the whole world but suffer the loss of his own soul?"

What will it profit you or me, if we make all the money in the world, if we reach the height of our professions, even if we earn honorary degrees, but we find ourselves indifferent and our lives narrow? What will it profit this university, if after all its good education, it graduates its students into irresponsibility?

I wonder what kind of education the Good Samaritan had? I suspect that those who passed by that miserable man who had been thrown among robbers probably had college degrees. Certainly they were busy with their professions— too busy to take responsibility for someone who was dirty, half naked, and half dead.

We all raise shields against the poor. Then we say that poverty is invisible. What President Johnson is asking us to do is very simple, but very hard. He is asking us to lower these shields. He is confident that once we see what needs to be done, we will do it.

The President's Task Force for the War on Poverty is going to do its part. Are you going to do your part? Are you, who are graduating today going to graduate into irresponsibility? Are you who stay on to study and to teach in the years to come going to practice responsibility right here at Georgetown? Or are you going to turn your back on the hungry and the poor and the strangers on our streets here in Washington?

If you on the faculty tell your students that their only

responsibility is to their academic studies, if you tell them to think of themselves solely as students, not as responsible citizens, then you are laying the pattern for a lifetime of irresponsibility. If today students are taught to use their books as shields, tomorrow they will find their professions or their family obligations just as effectively shields. That is what I mean by graduating as students into irresponsibility.

You might say that I am wrong here, that the student of today will join the Peace Corps tomorrow. I hope so—I have some applications handy. That is one way to put down your shields and serve your fellow man, full time, for a short period of your life. And when you come back home, I will try to recruit you for the war on poverty.

When we asked 230 of the first returned volunteers, four out of five said they were interested in the war on poverty. Over thirty percent said they were ready right away to volunteer for part-time, some even for full-time, service.

But do we need this period of service abroad to learn how to serve at home? If we do, then we are in serious trouble. Because the Peace Corps barely scratches the surface of our needs. Soon there will be 10,000 Peace Corps Volunteers. But there are half a million college graduates this year alone. There are over two million college and university students in our land. If 10,000 are to learn responsibility in the Peace Corps, and two million are to practice the irresponsibility of their specialties, then we are in deep trouble. If we do not commit ourselves to waging the War on Poverty, if you in our universities and student bodies and faculties do not commit yourselves to this, then the iceberg of poverty is going to bring real havoc to our cities, to our backdoors, yes, even to this university campus.

You of Georgetown have already taken a significant step in the right direction. That is, 300 of your students and faculty members have started on the "Road to Responsibility." They volunteered to give some time each week— to serve in twenty-four social action projects in this city.

From an office under the staircase in Healy lobby, they go out to work in slum neighborhoods and schools. They go out to work with the children of the slums—those behind in school, and those out of school and out of work. They do special tutoring, organize sports programs, assist in community organizations, serve in understaffed hospitals and settlement houses. They work Saturdays, on week-day afternoons, and throughout the summer vacation.

They are learning the hard way, but the real way, who the poor are—and what poverty means. For them statistics take on faces. The 60,000 faceless, functional illiterates of Washington have become people to them—boys and girls they are teaching to read. Poverty for them has become something personal.

Is this all a distraction from their true work as students? I do not think so. Far from subverting the educational process, this program, it seems to me, is helping to fulfill it. In accepting responsibility for poverty, and for the great social problems of our national life, these three hundred Georgetown Volunteers are pointing the way to a great new frontier in American education: The Frontier of Service! By serving in this way these men and women will not only be better Americans: They will be better doctors, better lawyers, better businessmen, better foreign service officers.

The very nature of a profession is service. But when do students learn this most essential part? Medical students are too busy with intensive studies in medical school. A course in professional, legal responsibility is usually offered in the law school curriculum, but not required. But what can be conveyed there about a lawyer's or a doctor's duty to the poor—compared with what these Georgetown volunteers are experiencing? These volunteers are learning the compassion without which no profession or person is complete—the compassion that keeps us from by-passing the poor.

Take Jules Clavadetcher, a Georgetown student who all this year worked five hours a week at All Souls' Unitarian Church with some hostile and potentially delinquent

Negro children. So marked was the good effect upon the children that the Jewish women's organization of B'nai B'rith awarded this Catholic student its yearly citation for enlightened civic action for youth. Jules learned a lot about the problems of race and poverty. Perhaps he learned something about the Ecumenical movement too.

The Chairman of your own Philosophy Department, Dr. Jesse Mann, tells me: "I would much rather have students in my class learning about the philosophy of man by working with underprivileged Negro children of this city than merely by reading dusty volumes of Philosophy 104 in Riggs Library." Any student who is giving up a beer party or a dance or a lazy Saturday afternoon in favor of this work is not subverting Georgetown. This program of university service is rather the extension of education—the broadening of education—the deepening of education which we must have if we are to find our way through the web of modern technology. We must find our way through our technical specialties into our full responsibilities as human beings.

Fortunately, the needs of American education and the needs of our War on Poverty meet at this point. For what you have begun here is what we must launch on a vast scale, if we are to win this War. And for this reason I call upon all of you, students and faculty alike, to follow in the footsteps of the 300 who have already gone beyond these walls to serve in that "other America" in our nation's capital. I call upon all the colleges and universities of America to join in this great effort. But this is a special call to all those colleges and universities, which like Georgetown, stand in the shadow of the Cross. For this war against poverty is America's "Holy War." And if you who represent Catholic education in America fail to respond, you will deeply wrong yourselves, your country, and your faith.

In our great Sacraments, we see the love of God for Man. Because His Word became flesh, we vow to try to make the word become flesh, in our own inadequate lives. There is another sacrament that can help us learn how to do this, a sacrament that can give us the strength to keep on trying to do it. It is the sacrament of service to Man-in-Need.

Christ considered this so important that He made our final judgment turn, not on the number of prayers we say, or the number of devotions we attend, but on whether or not we are too busy to help Him when He comes to us in the garments of the poor. "I was hungry, and you gave me to eat. I was thirsty, and you gave me to drink; I was a stranger and you took me in. As long as you did it for one of these, the least of my brethren, you did it for me."

Now it is time, as it has always been time, for us to lower our shields, and to see the sacrament awaiting us beyond the altar rail, outside the campus gates. It is this mission to which we are sent, when we leave the chapel that stands at the heart of this campus. *Ite missa est* does not mean our trivial translation, "It is finished; you can go." And this commencement today does not mean: "I've done my share, I can go and look after my other business." It means instead: "Go and fulfill your mission."

A Religious View of Poverty

WHILE the problem of poverty is as old as mankind, citizens of the United States have special reasons to be concerned over its prevalence here. We are considered to be the wealthiest nation in the world, yet one-fifth of our citizens are in want. We are compelled to spend billions for armament, although slums and blight disfigure our cities and countryside alike. As a matter of conscience the American people offer aid to developing and impoverished nations around the world. Such generosity is good, but it should not blind us to needs here at home. From our abundance we are able to give generously, both in distant lands and within our borders.

Our response should be from the heart, but it must not be purely emotional in nature. Sound programs will endure to the extent that they are based on principle rather than feeling. To aid in forming lasting convictions, the Social Action Department of the National Catholic Welfare Conference offers the following considerations on the Christian view of poverty, our personal response to this challenge, and the function of society as it confronts the problem of want in the midst of plenty.

I. The Church and Poverty

There is a paradox in the Christian teaching on poverty. The Holy Gospels teach us to respect poverty, but they also oblige us to help the poor in their misery. Our Lord called the poor blessed. He asked His followers to sell what they had and follow Him, advice that was followed literally by the first Christians. Jesus Christ could say that He had not whereon to lay His head, and He was buried in another man's tomb. St. Paul described the followers of Christ as the poor and the powerless.

"Consider your own call, brethren; that there were not many wise according to the flesh, not many mighty, not many noble.

STATEMENT OF THE DEPARTMENT OF SOCIAL ACTION, NATIONAL CATHOLIC WELFARE CONFERENCE, 1312 MASSACHUSETTS AVENUE, N.W., WASHINGTON, D.C., 20005. ISSUED FEBRUARY 28, 1964. REPRINTED WITH PERMISSION.

But the foolish things of the world has God chosen to put to shame the wise, and the weak things of the world has God chosen to put to shame the strong, and the base things of the world and the despised has God chosen, and the things that are not, to bring to naught the things that are; lest any flesh should pride itself before him." (I. COR. I, 26–29)

St. James could say: "Has not God chosen the poor of this world to be rich in faith and heirs of the kingdom which God has promised to those who love him?" (JAMES II, 5) The ministers of God were described as "poor, yet enriching many, as having nothing, yet possessing all things." (II COR., VI, 10). This was but a reflection of the life of the Master, "being rich, he became poor for your sakes, that by his poverty you might become rich." (II COR., VIII, 9)

The Church has been interested in the poor primarily because it sees every person as a child of God. While the world honors power, wealth, and achievement, the follower of Christ insists upon the moral worth of those who are neglected and even despised. He does not use worldly standards in judging personal excellence. A Saint Francis could cast aside his clothes as a symbol of complete freedom from worldly attachment. A Saint Vincent de Paul could devote his life to the destitute and the oppressed. A Saint Camillus could wash the sores of the abandoned sick. All these have been honored because their love of God led them to cast their lot with the least of Christ's brethren.

The Church has endorsed poverty be demanding it from those who have entered the solemn religious life. These give up the right to use and dispose of worldly goods. They do this, not because the world that God made is evil, but in order to cut their ties to all that might turn their gaze from God and lead them to concentrate on the passing and corruptible.

Yet, and herein lies the paradox of the Christian teaching on poverty, the Church also speaks of a form of poverty that hurts the soul, something totally different from religious detachment from worldly goods. There is a destitution that binds men to this earth, since it forces them to use every waking moment to keep body and soul together. There is want that breeds bitterness and resentment, even hatred.

Pope Pius XII, in his Christmas Message of 1952, talked

". . . of the consequences of poverty, still more of the consequences of utter destitution. For some families there is a dying daily, a dying hourly; a dying multiplied, especially for parents, by the number of dear ones they behold suffering and wasting away . . . sickness becomes more serious, because it is not properly treated; it strikes little ones in particular, because preventive measures are lacking.

"Then there is the weakening and consequent physical deterioration of whole generations. Whole masses of the population are brought up as enemies of law and order, so many poor girls gone astray, pushed down into the bottom of the abyss, because they believed that that was the only way out of their shameful poverty. Moreover, not rare is the case where it is wretched misery that leads to crime. Those who in their works of charity visit our prisons affirm constantly that not a few men, fundamentally decent, have gone to prison because extreme poverty has led them to commit some unpremeditated act."

_____

Pope Pius XII is but one of the great modern popes who, particularly in the last seventy years, have shown deep concern for poverty in our industrial society. There is an essential difference between the austerity of the Trappist monk who cultivates the field and prays to God in his simple cell and the wretchedness of those who live in the slums of our large cities. The monk is poor, but he has sufficient to eat; he has adequate clothing and needed medical care. He is a respected member of society.

But there are those in our slums who do not have enough to eat. Their clothing is worn and threadbare. They are overcrowded in wretched housing. They have no privacy, not even the mercy of silence. And, the greatest hurt of all, they feel rejected and unwanted. They could die, and no one would shed a tear.

This poverty, in the words of Pope Pius XII, often leads to

_____

"social conditions which, whether one wills it or not, make difficult or practically impossible a Christian life."
(SOLENNITA, JUNE 1, 1941).

Again this same pope states:

"the Christian must be ever mindful that the establishment of God's kingdom in men's hearts and in social institutions often requires a minimum of human development. . . . For this reason, the Christian will always be ready to work for the relief of every material distress. . . . In a word, he will be diligent to achieve the betterment of the poor and the disinherited." (ADDRESS, APRIL 25, 1957)

_____

What precisely did the Pope have in mind when he spoke of degrading social conditions? Let us listen to his description of slum living:

"Dilapidated, ramshackle houses without the most necessary hygienic installations sometimes yield a sizable income to their owners without costing them a penny. Inevitably, they neglect to make necessary repairs in them for years on end."

"Enough can never be said about the harm that these dwellings do to the families condemned to live in them. Deprived of air and light, living in filth and in unspeakable commingling, adults and, above all, children quickly become the prey of contagious diseases which find a favorable soil in their weakened bodies. But the moral injuries are still more serious: immorality, juvenile delinquency, the loss of taste for living and working, interior rebellion against a society that tolerates such abuses, ignores human beings, and allows them to stagnate in this way, transformed gradually into wrecks."

"Society itself must bear the consequences of this lack of foresight. Because it did not wish to prevent the evil and to provide a remedy in time, it will spend enormous sums to keep up an appearance of curbing delinquency and to pay expenses for prolonged confinement in sanatoriums and clinics. How many millions are authorized for the cure of evils that it would be easier and less expensive to prevent?"
(ADDRESS, MAY 3, 1957)

These words of Pope Pius XII make abundantly clear the

vital distinction between the poverty blessed by the Church and the wretched destitution that endangers soul and body alike. We must view abject poverty as we view physical sickness, as an evil that must be prevented when possible and certainly cured as soon as possible. Our Blessed Lord did not tell the sick that they were blind or deaf or crippled because of the unchanging laws of the universe. Rather He used His infinite power to heal, thus inspiring us to use both science and compassion in the service of the sick.

In the same way, His holy Church views poverty as a challenge, not merely to our compassion and charity, but also to intelligent social action aimed at eradicating the many causes of human failure. It is a tragic commentary upon the world today that nations are forced to spend billions for ghastly weapons of war, and yet cannot find the funds to eliminate slums. Our ingenuity can cope with the almost unbelievable difficulties of sending a rocket to the moon. But we seem unable to come up with workable plans to aid human beings created in the image and likeness of Almighty God.

To face this challenge intelligently, we must make some important distinctions in regard to those who are poor. There are some persons whose poverty stems from personal conditions that cannot readily be changed. They are not able to earn a living today, nor is it likely that most of them can ever produce enough to secure a proper livelihood. In this class are many of our aged, some who are physically or mentally handicapped, or mothers who are the sole support of young children. Such persons need help given in a way that fully respects their human dignity.

On the other hand, there are those who are poor largely because of external conditions that have prevented their earning a decent living. They have both the native ability to work and the desire for a good job, but they lack either the training or the opportunity to earn a fitting salary. Such persons include the uneducated and the unskilled, victims of racial discrimination, farmers without adequate resources and training, many unemployed persons over forty, and those who live in areas of declining industry. in these cases, we seek methods and techniques that will enable them to become productive members of our economic society.

Another important distinction concerns the method of affording assistance for each of these groups. There is a form of aid that is intensely personal. Here the stress is upon contact between individuals. Such help does not preclude organization and planning, yet it is basically a person-to-person apostolate.

There are other problems that must be met primarily by social action, whether this be private or governmental. Here the basic concern is the removal of social conditions that breed poverty and destitution. It is obvious, for example, that economic policies that stimulate the demand for workers will make it much easier to retrain and relocate the unemployed.

Whatever distinctions might be made, however, in the Christian understanding of poverty, in practice any attack on poverty must be universal. The heart of the true Christian goes out to all in need. For charity knows no limits. Such has been the pattern, for example, of the Catholic Relief Services. Not only is the entire world its area of operation, but all men, of all races and of all religions, are the beneficiaries of its programs of aid. The only criterion is their need. So, too, as we face this problem of poverty in our country, there must be no restriction of race, religion, or politics. Nor should there be any inhibiting of those who seek to help the poor, whether they be individuals, or private agencies or offices of government. In the spirit of the Good Samaritan, who taught us that every man is our neighbor, we must seek the opportunity to serve the stranger wounded in the struggle of life.

We wish to illustrate these principles by noting both the individual and the social responsibility of Americans confronted with poverty in an affluent society.

II. Individual Religious Commitment
What, then, does the Church ask of the concerned Christian, as it directs his attention to this basic problem of poverty in this wealthy nation? First, and above all, it asks

that we make this a matter of personal concern and involvement. In older and simpler societies, it was fairly easy for any person who wanted to help his neighbor to know what was needed. Today it is possible to live in our sanitary suburbs, rush to work without really seeing our city surroundings, spend our days in office or factory, and never even know what life is like for 35 million fellow Americans who live in poverty. We can discuss the question in the abstract, as a political, social or economic problem, and ignore the human tragedy involved. Pope Pius XII noted that many persons are misinformed about poverty:

"Persons of good faith who have only inadequate knowledge of the matter believe that the majority of those who live in slums or who must be satisfied with an income below the essential minimum are there through their own fault or negligence, and that welfare organizations are capable of helping anyone in need of it." (ADDRESS, MAY 3, 1957)

Secondly, the Church asks us to form a Christian conscience about the dignity of each person and our own responsibility to do all within our power to help them. When our Saviour was asked to illustrate the law of love of neighbor, He gave the parable of the Good Samaritan as His answer. Compassion is the mark of the Christian. Christ's description of the last judgment is clear and simple. The Lord confronts the just with these words:

"I was hungry, and you gave me to eat; I was thirsty, and you gave me to drink; I was a stranger and you took me in." And the just asked in astonishment when they did these things to the Lord. He replied: "As long as you did it for one of these, the least of my brethren, you did it for me." (MT. XXV, 34-40)

On the day that all men as sinners shall ask mercy, they will receive it to the extent that they showed mercy toward their fellow man.

Thirdly, we must realize that the best form of help, as was said over seven centuries ago by the great Jewish physician, Moses Maimonides, is to help people to help themselves. Giving food to the hungry, clothing to those who shiver in the cold, and shelter to families that lack decent housing is important, but it is only a first step.

Much more necessary is intelligent concern over the causes of indigence and destitution. To cite one example, racial discrimination is widely considered as an important source of poverty. The Catholic bishops of the United States noted in their 1958 statement on discrimination: "It is a matter of historical fact that segregation in our country has led to oppressive conditions and the denial of basic human rights for the Negro. This is evident in the fundamental fields of education, job opportunity, and housing. Flowing from these areas of neglect and discrimination are problems of health and the sordid train of evils so often associated with the consequent slum conditions." Certainly no Catholic with an informed conscience will remain aloof from the struggle for civil rights which is today one of our first domestic problems. Indeed, we Catholics must go beyond civil rights and be sensitive to human rights, whether or not these fall in the province of civil law.

While we give wholehearted support to civic projects for the relief of poverty, we do not feel that our Christian duties end with such endorsement. It is not enough to vote for sound policies, to pay taxes, and to contribute to charity. The dedicated Christian must be always ready to give of himself. As Pope John XXIII noted: "Tragic situations and urgent problems of an intimate and personal nature are continually arising which the State with all its machinery is unable to remedy or assist. There will always remain, therefore, a vast field for the exercise of human sympathy and the Christian charity of individuals. We would observe, finally, that the efforts of individuals, or of groups of private citizens, are definitely more effective in promoting spiritual values than is the activity of public authority. (*Mater et Magistra*, No. 120)

The list of possible personal projects to aid the poor and and the unfortunate is long. In many of our cities, college students have formed tutoring groups to aid children in slums. Retired teachers have volunteered to give their evenings to help the illiterate to acquire at least a minimum of reading and writing. There are settlement houses and neighborhood projects to bring hope and incentive to those who seem to have no future. One can visit the bed-ridden poor, clean their rooms, and shop for them. Adults can act as substitute parents for children who have no real home life. Such children can be invited into their homes to study and to have a warm evening meal. Many religious groups have free summer camps for deprived children. There are parish interracial visitation programs, for the purpose of promoting better understanding among the races. Some Catholic groups have established half-way houses for former prisoners, to ease their transition into normal communtiy life.

Such programs are many and diverse, but they have one point in common. Each calls for personal involvement. Each demands the most exquisite form of Christian charity, since each requires that we respect and honor the human dignity of the person who is poor and unfortunate. Such charity is strong and healing. It does not demean or de-grade, as sometimes happens with badly planned gifts of material goods alone.

III. A Social Challenge
In discussing social measures to relieve or prevent poverty, we shall present objectives and programs from a religious and moral point of view. It is not our concern as religious leaders to deal with problems that are purely economic, political, or technical.

If we are to help the poor to help themselves, we must above all be concerned about work. Avoiding job dis-crimination is but one step. It is equally vital to be sure that work is available and that the poor are educated and trained to do useful work. We are heartened at the concern of civil authorities, on every level of government, as they contemplate this problem. We pledge to them our full support in an unremitting war against poverty. But this struggle, to be fully successful, must adapt itself to the natural patterns of each community. It must use the schools, welfare agencies, and other community activities that are already doing good work in combatting ignorance, illiteracy, and demoralization. These local institutions should be assisted and supplemented, whether they be governmental or private in nature.

In the area of housing, we ask for sensitivity for the rights of the poor. Slum clearance and urban renewal programs are good in themselves, both as civil projects and as aid in the rooting out of poverty. But let us not approach these needs merely as engineering blueprints, ignoring the human element involved. It is heartless to uproot hundreds of families in the name of slum clearance, if no suitable alternate housing is available. Indeed, many experts today counsel us to salvage and renovate an area, if at all possible, so as to keep intact the thousands of human contacts that make life more bearable. As religious leaders, we hesitate to discuss such technical problems, except that social scientists themselves have warned of the moral factors involved in such planning.

Our special concern should be for young persons who lack the training and opportunity to secure useful work. Unemployment is tragic at any age, but lifelong damage can be inflicted when the young are unable to secure worthwhile jobs. Undoubtedly we must redouble our efforts to encourage such persons to secure at least a high-school diploma. We should seriously consider the worth of youth camps or special training projects directed to the need of young adults. Here we note the insight of Pope Pius XII, who observed that society spends millions because of crime and social demoralization, when timely measures of prevention would have prevented both the personal tragedy and the social waste.

We also note with concern the fact that nearly two million farm families, and hundreds of thousands of farm workers, are among the poorest of Americans. Great religious leaders, such as the late Pope John XXIII, have extolled the spiritual and moral value of farm living. But they also asserted that such values cannot compensate for grinding poverty. Our farming poor need different types of economic help. Some can be given the training and the finances which will enable them to become self-supporting in agriculture. Others may need at least part-time employment in industries located in poorer rural areas. Still others must seek urban industrial work, but they cannot secure this without adequate training. It is a commonplace among vocational advisers that good education pays its costs many times over in the average lifetime. Surely our society can afford such an investment.

It is not difficult to persuade a homeowner to repair a leaking roof, even when he feels he can ill afford the cost. He knows that rain can damage his house and furnishings irreparably, costing him far more than any preventive repairs. In the same way, citizens must realize that urban blight and decay; the myriads of evils surrounding our slums; the effects of delinquency, vice, and crime; and the results of human demoralization constitute heavy financial losses to our society, as well as poignant personal tragedies. They demand heavy outlays from tax funds and lead to losses in deteriorating property, as well as the loss of goods and services that could have been produced by the unemployed. What our consciences dictate as morally right, our economic judgment reinforces as socially profitable.

Yet it would be unfortunate, even in this area of social action, were we to confine our activity solely to approving legislation, paying taxes, and contributing to organized social-welfare programs. Many Americans have time and energy which they would willingly contribute to the needs of their fellow men, if they could see the chance to do this. There are retired persons who wish to be active and useful. Mothers of grown children may have time on their hands. Many of our teenagers wish to be challenged with something truly useful in their leisure time. The spirit and dedication that characterized our Peace Corps can also be used in domestic service by those who may not be willing or able to serve abroad.

In emphasizing the need for social action, we must at the same time pay deserved tribute to the many voluntary agencies, including especially our own Catholic Charities, the Saint Vincent de Paul Society, and others which have devoted so much to the service of the unfortunate in our society. Their workers know from firsthand experience the tragic problems caused by destitution and demoralization. Their wisdom and guidance will be invaluable in any campaign against poverty. New programs must supplement, not replace, what is being done so well by these dedicated groups.

America has been hailed throughout the world for its generosity, its willingness to come to the aid of those in need. When there is famine or natural disaster, we rush to help, using both governmental and private agencies. Without narrowing our worldwide vision of generosity and sympathy, let us also turn our eyes to the problems here at home. Of the early Christians it was said: "See how these Christians love one another." Can we think of a more fitting expression of the Christian renewal being worked out in Vatican Council II than a torrent of concern on our part for the poor in our midst? "As long as you did it for one of these, the least of my brethren, you did it for me." (*Mt.* xxv, 40)

SUPPLEMENTARY READINGS

Brown, Robert McAfee, Thomas Merton, Norman Counsin, et al. "Commentaries on PACEM IN TERRIS," SATURDAY REVIEW, Vol. 48 (February 13, 1965), 19–30.

DECREE ON THE CHURCH IN THE MODERN WORLD. Vatican Council II. Pope John XXIII. PACEM IN TERRIS.

Sheerin, John B., c.s.p. "Pacem in Terris, Magna Carta for Peace," CATHOLIC WORLD, Vol. 197, 1179 (June 1963), 148–51.

Shriver, Sargent. POINT OF THE LANCE. New York: Harper & Row, 1964. See "The War on Poverty," pp. 97–116.

POINTS FOR DISCUSSION

1. What is the significance of Pope John's having addressed Pacem in Terris to all men of good will? Is it proper for the Holy Father to so address himself to the entire world?

2. On what principles is the Church justified (obliged) to enter the temporal order?

3. What is our responsibility to other nations of the world? As the United States? As individual citizens? As Christians?

4. Is it possible for a Christian to adhere to an isolationist position?

5. In areas of world responsibility (food, economic help, immigration laws), to what degree should one nation assist another? Is there any moral obligation to do so? When? Explain your view.

6. What is your attitude as an American when you realize that some of the people to whom we give aid take international positions opposite to ours and do things which seem to jeopardize the common good? (Trade with Cuba, etc.)

7. Why do you think many countries dislike America even though they are being supported by us or at least helped? What is often missing from our foreign aid?

8. What are your ideas on the United Nations? What did Pope John say about a World Federation? About the Principle of Subsidiarity?

9. Does the Church favor any one type of government, for example, democracy?

10. Would you agree with this philosophy as expressed by Pope John. "The public authority of the world community must tackle and solve problems of an economic, social, political, or cultural character which are posed by the universal common good"?

11. Regarding Shriver's commencement address on the war on poverty. Whose responsibility is it to help the poor?

12. What Christian insight from words of Christ do we find in this regard?

13. What would you say is the definition of a good Christian?

14. How does a Christian in a large city go about living practically up to this image of a good Christian?

15. What is your attitude toward priests and nuns marching at Selma, in ban-the-bomb demonstrations, etc.?

16. Does adherence to the Christian and human principles of peace necessarily mean adherence to an anti-war, pacifist philosophy? Explain your position.

chapter 11
COMMUNISM

Ten years ago it was very common in certain segments of the press to speak of the "Communist menace." With the passage of the decade there also passed to a notable degree the somewhat exaggerated and rather heightened concern and fear of Communist infiltration into our American government and culture. There is no doubt that in the past there was good foundation for this concern and even fear. At the same time it should be stressed that there still exists today in the world generally and in America a real danger and a serious threat to freedom from communism. But it does not evoke the same kind of antagonisms and fears which it did formerly. Questions of "peaceful co-existence" are currently being explored. Hints of a thaw in the "cold war" are periodically circulated especially in this nuclear age when a "hot war" could mean the total destruction of all sides engaged in the conflict.

This newer approach to communism is seen not only in the political arena of world opinion but also in religious circles. It is a fact, surprising to some within as well as outside the Church, that in the Decree of Vatican II on the Church in the Modern World there is no explicit condemnation made of communism and its atheistic philosophy. This is in keeping with all decrees of this Council which studiously avoided all anathemas and similar condemnations. Still the Church remains unalterably opposed to the false tenets of communism, so it is fitting for you to consider now some of the basic conflicts between communism and Christianity, both in order to be able to evaluate communism critically, with an understanding of something of its basic appeal, and to have a more positive attitude toward Communists as opposed to communism. The article included here, *Communism, Pipe Dream of Utopians,* is written by a man who spent many of his mature years in the Communist Party as editor of the London Communist newspaper *The Daily Worker.* The article is still acknowledged to be one of the finest brief presentations of the Communistic view of life.

Communism
Pipe-Dream of Utopians
DOUGLAS HYDE

THE COMMUNISTS think they can realize their goal — a Communist world — in our lifetime. Every Communist believes that if he and his comrades work hard enough and are able to seize the opportunity when it comes, then they will live to see the victory of Communism throughout the entire world. They have, further, well-laid plans to bring this about.

Today's Communists believe that Asia, Africa and Latin America are the areas of promise in the years immediately ahead. If they can win for themselves those three they plan to by-pass the West and confront us with a situation where a majority of mankind already lives under Communism.

They also believe that some day an economic crisis must come to the West, just as one came in the late 1920s and early '30s. When it comes, it will start in America. A chain reaction will be set in motion through all the capitalist countries of the West. The weakest links in the capitalist chain will break. . . .

How do I know all this?

I joined the Communist Party in 1928 just before my 18th birthday and I left it in 1948, 20 years later. That means that I spent the whole of my late adolescence and early manhood doing almost everything that a man can do for the movement.

Communism was my life. I worked as a local organizer, district organizer, and later on as a member of the London Secretariat of the British Communist Party. I am a writer and I became news editor of the Party's national paper: "The Daily Worker."

Learn from the Enemy
When I left the Party, I knew that Communism was evil.

I saw this in the lives of the people around me and in my own life too. But I also recognized that there are many things to learn from the enemy.

You cannot understand Communist successes over the last 40 years unless you understand the people who make up the movement. *Communists see this world as one,* each country linked with every other and mutually dependent, and all mankind linked together in the same way. It is true that they divide the world into classes and so make nonsense of their claim to be internationalists. But nonetheless that world concept, that realization of the interdependence of peoples which they have is something we should appreciate and emulate. Isn't it a part of our Christian inheritance?

Since I left the Communist Party I have traveled as a commentator on world affairs in almost every part of the world. I have been able to maintain contact with Communists and Communism over the years. In my experience, the things which attract a person to Communism in Europe are much the same as those which attract another individual on the other side of the world.

Some time ago, I had the opportunity to share many long conversations with the supreme commander of the Hukbalahap, the Communist guerrillas in the Philippines. He was in jail and I asked the Philippine Government if I might be sent to jail as well—to share his conditions and to share his mind. I used to spend 16 hours a day in his cell, arguing with him from 6 in the morning to 10 at night.

As we talked I immediately realized that our minds could meet, even though he was a leader of Asian peasant origin, and I, a so-called "Western intellectual." We had been moulded in the same way. We had been put through the same process. The things that brought him to Communism were *the same bad social conditions and injustices* which had made me a Communist as a boy of 17. He had suffered under them, while I had been a mere observer. These problems, which should be the concern of all mankind, led both him and me into Communism. Gradually I was able to win him from Communism and help him back to his ancestral Faith.

Inside the Marxist Mind

When I talk to you of Communists, therefore, I am not talking of some particular sort of British Communist. I talk of a type to be found all over the world. I would like to take you inside the mind of a Communist. I don't think I need tell you that Communism looks different to the Communist from the way it looks to those in the opposite camp.

To the overwhelming majority of Communists, Communism first and foremost is an ideal, *a dream of a good society.* There is nothing intrinsically evil in dreaming of good societies. Saints of the Church have done the same.

Almost always the people who go to Communism are young. Youth is a period of idealism. It is right and proper that young people should be dreaming of good societies. When we become older and our arteries begin to harden, we get impatient with the idealism of youth. The Communists take this vital force and use it for their own purposes. Too often we have neglected it.

Secondly, Communism is a revolt against real evils, not imaginary ones. Communists do not have to create the evils against which they campaign. These exist already.

Social and racial injustices outrage people with a strict sense of justice. The natural rebel has a sensitive social conscience, and feels constrained to speak out against evil when he sees it.

Consequently, flowing into the Communist Party all over the world is a constant stream of young idealists and natural rebels, anxious to change the world, to make an end of evil, believing that no one else cares about the scorned and the rejected. This is something which should exercise our minds as Christians.

Communism provides, thirdly, *membership in a world-wide organization* which cuts across the narrow frontiers of our time, has a common aim and purpose, and a common philosophy. It pools all of its experiences, and learns from its mistakes.

Those who join feel that they are part of a great international movement which *knows where it is going and how to get there.* This gives them a feeling of strength. Any psychiatrist will tell you that many people in the world today feel they "do not belong." Buttressed by this awareness of the international character of the movement, Communists are made to feel they do indeed "belong." In a curious sort of way, the internationalism of Communism is an inversion of the Catholicity of the Church— this desire of men to be united regardless of race or nation, in a common faith, and with a common aim which embraces the whole world.

Everything Must Go
Communism aims to overthrow everything for which civilization has stood for the past 2,000 years. I say this, not in a propaganda sense. I mean it exactly. The Communist believes that you cannot graft Communism onto a Capitalist society. You must destroy the existing social order completely—its ideological superstructure, its culture, ideas, everything which has grown out of it. Only then can you build a Communist society.

The philosophy is militantly atheistic. It not only says there is no God but also declares that this is a purely material world and man is a purely material creature. The very memory of the name of God must be wiped from the mind of man before Communism can succeed.

Communism, fourthly, is a religion. The Communist will deny this, since he is opposed to all religion. But I believe that you can explain the lives of Communists themselves only in terms of spiritually hungry people who are giving everything to Communism—what men in other times and in other circumstances have given to God. They live for Communism and if necessary they will die for it too.

Not very long ago, the British Communist Party advertised a series of lectures in the "Daily Worker" under the general title of *"A Faith for a Modern Man."* I believe that that is precisely what the Communists are trying to make of their Communism. They demonstrate in their own lives, and in their international movement, that if you deny men a good

353

faith, they will turn to an evil one. Here in what was once called Christendom, we have produced large numbers who have no faith, nothing to live for, and nothing to die for. They don't believe in God. They don't believe in themselves. Life is purposeless. *It is inevitable that men should revolt against this unnatural situation and seek some substitute.* It is for this reason that Communism does not attract the worst of people with the worst of qualities. Instead, it takes the best of people with the best of qualities and uses them for evil purposes. It demands loyalty, devotion, and willingness to sacrifice.

All over the world this process has helped to give the movement a great inner strength. It uses what is good in men. It uses what is evil too, such as a hatred of society which they feel has perhaps cheated them or cheated others, their resentments and frustrations, their desire for vengeance on a community which has not given them the opportunity they had hoped to have.

Red Martyrs, Too

Communists often shame those of us who call ourselves Christians by their zeal and enthusiasm, their dedication and readiness to sacrifice. A little time ago I was traveling around the jungle of Malaya. I went into an area which was still in the hands of Communist guerrillas. When I got there, I inquired about a group of men whom I had known years ago. They were leaders of the Malayan Communist Party. Almost all were graduates. All had professions into which they might have gone. Instead, at the call of Moscow they took to the jungles.

I found that only one of them was still alive. He was on the border between Malaya and Thailand, hunted like an animal, with a big price on his head. In bad shape physically, he was living in a part of the jungle which was so dense that he was getting hardly any sunshine. The others were dead. To the security people who shot them they were so many Communist terrorists—the enemy. But to other Communists all over the world they were martyrs.

That is what I mean when I say that Communists often shame those of us who are Christians.

Often it is the small sacrifices which go on day after day, year after year, which make the biggest demands upon people, and are the biggest test. I saw these being made over and over again in my experience as a Communist.

Red 'Blood Cell' Plot

I remember for example, how at one time we who were employed by the "Daily Worker" wanted to spread Communism in the area around the Daily Worker building. Already a Communist Party group existed in every nearby factory. The only large concentration of employees amongst whom there was no Communist cell was in a large hospital.

As leader of the Communist group in the "Daily Worker," I checked and found that no one on our staff had any contact inside that hospital. I called a meeting and asked for suggestions. London was being bombed almost daily, and every hospital was crying out for blood for transfusions. *"Why don't we volunteer to give our blood?"* one member suggested. "If we do that we could go back to the hospital time after time, meeting the doctors and nurses. We could make friendships, and out of friendships, converts."

I called for *volunteers*. There were 200 members of the "Daily Worker" staff. *I got 200 volunteers.* My staff queued up outside the hospital time after time. Often, in fact, when I wanted a reporter to go out on assignment, I had to send a messenger to fetch him from the blood-line.

One night, as the last edition was going to press, the man responsible for the technical production of the paper collapsed on the job. Our staff doctor examined him and said: "This man has given too much blood, he has nearly drained himself white." He had done this in his anxiety to make recruits.

This story has two sequels. As a result of that operation we made our first contacts inside the hospital. A Communist Party cell still exists inside it, among the doctors and nurses, today.

Mao Gets a Leader

Some years later, secondly, Mao Tse-tung got in touch with the British Communist Party, soliciting a trained journalist, public relations man and tough Communist for his staff, to move around with them and interpret the mind of the West to Mao and Mao's mind to the West. I was asked to select the man. I chose the man who collapsed on the job, because I knew he was dedicated.

When the Korean War began—by which time Mao and his comrades had become the rulers of China—my Communist-elect went with the Chinese forces into Korea. He was one of the men who helped to indoctrinate British, American and other English-speaking prisoners-of-war in Communist and Marxist ideas. As a consequence a demand was made in the British House of Commons that he should be charged as a traitor.

There is something of the tragedy and the evil of Communism. On the one hand, a man who was prepared to give his blood for a cause until he collapsed; and on the other, that cause so rotten that he dared not return to his own country lest he be charged as a traitor.

Communists believe that if you make little demands upon people, you will get a little response and that is all you deserve. *But if you make big demands upon them you will get an heroic response.* As a Catholic writer for the last 12 years I experienced the same with Catholics. This desire for dedication and self-sacrifice is not exclusive to Communists.

But Communists also know that it is not sufficient *just* to have dedication and enthusiasm. If people are to be effective, they *must be well instructed.* The life of every hard-core Communist consists of continual instruction, which serves as ammunition for a fight in which he is already engaged.

They believe, too, that people can be immensely more successful if trained in *leadership techniques.* You see this demonstrated in many factories. It only takes a handful of Communists to make an enormous impact upon a giant plant or upon an entire locality.

How Reds Train Leaders

Communists say that they can train anyone who is willing to be a leader. I believed this, and proved it, when I was tutoring leadership courses.

On one occasion, a member of the class presented the biggest challenge I ever had to meet.

He was very short and grotesquely fat. He had a flabby white face, with a cast in one eye, and a most distressing stutter. I am not making fun of the man when I tell you that he said to me: "C-c-c-comrade I w-w-want you to to to take me and to train me and to turn me into a leader of m-m-men."

I wondered how I was going to do it. But I had told my class that we could take anyone who was willing, and he was pathetically anxious. So I set about the job.

According to Communist practice, the first thing to do to turn a man into a leader is *to give him confidence.* The second is to give him *something to have confidence about.*

As I looked at him, I thought, "Well, he does not have much to be confident about." So we had to give him self-confidence. I told him: "If you will attend classes and learn the things which we can teach you, we will give you the answers to all the great questions which are troubling the mind of modern man. We will explain the universe to you, what man has been trying to do throughout the ages. We will show you that the whole of history has been working towards revolution and the ultimate victory of Communism. We will show you how the very laws of the universe are on our side. *This is the essence of dialectical materialism* — that the very laws of the universe work for Communism; in particular, *the law that all progress comes from conflict.* Then sooner or later you will become one of the small group of people who understand the nature of change. And when the right moment comes, you will be one of those who will overturn this rotten old world in which we live and build a grand new world instead."

The "Messianic Complex"

Even though he came to us with an inferiority complex,

it was not very long before we had given him a messianic complex. With a new-found belief in himself, his personality began to unfold. After some months of instruction *I told him that he ought to be a tutor.* He was terrified. He said: "Wh-wh-what, m-m-me?" I replied: "Yes, because when you came to the Party through one of its campaigns, you knew nothing of Communism as a theory. But you have learned a lot in recent months and the people who are now just coming to Communism know as little as you knew some months ago. The whole art of teaching is to know a little bit more than those whom you are trying to teach. If you have that you can get away with it.

"You should be a teacher," I told him. "If they ask you questions you don't know how to answer, *go to your textbooks and find the answers.* You will learn that way and you can give them the answers later on." So he became the tutor of a small group.

This was an essential part of his training. He had to formulate and get some order into his own ideas, then pass them on to others in simple language—first to a small group, then to a larger group. Later we put him through a public speaking course.

We did not turn him into a great orator, but we did make him an effective agitator and propagandist. Although we did not cure him of his stutter, it became very much modified in the process, as he gained confidence. We also taught him parliamentary procedure—how to chair a meeting, how to move a resolution or an amendment. Then we told him to become active in his union and *to accept any responsibility that came his way.* Today he is a leader in Britain's only Communist-controlled union.

The Communist Party regularly takes such unpromising human material and uses it effectively. The secret of our success was this: we did not ask him, a worker, to teach dialectical materialism to nuclear physicists. We taught him to put over simple ideas to simple people—and that is what I believe we Christians need to do. *We, too, can use men effectively if we will get them to work with people at their own level.* Because Communists succeed in training leaders they are able to make an immensely more effective impact than would otherwise be the case.

Conflict Essential
Communist Party leaders see the world in terms of conflict. They believe that they should fight for Communism as if they were fighting a war; that they must use the techniques and tactics of war. They must be prepared to destroy the enemy from within. That is why they infiltrate every sort of organization. They are taught that they should use allies as long as they serve the purposes of Communism, then turn against them, reject them and destroy them if necessary.

I recall how in 1928, a new line came from party headquarters. Until then we had been attacking Left-Wing Socialist leaders; the new line was that we should try to make allies of them instead. The branch of the Communist Party to which I belonged didn't accept this. We thought it much more fun attacking people than being friends with them. One of the leaders came from headquarters to try to convince us. For a long time it looked as though he would not succeed. Then he said: *"Comrades, we must be ready to take these people by the hand in order to take them by the throat."* This was such obviously good Marxism that we accepted the new line without further discussion.

I think this is a point to remember, because in the period ahead of us, we are going to have a lot of Communists, open and underground, trying to make allies. They will *say: "We are agreed on short-term objectives.* Forget about our long-term aims, we are all for peace, we are all for social justice, why shouldn't we travel hand in hand?" It is necessary to remember at such times that when they take you by the hand they want to be able in due course to take you by the throat.

Espouse Popular Fronts
Communists believe that by the creation of national and popular fronts they can win support. If they can espouse popular causes then they should be able to build sympathy, and from that make many new recruits, as they did in the 1930s all over Europe. The seeds of treason which we wit-

nessed during the 40s and 50s were sown in the 30s when Communists were recruiting students in universities all over Europe and North America.

Communists, of course, will look for popular causes everywhere and in particular in underdeveloped countries. Also they try to identify themselves with the demand of landless peasants for land, with the demand for land reform and social reform of every sort.

They believe too that they should use this period to build up the Party itself. They are always on the look-out for potential leaders. But the anticipated period of peace (they feel that time is on their side now), the period of popular fronts, call for a particular type — an educated man. When fighting for Communism with the gun, the peasant or uneducated worker may be just as valuable as the educated man. But when the battle is one of doctrines and of ideas, it is the educated who count.

I believe that the success of the Communists is a measure of the Christian's failure. The things for which they campaign are so often the things which we should be taking up. The Communists of China did not obtain victory by going to the peasants of China and teaching them dialectical materialism. They talked about producers' co-operatives; they promised to break the strangle-hold of the money-lender, the landlord, and the merchant who had dominated their lives for generations. It was simple things like these that brought the Communist cause support.

The Christian Lag
Those are the things we might well be doing. Wherever an attempt is made to apply the Church's social teachings to rural and backward conditions, this takes the form of producers' cooperatives, credit unions, land reform and attempts to teach people to help themselves. We ought to be giving a great deal of attention to that sort of activity wherever possible.

The peoples of the underdeveloped areas are the great challenge to us today. The *moral principle* to be applied in the 20th century is that *the rich nations of the world have a responsibility towards the poor ones*: not just to give doles and handouts, useful as these may be as first aid and good as they may be for our own consciences, but *to help the people of the poorer countries to help themselves*. If we can do that, then I believe that any people faced with the choice between living as practicing Christians or as Communists will choose the Christian way every time. Too often they choose the Communist, because they believe no one else cares.

When I was talking to Luis Taruc, the Communist rebel leaders in the Philippines, and outlining Catholic social teaching to him, his first reaction was: "Why did no one tell me about this when I was young? I knew nothing about it. I used to go to church on one side of which was St. Joseph and on the other side St. Isidore. Yet no one ever told me anything about the Church's social teachings, which those two saints represented. If I had known about them when I was a boy in the barrio, I would have gone out and tried to do something about it. But when I joined the Communists, *I thought that the Church had nothing at all to say on the social question*." But what does he (you) do?

World Needs Leaders
This has happened time after time. But it is up to Christians to see that it does not happen. We should be turning out from amongst both priests and laity, leaders who are equipped to pass on the good things we have to others, who understand leadership techniques, and who have that attitude of mind which is the secret of leadership. I would say that creating that attitude is really the most important.

You can go through a seminary, you can go through a college and never really see the point of it all in terms of action.

From our Catholic universities and colleges we may turn out successful professional people. *But they are not effective leaders unless* we have taught them to *apply* the teachings of the Church to the society in which they live, to the profession in which they will work, to every aspect of life which touches their own lives.

Men today are absolutely hungry for *leadership*. All over the world, people are seeking answers, looking for the truths we profess. Millions in recent years have been taken out of their traditional background, thrown into great cities, there becoming rootless proletarians with no sense of purpose or direction. These will turn to anyone who offers leadership.

A tremendous need exists for *lay leaders* today, men who are prepared to see their job as not only one of trying to Christianize themselves (and heaven knows that is a big job in itself) but to Christianize the society in which they live as well—all its institutions, its organizations, its professions and trades, viewing everything in terms of cooperation with God, cooperating with the Church in an attempt to bring all mankind to Christ's kingdom.

Challenge to Christians
It is tragic that so many people in the past have been "sold" under the fase belief that only Communists care about social and racial injustices. This has helped to create an explosive situation—poverty in the midst of plenty, poor nations getting poorer and rich nations getting richer. Side by side with that, exists a group of faithless people who have a spiritual vacuum in their lives which must be filled. In that mixture is dynamite.

We must not be satisfied simply to produce Christians who know the first commandment—that they must love the Lord their God—but who know nothing about the second—that they must love their neighbor as themselves. When they begin to apply the second one, they begin to play a part in the battle of our time *directly* and *effectively*.

Communism could spread across the world. The Communists believe that. There is plenty of evidence to suggest that it could happen. But it need not. Whether it happens or not will depend on people like *you*, and whether *you* are prepared to accept the responsibilities which history is thrusting upon your shoulders.

If *you* fail to meet the challenge of our time, Communism may overwhelm us all. If you meet that threat of Communism and defeat it, you will not only end a great threat to the Church, you and today's society will emerge from this titanic struggle strengthened in purpose and purified in the process.

SUPPLEMENTARY READINGS

CATHOLICS AND COMMUNISTS: ELEMENTS OF A DIALOGUE. *Political Affairs Publishers, 23 West 26th Street, New York, New York 10010.*

Hyde, Douglas. I BELIEVED. *New York: Putnam, 1950.*

Morgan, Everett J., s.j., and Twomey, Louis J., s.j. (eds.).

THE SOCIAL CONSCIENCE OF A CATHOLIC; THE SOCIAL DOC-TRINE OF THE CHURCH APPLIED TO PROBLEMS OF OUR CONTEMPORARY SOCIETY. *Berkeley: McCutchan Publishing Company, 1964. Distributed by Marquette University Bookstore. Many significant references to fundamental ideas of Communistic philosophy and its causes and effects are listed in the Index on page 300.*

POINTS FOR DISCUSSION

1. What sound insights and principles can Christians derive from some of the basic tenets of communism?

2. What are the main circumstances and motivations which draw many people into the Communist party?

3. Mr. Hyde refers to communism both as "militantly atheistic" and as "a religion." How do you explain this apparent paradox?

4. What are the attitudes of Cummunists toward the development of leadership pontential within the party? How do they achieve this goal? In your estimation, are they more effective in this area than Christians seem to be? Why? Why not?

5. Comment upon this statement from a Communist leader and apply it to concrete experiences of past and present history: "Comrades, we must be ready to take people by the hand in order to take them by the throat." How does this differ from the Christian principle voiced by St. Ignatius Loyola: "We should be ready to go in their door to bring them through ours."

6. Give your observation and judgment on the following statement of Mr. Hyde: *"I believe that the success of the Communist is a measure of the Christian's failure."*

7. *What is your reaction to the new developments in the Vatican's approach to Communist peoples? Do you think that peaceful co-existence between the free world and the Communist world is possible? Desirable? On political grounds? On religious grounds?*

8. *What is your reaction to the statement: "Better Red than dead"?*

chapter 12
THE CHURCH AND THE CIVIC COMMUNITY

On the local level of the civic community the Church also has its God-given responsibility to be of service as the "called community." In the past decade there has been a progressive and gradual development of the Church's active awakening to this responsibility in practice as well as in principle. This openness toward, concern for, and active participation in common problems, affecting the entire civic community, and not only the Catholic segment of the community, should be cultivated by all Catholic citizens and this responsibility should be realized under both aspects of one's life, the civic and the religious. It is most important that you see your involvement in these problems within their religious context as well as in the context of good citizenship. The brotherhood fostered by Christian love for the world community and for the civic community within the people of God should deepen the highly praiseworthy human concern of good neighborliness from merely natural motivation.

The areas of civic concern which can be explored and discussed in class are many and varied. Since some will be more applicable in different localities than others, each class, together with its teacher, should select those particular problems for consideration which are currently of special interest and concern to that locality. The article which follows from the Office of Economic Opportunity in Washington deals specifically with the war on poverty and it presents many guidelines for community action. It is hoped that through exploration and discussion of these civic problems you will be moved to take an active part in community action programs to the extent that you are able both now and in your future lives.

The War on Poverty
— A Hometown Fight

"THERE ARE MILLIONS *of Americans—one fifth of our people— who have not shared in the abundance which has been granted to most of us, and on whom the gates of opportunity have been closed."*

LYNDON B. JOHNSON
THE WHITE HOUSE
MARCH 16, 1964

How Do You Start the Anti-Poverty Battle at Home?

You do it with Community Action. The Community Action Program will provide technical and financial assistance for urban and rural communities to fight poverty. Individual communities will decide how to do the job with private and public resources that will be augmented by this new Federal assistance.

The problems of poverty are a network of social ills like illiteracy, unemployment, poor health and dilapidated housing. To alleviate them will require a network of anti-poverty attacks that are varied while they are coordinated. This combination—fashioned by local talent and leadership—is the major aim of the Community Action Programs.

Specifically, remedial reading, literacy courses, job training, employment counseling, homemaker services, job development and training, vocational rehabilitation, health services are only some of the individual programs that can be supported and coordinated with a detailed local anti-poverty program.

In the past, many of these separate programs have been scattered and un-coordinated. A remedial reading program, for example, has limited effect if there is no comparable course to permit the parent to guide and help his child. Both programs have limited effect if the parents have no marketable skills and live in squalor. A program that addresses all of these difficulties in a systematic fashion will truly help that child and his family to remove

ISSUED BY THE OFFICE OF ECONOMIC OPPORTUNITY, PUBLIC AFFAIRS, WASHINGTON, D.C.

the shackles of poverty. And this is the intent of Community Action.

The Federal Government will help local communities to develop and support these anti-poverty programs. However, Federal assistance will depend on the community's determination to:

1. Mobilize its own public and private resources for this attack.

2. Develop programs of sufficient scope and size that give promise of eliminating causes of poverty.

3. Involve the poor themselves in developing and operating the anti-poverty programs.

4. Administer and coordinate the Community Action Programs through public or private non-profit agencies or a combination of these.

In smaller communities and in those with more limited resources local leaders can begin a Community Action Program in stages. For example, a community might start with a pre-school program coupled with a health service clinic for these youngsters. These should be followed by other specific programs all linked to each other in a coordinated campaign.

All local programs should use the talents of persons living in and affected by the poverty stricken neighborhoods in planning and operating programs. As workers in projects, they could be used as aides to professionals, as recreational and day care assistants and as helpers in homemaker and health services. Some other examples are community research aides, library aides, tutoring assistants, probation aides and family service workers.

Further, Community Action Programs should see that existing local, State and Federal programs are linked to each other in a concentrated drive against poverty. Assistance now available to States and local communities under the Manpower Development and Training Act, the 1962

Public Welfare Amendments, vocational education and the various programs under the Housing and Home Finance Agency all should be joined with any total community anti-poverty effort.

Community Action Programs, in short, will fuse the old, scattered programs while providing the technical and financial assistance to initiate the new attack against the varied problems that have ensnared the poor.

What Kind of Programs Might Be Developed:
Community Action Programs will vary as the needs of the people vary in different parts of the nation. They must be part of a total effort to help people escape poverty, not to make it more bearable. Here are some illustrations that might be part of a Community Action Program:

1. Providing special and remedial education, with particular emphasis on reading, writing, and mathematics.

2. Providing academic counseling and guidance services and school social work services.

3. Providing after-school study centers, tutoring, and summer, week-end and after-school classes.

4. Establishing programs for the benefit of pre-school children.

5. Reducing adult illiteracy.

6. Developing and carrying out special education or other programs for migrant or transient families.

7. Improving the living conditions of the elderly.

8. Arranging for or providing health examinations and health education for school children.

9. Rehabilitating and retraining of physically or mentally handicapped persons.

10. Providing health, rehabilitation, employment, edu-

368

cational and related services to young men not qualified for military services.

11. Providing community child-care centers and youth activity centers.

12. Improving housing and living facilities and home management skills.

13. Providing services to enable families from rural areas to meet problems of urban living.

14. Providing recreation and physical fitness services and facilities.

How Do You Tell What Is Needed In Your Community?
The problems of the poor must be assessed in more than money terms. Simply enumerating the low income families will not permit you to select a priority list of projects. Here are some of the factors you should sort out:

1. The number of low-income families, particularly those with children.

2. The extent of persistent unemployment and under-employment.

3. The number and proportion of people receiving cash or other assistance on a needs basis from public agencies or private organizations.

4. The number of migrant or transient low-income families.

5. School dropout rates, military service rejection rates and other evidence of low educational attainment.

6. The incidence of disease, disability, and infant mortality.

7. Housing conditions.

8. Adequacy of community facilities and services.

9. The incidence of crime and juvenile delinquency.

Who Will Pay For The Programs?

Federal money will be available (1) to help establish Community Action Groups, (2) to assist in developing programs, (3) to support those programs, (4) for technical aid, (5) for special research and demonstration projects, and (6) to train persons to work in Community Action Programs.

The Federal Government will pay up to 90% of the cost of Community Action Programs in the first two years. The balance, to be furnished by local Community Action groups, can be in cash or in kind, such as services and facilities, to support local programs.

How Do You Begin?

1. Bring together the appropriate voluntary and government agencies in welfare, health, housing, education and employment as participants in developing a Community Action program. Include leaders from the areas in which the program will operate.

2. Assemble all available information on the poverty problem. Identify the extent of poverty in the community and begin to determine major characteristics. List the problems in order of priority.

3. Develop a set of proposals to attack the causes of poverty. Determine what local resources are available to support such programs.

4. Decide on a specific geographical area for the program.

5. Form a local Community Action organization that includes not only government and voluntary organizations, but business, labor and other key civic organizations as well.

6. Ask for technical help if it is needed to plan your programs. This help can come directly from the Office of Economic Opportunity or from those States which have received technical assistance funds.

7. Contact the State Government to determine how its

agencies and programs can help and can be integrated into the total local anti-poverty effort.

8. Develop projects in order of importance and ability to carry them through.

9. Apply to Community Action, Office of Economic Opportunity, for the detailed forms to submit your application.

COMMUNITY ACTION
OFFICE OF ECONOMIC OPPORTUNITY
WASHINGTON, D.C. 20506

Harrington, Michael. THE OTHER AMERICA. New York. Macmillan, 1962.

Morgan, Everett J., s.j., and Twomey, Louis J., s.j. (eds.). THE
SOCIAL CONSCIENCE OF A CATHOLIC. Berkeley: McCutchan
Publishing Company, 1964. Distributed by Marquette University
Bookstore. This book contains much excellent material for the
consideration of different problems affecting the civic community
with attention to a Catholic's responsibility. Consult the Index
for references to different problem areas.

POINTS FOR DISCUSSION

1. The following procedure for study-discussion sessions may
be used in pursuing any of the civic problems most relevant
to the local scene—poverty, care of the sick or aged, low standard of education, housing, minority groups, etc.*

Step I. Presentation of the Problem (15 minutes). Explanation
of the main question or questions involved, given by a student
or by the teacher, with some relevant facts needed to understand
it and work toward solution.

Step II. Practical Discussion of Problem in Buzz Groups (30
minutes).

Three phases:
a. OBSERVE. What are the facts as we see them?

b. JUDGE. How should things be? Evaluation of the fact situation. What should goals be in order to handle problem?

c. ACT. What should be done? Plan ways of meeting the problem and achieving objectives.

* WE ARE GRATEFUL TO FATHER JOSEPH GRAU, s.j., PRESENTLY OF MARQUETTE UNIVER-
SITY, BUT FORMERLY A RELIGION TEACHER AT MARQUETTE HIGH SCHOOL, FOR HIS KIND
PERMISSION TO INCLUDE THIS USEFUL MATERIAL IN THIS BOOK OF READINGS.

NOTE: In these buzz groups this three-phase development is used not as a formal planning process in order to meet the needs but as an *exploratory* process to help make clearer the complexity of the problems with which we are dealing. The approach would be: "If you were an adult, with these responsibilities, how would you handle them?" If some attempt has been made to sketch provisional solutions, then when we see what is actually being done, as explained by someone working in the field, we will have a better appreciation of the problem and of the present solution. We will also be better equipped to question and to further expand our knowledge. (There is no formal recorder for these buzz sessions; each participant keeps hsi own notes for questions he will want to ask later and for suggestions he may want to make to the group.)

Step III. *Explanation of present solution to the problem with indication of religious dimension involved therein (20 minutes). Main speaker (in religion class it could be a guest lecturer or the teacher or another student) presents how the problem is being met at the moment in the community.*

Step IV. *General question-discussion period (20 minutes). Here participants are to ask questions that have resulted from buzz sessions and to listen to the main speaker's explanation of the situation. Some practical suggestions for action should be put forth.*

2. *An outline as a guide for discussion of community needs and services.*

Stating the Problem. *Some fundamental elements in the entire social picture of the civic community.*

1. In a set of urban communities of over 1,000,000 people (number is relative to locality) how should we care for:

a. the sick and handicapped (physically and mentally)
b. the poor
c. social misfits (delinquents, juvenile and adult)
d. disintegrating families
e. minority groups of different racial and cultural backgrounds.

II. How to coordinate and evaluate what is actually being done at the present time — how to judge the effect of present agencies in meeting the present needs of the above classes of people.

III. How should all of this be carried out with due attention to:

a. *proper emphasis on most serious problems.*
b. *best use of modern developments in medicine, psychology, social work, etc.*
c. *preventive and not merely remedial measures.*
d. *meeting these human problems in a genuinely human way, in conformity with the personal dignity of all involved, both the persons helped and helping.*
e. *different and sometimes opposing views concerning priorities and methods, caused by the different value systems in our pluralistic society.*

NOTE: The following points should be kept in mind during these discussions: All questions have not been answered in these discussions. In fact a great many have not even been asked. Some answers seem inadequate, incomplete, and disappointing. Much of the material presented calls for thinking and re-thinking. But what good is it all? One answer is that we all now have a better knowledge from the experience of these discussions that what we have done has been only an introduction, a scratching of the surface, of these problems. That is true, but it is also true that for many the surface was pretty smooth before and it is about time that it was scratched. For others, the scratches have gone deeper. What can now be done to continue the digging process and to work at laying a better foundation for an active and intelligent role as responsible citizens, motivated by genuine charity and justice, on a supernatural as well as a natural basis, as Christians as well as Americans or Canadians, etc.?

3. The following questions furnish subjects for personal essays or for further group discussion:

a. *Of the problems examined and discussed, which do you feel is the most important and why? Which touches you most significantly?*
b. *What do you think you can do at this time to help meet these problems? Even if there is not much you can actually do, what*

should your attitude toward the problems be, and toward those who are working for a solution?

c. In view of the complexity of the problems, what further preparation would you want to receive both in and out of school and religion class?

d. What basic Catholic teachings have a bearing on these problems, on the attitude you should have toward them, and the manner in which you should cooperate with others, Catholic and non-Catholic, in working toward their solution?